GLOBAL SOCIAL MOVEMENTS

GLOBAL SOCIAL MOVEMENTS

Edited by
ROBIN COHEN and
SHIRIN M. RAI

THE ATHLONE PRESS
LONDON AND NEW BRUNSWICK, NJ

First published in 2000 by
THE ATHLONE PRESS
1 Park Drive, London NW11 7SG
and New Brunswick, New Jersey

© Robin Cohen, Shirin M. Rai and The Athlone Press 2000

Robin Cohen and Shirin M. Rai have asserted their right
under the Copyright, Designs and Patents Act, 1998,
to be identified as the editors of this work

British Library Cataloguing in Publication Data
A catalogue record record for this book is available from the British Library

ISBN 0 485 00419 4 (HB)
ISBN 0 485 00615 4 (PB)

Library of Congress Cataloging-in-Publication Data
Global social movements / edited by Robin Cohen and Shirin Rai.
   p. cm.
   Includes bibliographical references and index.
   ISBN 0–485–00419–4 (cloth : alk. paper) – ISBN 0–485–00615–4 (pbk. : alk. paper)
   1. Social movements. I. Cohen, Robin. II. Rai, Shirin.

HN17.5.G568 2000
303.48'4–dc21   99–087577

Distributed in the United States, Canada and South America by
Transaction Publishers
390 Campus Drive
Somerset, New Jersey 08873

Typeset in Garamond by
Aarontype Limited, Easton, Bristol
Printed and bound in Great Britain by Bookcraft (Bath) Ltd

CONTENTS

CONTRIBUTORS AND EDITORS

Sarah Ashwin worked between 1991 and 1993 as the research officer for the Central and East European desk of the International Confederation of Free Trade Unions (ICFTU). She left this post in order to do doctoral research on the Russian workers' movement in the Sociology Department of Warwick University. She is now a lecturer in Industrial Relations at the London School of Economics. She is author of *Russian workers: the anatomy of patience* (1999).

Upendra Baxi was Professor of Law and Development (1973–96) and Vice-Chancellor (1990–4) of the University of Delhi. He has held many other appointments in the USA and India and is currently Professor of Law at the University of Warwick. He has published widely on the Indian legal system and on human rights. His books include: *Towards a sociology of Indian law* (1985) and *Human rights for a changing world* (1994). He is also author of *The future of human rights* (1999).

James A. Beckford is Professor of Sociology at the University of Warwick and was Vice-President of the International Sociological Association, 1994–8. His research is concerned with civic religion, chaplaincies and with the relationship between religion and politics. His main publications in the sociology of religion include *The trumpet of prophecy: a sociological analysis of Jehovah's Witnesses* (1975), *Religion and advanced industrial society* (1989) and (with Sophie Gilliat) *Religion in prison: equal rites in a multi-faith society?* (1998).

Cynthia Cockburn is Research Professor in the Department of Sociology, City University, London. Her earlier research was concerned with local government, gender in technological change and equality in organizations, particularly in trade unions. Publications from this period include *Machinery of dominance: women, men and technological know-how* (1985) and *In the way of women: men's resistance to sex equality in organizations* (1991). Her current research theme is women's international networking in relation to issues of peace and war. Her most recent book is *The space between us: negotiating gender and national identities in conflict* (1998).

Robin Cohen is Professor of Sociology and Senior Research Fellow, Centre for the Study of Globalization and Regionalization, University of Warwick. He has published widely on migration, globalization and social identity. His books include *Frontiers of identity: the British and the others* (1994) *Global diasporas: an introduction* (1997, 1999) and (with Paul Kennedy) *Global sociology* (2000). He is also editor of *The Cambridge survey of world migration* (1995). In association with the Economic and Social Research Council's Transnational Communities Programme he is working on the themes of transnationalism and cosmopolitanism.

John Forrester is a Research Associate in the Stockholm Environment Institute at the University of York and an associate research fellow of the Department of Sociology. He holds a Social Anthropology degree and PhD from Queen's University Belfast and has worked for around ten years on cultural sustainability and participatory environmentalism. Most recently he has concentrated primarily on issues relating to Local Agenda 21 and around community participation in environmental assessment.

Paul Havemann has been Professor of Law at University of Waikato, New Zealand since 1990. He has also worked at universities in the UK, Australia and Canada where he was head of the School of Human Justice, University of Regina. He teaches in the areas of law and society, criminology, First Peoples and public law and rights theory. He has co-authored *Law and order for Canada's indigenous peoples* (1984) and edited *Indigenous peoples rights in Australia, Canada and New Zealand* (1999). His research interests are currently focused on social rights, citizenship and empowerment in the context of advanced modernity.

Paul Lubeck is Professor of Sociology and History and Director of the Center for Global, International and Regional Studies at the University of California, Santa Cruz. He has conducted field research in Nigeria, Malaysia and Mexico and won the Herskovits prize for his first book, *Islam and urban labor in Northern Mexico* (1986). He has published widely on Islam, on the spread of capitalist social relations and on comparative sociology. He is currently completing two books, titled *Globalization, Islamism and contested modernities* and *From Silicon Valley to Silicon Island: Penang's role in the global electronics industry*.

John Mattausch is Lecturer in Sociology at Royal Holloway College, University of London. His current research concerns the long historical association between Britishers and Gujaratis, the latter now a significant UK minority ethnic community. He also retains an interest in issues over nuclear militarism. His publications include *A commitment to campaign: a sociological study of CND* (1989); 'A "penury of books": The printing press and social change, in an Indian setting', *South Asia* 19 (2), 59–83, and 'From subjects to citizens: British East African Asians, 25 years on', *Journal of Ethnic and Migration Studies*, 24 (1) 1998. He has been working on a theory book the chief theme of which is the influence of chance upon social affairs.

Ronaldo Munck is Professor of Sociology at the University of Liverpool has been previously Professor of Sociology at the University of Durban-Westville, South Africa. He is author of many books. His latest are *Marx @2000: late Marxist perspectives* (1999) and *Critical development theory: contributions to a new paradigm* (1999) and *Labour worldwide in the era of globalisation: alternative union models in the New World Order* (1999).

Peter Newell was a Lecturer in International Studies at the University of Warwick and is now a Research Fellow at the Institute of Development Studies, Sussex, exploring the links between globalization, governance and environmental politics. He has a book forthcoming with Cambridge University Press on the global politics of climate change, a co-authored book with Macmillan on EU environmental policy and has published a number of other book chapters and articles in these areas.

Shirin M. Rai is Reader in Politics and Women Studies at the Department of Politics and International Studies at the University of Warwick, UK. She is the co-author of *Chinese politics and society: an introduction* (1997), and the co-editor of *Women in the face of change: Soviet Union, Eastern Europe and China* (1992) and *Women and the state: international perspectives* (1997). She has written extensively on the area of women and democratic politics in the Third World, and is currently writing a book on the politics of gender and development.

Deborah Stienstra is Associate Professor of Political Science and Women's Studies at the University of Winnipeg, Canada. She has published two books: *Women's movements and international organizations* (1994) and, with the late Barbara Roberts, *Strategies for the Year 2000: a woman's handbook* (1995). She has also written articles on prostitution, foreign policy, information and communications technologies, and disability rights.

Steven Yearley holds the Chair in Sociology at the University of York. Since the late 1980s he has been working on environmentalism and on overlaps between the sociologies of science and of the environment. Most recently, he has studied the globalization of environmental campaigning. This led to his latest book *Sociology, environmentalism, globalization* (1996). He has also carried out research on public responses to computerized environmental modelling. In connection with the latter, he currently holds an ESRC Fellowship in the public understanding of science.

ACRONYMS

AFL–CIO	American Federation of Labour–Council of Industrial Organizations
Alt-WID	Alternative Women in Development
APC	Association for Progressive Communications
APCWD	Asian and Pacific Centre for Women and Development [of the United Nations Economic and Social Commission for Asia and Pacific]
APEC	Asia–Pacific Economic Co-operation
ATSIC	Australian Commonwealth's Aboriginal and Torres Strait Islander Commission
BARC	Bhopal Action Research Center
BGPMUS	Bhopal Gas Peedit Mahila Udyog Sangathan
BJP	Bharatiya Janata Party [Indian People's Party]
BP	British Petroleum
BPEO	Best Practicable Environmental Option
CEO	Chief Executive Officer
CERES	Coalition for Environmentally Responsible Economies
CIS	Commonwealth of Independent States
CND	Campaign for Nuclear Disarmament
CONGO	Coordinating Body of Non-Governmental Organizations
CRZZ	Central Council of Trade Unions [Poland]
CSW	Commission on the Status of Women
DAWN	Development Alternatives for Women for a New Era
ECOSOC	Economic and Social Council [of the United Nations]
EDF	Environmental Defence Fund
END	European Nuclear Disarmament
ENGO(s)	environmental non-governmental organization(s)
ETUC	European Trade Union Confederation
EU	European Union
EUROSTEP	European Solidarity towards Equal Participation of People

FIFA	Fédération Internationale de Football Association
FINNRET	Feminist International Network on New Reproductive Technologies [later known as FINRRAGE]
FINRRAGE	Feminist International Network of Resistance to Reproductive and Genetic Engineering
FSC	Forestry Stewardship Council
FTUI	Free Trade Union Institute
FWBO	Friends of the Western Buddhist Order
GAATW	Global Alliance Against Trafficking in Women
GCC	Global Climate Coalition
GSM(s)	global social movement(s)
GSMO(s)	global social movement organization(s)
IAW	International Alliance of Women
ICC	International Chamber of Commerce
ICEM	International Federation of Chemical, Energy, Mine and General Workers' Unions
ICFTU	International Congress of Free Trade Unions
ICJIB	International Coalition of Justice for Bhopal
ICTs	information and communication technologies
IGO(s)	inter-governmental organization(s)
ILO	International Labour Organization
IMF	International Monetary Fund
INAC	Indian and Northern Affairs Canada
INGO(s)	international non-governmental organization(s)
IPR(s)	intellectual property rights
ISI	import substitution industrialization
ISIS	International Women's Information and Communication Service [Not a literal acronym. Later the body was known as ISIS International]
ISIS-WICCE	Women's International Cross-Cultural Exchange
ISKCON	International Society for Krishna Consciousness
ITS(s)	International Trade Secretariat(s)
IUF	International Union of Food and Allied Workers
IWTC	International Women's Tribune Centre
MAD	mutually assured destruction
MAI	Multilateral Agreement on Investment
MENA	Middle East and North Africa
MIC	methyl isocyanate
MIF	Miners' International Federation
MNC	multinational corporation
MNE(s)	multinational enterprise(s)

MOSOP	Movement for the Survival of the Ogoni People
MTI	Islamist Party [Tunisia]
NAC	National Action Committee on the Status of Women
NAFTA	North American Free Trade Association
NATO	North Atlantic Treaty Organization
NGOs	non-governmental organizations
NIDL	new international division of labour
NPG	Independent Miners' Union [Russia]
NRM(s)	new religious movement(s)
NSM(s)	new social movement(s)
NVLA	National Viewers and Listeners Association
OECD	Organization for Economic Co-operation and Development
OPEC	Organization of Petroleum-Exporting Countries
OPZZ	All-Poland Trade Union Alliance
OS(s)	operating system(s)
PPM	political process model
PUCL	Peoples' Union of Civil Liberties
PUDR	Peoples' Union for Democratic Rights
PVC	polyvinyl chloride [a thermoplastic material]
RSS	Rashtriya Swayamsevak Sangh
RTZ	Rio Tinto Zinc
SAP(s)	structural adjustment programme(s)
SCLC	Southern Christian Leadership Conference
SMO(s)	social movement organization(s)
TAPOL	an Indonesian human rights campaign
TNC(s)	transnational corporation(s)
TRIPs	Trade Related Intellectual Property Rights
TSMO(s)	transnational social movement organization(s)
TUI(s)	Trade Union International(s)
TWMAEW	Third World Movement Against the Exploitation of Women
UBINIG	acronym of Bengali name for Policy Research for Development Alternatives
UN	United Nations
UNCED	United Nations Conference on Environment and Development
UNCTAD	United Nations Conference on Trade and Development

UNCTC   United Nations Centre for Transnational Corporations
UNIFEM   United Nations Development Program for Women
UNNGLS   United Nations Non-Governmental Liason Service
USAID   United States Agency for International Development

VHP   Vishwa Hindu Parishad [World Hindu Council]
VKP   General Confederation of Trade Unions [Russia]
               [formerly the VTsSPS]

WBCSD   World Business Council on Sustainable Development
               [formerly Business Council on Sustainable Development]
WCL   World Confederation of Labour
WEDO   Women's Environment and Development Organization
WFTU   World Federation of Trade Unions
WIB   Women in Black
WICZNET   Women and Conflict Zones Network
WIDE   Women in Development Europe
WILPF   Women's International League for Peace and Freedom
WIN   Women's International Network
WMS   Women for Mutual Security
WTO   World Trade Organization
WWF   World Wildlife Fund

ZGKSM   Zahreeli Gas Kand Sngarash Morcha

1

GLOBAL SOCIAL MOVEMENTS

TOWARDS A COSMOPOLITAN POLITICS

Robin Cohen and Shirin M. Rai

This opening chapter serves both to introduce this book and to advance some arguments about the possibilities of new forms of global politics that go beyond the specific claims made by our authors. We start by defining the expression 'social movements', describe how 'new' social movements emerged in the 1970s and explain why it is important to recognize that 'global social movements' (GSMs) are now altering earlier agendas for social change and political engagement. Next, we explain why we selected the examples of GSMs contained in this book. Finally, we will develop the argument that political life is now moving beyond the confines of the territorially bound nation state to take on new global and cosmopolitan dimensions. A short conclusion follows.

DEFINING SOCIAL MOVEMENTS IN GENERAL

The expression 'social movements' has gone in and out of fashion in sociology and political science, possibly in response to the unrealistic demands on the notion made by some scholars. As Wilson in his early impressive account observed (1973: 13) scholars had over-reached themselves to include fraternities, youth groups, political parties, sects, nudists, voluntary associations, guerrilla organizations, cool jazz or beat literature – all under the rubric of 'social movements'. On the other hand, as he also pointed out (p 5), it was impossible to ignore the influence of the Chartist, the Suffragette, the Abolitionist, the Prohibitionist, the Pentecostal, the Black militant, the John Bircher or the peace marcher. Even the flying-saucer spotter, the flat-earther, the sabbatarian and the Satanist have managed to attractive sizeable numbers of dedicated followers. 'Social movements' is the one expression that can hold these diverse phenomena together.

Using an earlier model developed by Aberle (1966), Wilson (1973: 14–29) favoured a typology that recognized four kinds of social movement – transformative, reformative, redemptive and alternative. *Transformative* movements seek to change the total social structure often by violent means or in anticipation of some cataclysmic change. This category could include movements of the political left, to which we will return later. But such a category alluded principally to millennial and fundamentalist religious movements. As Beckford makes clear in his contribution to this book, treating such movements as deviant, strange organizations led by charismatics and joined by fanatical followers is not particularly productive. What is required, he suggests, is an approach 'which is sensitive to the diversity of participants, the reticulate character of movements' social organization, and the diffuseness of ideas and sentiments at play in many mobilizations'. By adopting a 'fluid' approach to religious movements, their more diffuse influence on social relations and culture can be plotted. In his chapter on Islamic movements, Lubeck is also concerned to refute the conventional wisdom that Islamicism is pre-modern or even atavistic. Instead the 'Islamists' in his account embrace science and technology, are recruited from the middle classes and the universities and do not come from the old clerical orders or Sufi brotherhoods.

Wilson's second type of social movement is described as *reformative* – aiming at partial change to try to offset current injustices and inequalities. The adherents and followers of such movements believe that positive change to remove such features will create a more just social order and a more effective and viable polity. Typically, such a movement concentrates on one issue, though often a vital issue like the position of women or the possession of nuclear arms. In the first case, Stienstra shows in her contribution how strategies of 'disengagement' (see the 'alternative type' below) gave way to an attempt by many women's groups to 'mainstream' their activities. In other words while there are always elements in all social movements that wish totally to reject or ignore current social arrangements, the international women's movement is reformative insofar as the bulk of its activities is intended to secure votes for women, produce equal pay, secure equal civic rights and generate equal access to goods, services, social esteem and political power. Again, in his chapter on the peace movement, Mattausch insists that the Campaign for Nuclear Disarmament (CND) did not comprise a group of people seeking to build 'a radically new social order'. In terms of their actions, while some demonstrations were confrontational most were well-ordered affairs.

Wilson's third type, *redemptive* movements, involves the total change of an individual whose problems are divorced from their social context and reduced to the issue of personality change and personal betterment. Again, the religious movements, including so-called new religious movements (NRMs), provide rich examples of this form. The Soka Gakkai starting in Japan, L. Ron Hubbard's Scientology movement starting in the USA and Transcendental Meditation started by the Maharishi Mahesh Yogi in India, all rapidly spread out of their home bases, thus demonstrating Beckford's point (below) that the emphasis on the individual's well-being is not incompatible with the global ambitions and wide reach of such movements.

Finally, Wilson uses the expression *alternative* movements, though not in the sense that we will adopt here. By 'alternative' we allude to the countercultural values, the rejection of materialism and the development of unconventional life-styles characteristic of some Western youth, a phenomenon often dated from the 1960s. Environmental social movements often contain the contemporary equivalents of those espousing similar 'life-style politics'. The adherents to such movements do not necessarily want to change the system, nor do they necessarily seek to reform it (though conventional 'green politics' has become more common in Scandinavia and Germany since the 1980s). Many seek rather to develop viable, sustainable alternative life-styles, conserving of energy and scarce resources and more in touch with spiritual values.

The sheer diversity of the examples so far adduced signals that social movement theorizing is bound to be a hazardous business. The four-fold typology we have initially introduced has to be surrounded with the usual cautionary notices. No one social movement fits exactly into each box; movements change over time and they contain diverse elements. There are also likely to be significant differences in the outlooks and motivations of the leadership, core adherents, followers and those influenced by social movements. It is thus very difficult to reduce such heterogeneity to a single definition without appearing bland or obvious. Indeed, this is the danger of Wilson's (1973: 8) prosaic definition: 'A social movement is a conscious, collective, organised attempt to bring about or resist large-scale change in the social order by non-institutionalised means.'

Although it is acceptable in a formal sense, probably the worst aspect of such a definition is the loss of sensitivity to the social and personal characteristics of many active participants in social movements. This loss is akin perhaps to saying that an apple is an edible, generally spherical fruit, green or red in colour of about 25–30 cm in circumference, without also saying that it is juicy, crunchy, delicious, but sometimes bruised, tart or floury. To give him his due, Wilson (1973: 5) senses this lack of 'taste' and 'colour' himself and supplements his definition with a more imaginative description:

> Social movements nurture both heroes and clowns, fanatics and fools. They function to move people beyond their mundane selves to acts of bravery, savagery, and selfless charity. Animated by the injustices, sufferings, and anxieties they see around them, men and women in social movements reach beyond the customary resources of the social order to launch their own crusade against the evils of society. In so doing they reach beyond themselves and become new men and women.

These somewhat unconventional aspects of social movements are also reflected in more recent discussions, including that of Byrne (1997: 10–11). For him social movements are:

- *unpredictable* (e.g. women's movements do not always arise where women are most oppressed);
- *irrational* (adherents do not act out of self-interest);
- *unreasonable* (adherents think they are justified in flouting the law); and
- *disorganized* (they avoid formalizing their organization even when it seems like a good idea to do so).

Finally we can refer to Zirakzadeh (1997: 4–5) who suggests that contemporary social movements:

- comprise a group of people who consciously attempt to build a radically new social order;
- involve people of a broad range of social backgrounds and provide an outlet for the political expressions by the non-powerful, non-wealthy and non-famous; and
- deploy confrontational and socially disruptive tactics involving a style of politics that supplements or replaces conventional political activities like lobbying or working for a political party.

'NEW' AND 'OLD' SOCIAL MOVEMENTS

Perhaps we have now reached the point where we have a working understanding, if not a watertight definition, of the phenomena those using the expression 'social movement' seek to uncover and depict. But this will not end our theoretical quest. For even if we accept that all social movements evolve and mutate, we have to consider the argument that there was a radical break, starting in the 1970s, between the 'old' and 'new' social movements. The basis for this thesis is enunciated, for example, by Boggs (1995: 331): 'The themes that permeated and galvanized the New Left [during the period 1968–70] – participatory democracy, community, cultural renewal, collective consumption and the restoration of nature – have been typically carried forward into the modern ecology, feminist, peace and urban protest movements that have proliferated since the 1970s.'

Boggs is predominantly concerned with defending the argument that the politics of the 1960s were not irrational, destructive, hedonistic and futile against the contrary assertions of a number of conservative US political commentators. His contention is structured around the proposition that there is an enduring legacy of the New Left that remains distinct from conventional class politics and Marxism on the one hand and is politically effective in challenging bureaucratization and centralized power on the other. He emphasizes how *local* struggles for empowerment, particularly in the ecological and feminist movements, 'take on particular significance here, insofar as they both represent, in different ways, efforts to overcome alienation, a sense of imbalance and domination. These movements ideally embellish not only democratization but also a recovery of the self in a world in which politics has been deformed' (p 349). (This emphasis on *local* struggles is characteristic of the literature on 'new' social movements and we will return to this feature shortly.)

Boggs's depiction of left politics in the USA can be usefully contrasted with European social theorists who also suggested, though in a subtly different way, that 'new' social movements had emerged out of the wreckage of the 'Events of May, 1968', when the French state appeared virtually to collapse in the face of street demonstrations and strikes. 'Everyone', the eminent French sociologist Raymond Aron said, 'was in the grip of a kind of delirium. The French people, and certainly the people of Paris, felt that the state had disappeared, that there was no more government and that once more anything was possible' (quoted in Caute, 1988: 239). The decisive reassertion of state power buttressed by conventional military and police power and the old-fashioned nationalist rhetoric of de Gaulle, profoundly depressed and incensed the constellation of progressive forces that had engendered the mood of delirium. Unlike in the USA, in Europe organized labour had formed an important part of the progressive front. The student body, which provided so much oppositional energy in 1968 was less anarchic, less affluent and less cut off from the working class than its US equivalent.

Frustrated by their defeat, the radical and left intelligentsia in Europe denounced the 'betrayal' by the 'old left' and consigned the labour movement to the ranks of an 'old' social movement. The 'old left' was said to be preoccupied merely with 'emancipatory/rights politics' and unable to comprehend the 'life politics' of the 'new social movements' (Giddens, 1990). As Munck adds later in this book other distinctions were equally boldly articulated. Whereas the struggles of labour, for national self-determination and civic rights were located 'merely' within the polity, the 'new' social movements were said to operate within civil society at large. Whereas the 'old' social movements were thought wedded irremediably within the dominant political system, the 'new' social movements wanted changes in social values or life-styles. Again, whereas 'the worker's movement has usually stressed political mobilization, the "new" social movements often went for direct action and/or daring attempts at cultural innovations' (Munck, below).

As Havemann argues in his contribution, the notion of 'new' social movements also echoed the post-modernist and post-structuralist accounts of the time. Meta-narratives, such as Marxism, liberalism and socialism were rejected in favour of 'the radical contingency of structures and events'. This stress on particularistic responses opened the way for pluralist, identity politics, and local challenges to dominant political discourses and structures at the level of neighbourhoods and local communities. Grassroots, bottom-up, network-based modes of organization were said to parallel and thought bound to replace the formal, hierarchical structure of the 'old' political and labour movements (Touraine, 1981; Melucci, 1989).

It would be a gross exaggeration to suggest that the distinction between 'old' and 'new' social movements was vapid or did not reflect some real shifts in the nature of political opposition. The 'new' social movements introduced a number of tactical and organizational innovations, using the newly recognized power of the media and the expanded circuits of communications more generally. They also spoke to a new audience in a different way with a different voice. The audience was no longer simply a local or national one: it became global. The modes of communication changed with widening access to the Internet, especially in Western countries, as did the speed at which information was exchanged through e-mail. While, arguably, the 'old' social movements spoke primarily to or against the nation state, the voice of the 'new' movements reached beyond the borders of the nation. There has been an attempt to enclose within their message sensitivity to the localized differences among their constituents, as well as universalized demands – on the grounds, for example, of humanity, ecology or generational sustainability. These changes have not followed any predictable patterns. Take, for example, Zirakzadeh's description (1997: 57) of the women's movement in West Germany during the 1970s:

> [Earlier] the vast majority of politically active women who were concerned with the problems of women at work and in the home tended to place their faith in parties especially the Social Democratic Party. In contrast the new women's movement was a current of women's politics that sought to liberate women by creating 'autonomous spaces' (that is, spaces from which men were excluded) where women could comfortably discuss issues relating to sexuality, child rearing and home life.

As contrasting examples in the UK and India, the politics of disengagement has gone into reverse. While the earlier women's movements were suspicious of any involvement with the state and its institutions, this position has shifted in the last decade, allowing women's groups to participate more fully in institutional politics (McBride and Mazur, 1995; Rai, 2000). The limitations of disengagement were also more apparent as soon as Western feminists sought to internationalize and reach out to their sisters in other countries. As Stienstra and Cockburn show in their contributions to this book, it was apparent that the denial of civic and political rights, social repression and economic inequality (the 'old' emancipation agenda) were the defining conditions of most women in most parts of the world. The mere fact of being a woman was an inadequate glue to fix a single identity, as 'new' social movement theory assumed. Instead, Cockburn maintains, women's groups will act together with a shared purpose 'only by means of conscious and careful processes of boundary-crossing, agenda-setting and alliance-building'. Her analysis of women's projects in three conflict-torn countries under the aegis of Women Building Bridges provides evidence of how tortuous was this process of linkage and solidarity.

Similarly, a review of the history, complexity and subsequent evolution of other social movements eludes any simple bisection into 'new' and 'old'. Let us take two cases in support of this proposition, starting first with the labour movement. For the European intelligentsia, who made most of the theoretical running, the 'old' social movements were often reduced to the labour and socialist movements. However, as we have shown by reference to Wilson's classic account (1973), the American tradition was more diverse and *included* social movements that were concerned with 'life politics' and 'identity politics'. Utopian communes, cargo cults, the Black Panthers and the Women's Christian Temperance Union all make an entrance in his account while, by contrast, the labour movement simply does not appear. Again, as Munck and Ashwin demonstrate in this book, the labour movement had itself mutated to take on some aspects of the new social movements (thus the expression 'social movement unionism'). It had consciously began to reach out towards tactical and strategic alliances with other social movements – a tendency to which we will return.

Secondly, and oddly, one of the most potent of contemporary social movements, the human rights movements, was virtually elided from the accounts provided by the 'new' social movement theorists. As Baxi points out in his contribution to this book, the human rights movement straddles the distinction between 'old' and 'new' social movements. This movement and its sub-movements (e.g. the anti-racist, indigenous peoples, pro-refugee, anti-apartheid, anti-torture movements and campaigns against corporate social irresponsibility) layered beneath the human rights rubric seek *both* political change and social transformation. They are thus concerned both with life- and emancipatory politics. The human rights movement in particular revealed the real limits of adopting oppositional stances to oppressive structures only in the form of local, anti-bureaucratic and participatory activities. By its very nature 'human' implied a universal, global view and linked back to the emancipatory traditions of the 'old' social movements.

THE RISE OF GLOBAL SOCIAL MOVEMENTS?

It short, we argue that the distinction between 'old' and 'new' social movements is less salient and less convincing than many scholars believe. We present this argument rather forcibly partly because we sense that the continued theoretical investment in gnawing again and again on this bone of contention is producing rapidly diminishing returns. Such a debate also misses the crucial datum that the world has moved on since the 1970s and 1980s and a number of important social movements have moved on with it. A related point is made by Lynch (1998: 149), who argues that because new social movement theorists wanted to reject 'old' forms of politics that were thought too class-based, there was 'a discursive demobilization of movements on questions of economic praxis'. Social movements have thus been late in articulating a normative challenge to the looming reality of globalization.

Even if their discourse has been deficient, in practice the mobilization of capital on an increasingly global scale has forced a number of social movements to move rapidly away from the national, let alone local, scale of opposition and confrontation. The description of certain social movements as 'global' or 'transnational' is increasingly common, though the shift of social movements to a world scale has thus far been weakly theorized. In a pioneering collection on this change, Jackie Smith *et al.* (1997: 59–60) provide the following portrayal:

> Social movements may be said to be transnational when they involve conscious efforts to build transnational cooperation around shared goals that include social change. Through regular communication, organizations and activists are able to share technical and strategic information, coordinate parallel activities, or even to mount truly transnational collective action. Like national social movements transnational ones incorporate a range of political actors including individuals, church groups, professional associations and other social groups. Movements are distinguished by the actors and resources they mobilize and in the extent to which they communicate, consult, coordinate and cooperate in the international arena.

It may be that we again need to add some 'taste' and 'colour' to this definition. To do so we consider a number of circumstances that impel or permit some movements to 'go global'.

First, a global age needs global responses. Increasingly, policies are being made and decisions taken by political units outside the nation state. (This is not, by the way, naively to proclaim the state's imminent demise.) Some figures are illustrative. In 1993 there were over 15,000 transnational institutions of all kinds, 90 per cent of which had emerged since 1960. The number of international non-governmental organizations (INGOs) with consultative status at the UN increased five-fold over the period 1970–95. The world summits on the environment, social development, population and women in the 1990s each involved several thousand participants. Table 1.1 provides some additional indicative data on this tendency for some parts of political life to locate outside the nation state system.

Second, the development of cheap 'real time' communications networks (the telephone, fax, Internet and satellite transmissions), together with affordable travel opportunities and denser links between countries, have provided a permissive factor allowing organization of social movements on a global scale.

Third, as globalization has advanced the capacity for powerful transnational actors, like the transnational corporations, to mix and match flows of minerals, raw materials, manufactured goods, information and services from many sites worldwide has outstripped the capacity of local or national social movements to oppose and contest their plans. Political activity has thus to adapt to a larger terrain, particularly in the case of the international labour movement and movements allied with it.

Fourth, a global logic has been forced notably too on the environment movement, much as it had been on the peace movement in earlier decades. Nuclear fall-out does not respect state frontiers while MAD (mutually assured destruction) at the height of the Cold War was predicated on the destruction of the world several times over. In the environmental field, the destruction of the forest cover in Brazil affects the global climate, Indonesian forest fires have

Organization	Date	Support	Density	Other comments
IGOs	1980s	No. 700	5,000 meetings a year	e.g. Universal Postal Union, NATO
INGOs	1990s	No. 23,000 (five-fold growth 1970–95)	Spend 15–20% of OECD funds to the South	INGOs provide support to 100,000 NGOs in the South serving 100 million people
Greenpeace International and Rainbow Warrior campaign	1985	3 million members in 158 countries	5 million sign petition on anti-nuclear testing campaign	15,000 in Tahiti force French to allow the docking of Greenpeace ships
Worldwide Fund for Nature	1990s	4.7 million members	In 31 countries including 12 in the South	Projects in 96 countries
Friends of the Earth	1990s	1 million members	In 56 countries, 23 in the South	Six large UK retail chains boycott rain-forest timber

Table 1.1 *Indicative data on international organizations and global social movements*

regional effects, emissions from many countries thin out the earth's ozone layer, while chemical waste discharged from one country's shore washes up on another. Without transnational coordination environmental movements simply are impotent (Cohen and Kennedy, 2000: Ch. 18).

Fifth, in the case of the labour, human rights and women's movements, there is an implied universal logic, such that sub-national, national or regional struggles can only be considered tactical, not strategic, interventions. Workers of the *world* are enjoined to unite not just the workers of Italy or Brazil. People have rights by virtue of their *human* qualities, not because of their ethnicity, civic status or nationality. Women are oppressed by patriarchy and gender inequality *everywhere*, despite the fact that the level of oppression will vary considerably. The case of religions is somewhat different. Some, like Zoroastrianism or Judaism, are non-proselytising – therefore their demands are for recognition or protection (a human rights issue). Others, like Christianity or Islam, seek universal conversion so often demand the right to preach, pray and convert in contexts where the state represents a rival and hostile source of authority. The universal claims of Catholicism (for example), which pre-dated the rise of the nation-state system, are also now being increasingly asserted or reasserted.

Finally, globalization at the level of politics, economics, environmental challenges and religious belief are paralleled by a certain convergence in values, though this is far from complete. Kriesberg (1997) lays particular emphasis on the spread of democratization, though he accepts that only 20 per cent of the world's population live in 'free' countries. The point is perhaps better made by suggesting that aspirations towards democratization are becoming more universal and further that states (in the liberal tradition the guarantors and founts of democratic liberties) are now often the source of despotism. GSMs often provide alternative fora for democratic impulses and activities.

THE CONTENT OF THIS BOOK

As editors of this book we decided that the principal cases of movements that had moved along a global path were the human rights, women's, environmental, labour, religious and peace movements and, with the exception of the last, we solicited two contributions on each social movement. Visibility, resurgence, 'importance', influence and numbers of supporters and followers identified at least two in the list – the women's and environmental movements. We thought it important to recognize the human rights movement, perhaps even more than in the first three cases mentioned, for at least three reasons. First, as has been stated, this movement has been poorly integrated into the social movements, particularly the 'new' social movements literature, despite its inherent and increasing importance. Jackie Smith (1997: 47) estimates that, by 1993, 27 per cent of the 631 global social movement organizations listed in the Yearbook of International Organizations were in the human rights sector. Second, we suggest that the human rights movements is an umbrella category for a number of other important component movements. Within the human rights movement, we might like to recognize, for example, the movement for indigenous peoples, the anti-apartheid movement, movements to protect political prisoners or refugees and the anti-racist movements. Finally, to supplement Baxi's general discussion of the human rights movement, we found that Havemann's treatment of the indigenous people's movement was particularly illustrative of the ways in which the 'local' and the 'global' have now become intermeshed. The heart of the paradox is that indigenous movements can only gain their support by asserting their difference, but they cannot succeed in the quest for recognition without showing their similarly to other oppressed peoples in other settings.

In the case of the two contributions on the women's movement (Steinstra and Cockburn), we have already shown how the internationalism has fused 'old' and 'new' agendas and linked local and global struggles. Environmental movements also draw their energy from conjoining the local and the global, though our contributors rather differ on the extent to which they think the Green's global credentials are opportunistic, exaggerated or deleterious. Yearley and Forrester are concerned to prick the moral smugness of the environmental spokespersons. They find their assertion that they can speak on behalf of humanity leads to utopianism and a bias towards the agendas set by activists in the North.

Environmentalists in the North take on the easy targets like the unpopular oil company, Shell, while avoiding more contested discussions that may involve taking on board the claims and needs of those in the South. Newell takes a different view, commencing with the apparent evacuation of the role of regulating the big polluting companies by national states. For him, 'the retreat of the state' and the states' failure effectively to police the environmental impact of the companies' activities has propelled environmental NGOs to fill the political vacuum – forging alliances with consumers, adopting high-profile unconventional tactics, seeking to influence institutional investors and occasionally co-operating with the companies themselves.

We have mentioned before the question of the international labour movement. It is undoubtedly the case that the distinctive history and symbolic importance of the labour movement often placed it in a category of its own. For Marx and Marxists, the proletariat was not merely a segmented, special interest group but 'the general representative' of humankind. The struggle of the worker against the capitalist was to be the final struggle, not one among many. Labour activists who followed this tradition were often dismissive of other theatres of contestation. They defined themselves as outside of the phenomenon of social movements or thought themselves only able to co-operate with other progressive forces from a privileged position. The experience of May 1968, the collapse of official communism and the rampant march of economic globalization have humbled and reformed the labour movement. As Ashwin and Munck show in this book the goals of the international labour movement are now more modest and more achievable, and many activists are able to recognize their affinity and resemblance to other social movements, while links particularly with women's and democratic movements are now common, accepted and welcomed (see also Waterman, 1998).

Like the labour movement, religion (conceived as a single social force) was not conventionally treated as a social movement, though the analysis of many individual sects and churches and tendencies were central to the American tradition of social movement theorizing. However, the link between religion, GSMs and globalization generates major new insights, as we see in our contributions by Beckford and Lubeck. The evolution and diffusion of the big global religions are vital parts of the process of globalization. Religious movements and GSMs are intimately linked. Finally, globalization has had a major impact on the character and spread of religious movements, new and old. So religion is simultaneously cause, part and consequence of globalization.

The final GSM we consider is the peace movement. Though this movement has been relatively quiescent since 1987 when the Intermediate-range Nuclear Treaty was signed, the real achievements of the movement remain important. Continuing pressure fostered the subsequent signing of the Non-Proliferation Treaty and the Comprehensive Test Ban Treaty. In his retrospective treatment of the CND, Mattausch insists 'the peace movement has been largely reactive in character' and often involved a remarkably restricted range of supporters in terms of their class and educational backgrounds. Nonetheless, the movement developed 'campaigning skills, experience, knowledge and inspiration', adding to a 'growing repertoire of tactics and strategies from which future campaigners may select'. Today, as Lynch (1998: 152) reminds us, there are still dangerous and potent issues to be addressed in the field of peace. The deregulation of arms in the post Cold War era has placed weapons in the hands of a wider group of political actors. Moreover, the campaigns to ban anti-personnel land mines has gained force in the wake of civilian injuries in former theatres of war in Vietnam, Cambodia, Laos, Mozambique, Somalia and Bosnia, among other places.

Naturally the authors of our chapters on the six selected GSMs have provided examples of the campaigns and activities of particular organizations within the broader rubrics they have chosen. This immediately raises the question of the manifold relationships that might arise between the overarching movement and its component or allied parts. Even the vocabulary describing these elements is unstable. We have adopted 'global social movements' in marginal preference to 'transnational social movements', though the expressions appear largely inter-changeable. Do we want further to make distinctions between non-governmental organizations (NGOs), international non-governmental organizations (INGOs), social movement organizations (SMOs) and transnational/global social move-ment organizations (TSMOs/GSMOs) (see Kriesberg, 1997: 13)? On the whole the contributors to this book came to a simple, working solution. We conceive smaller and more structured organizations like INGOs as *imbricated* within the larger GSMs. 'Within' rather than 'below', as the scales of a fish or the slates on a roof are not hierarchically arranged.

The particular arrangement of the slates would be contingent, changing and specific to a particular GSM. Some like Amnesty International, would follow the international lines of the nation-state system – with branches established in particular national jurisdictions. Other lines of slates would be deliberately based

Global social movement	*INGO (two examples of each discussed in this book)*
Human rights	International Coalition of Justice for Bhopal/Movement for the Survival of the Ogoni People
Women	Development Alternatives for Women for a New Era/Women in Black
Environment	Friends of the Earth/Coalition for Environmentally Responsible Economies
Labour	International Confederation of Free Trade Unions/World Federation of Trade Unions
Religion	Jehovah's Witnessess/Family Federation for World Peace and Unification (The Unification Church)
Peace	Campaign for Nuclear Disarmament/European Nuclear Disarmament

Table 1.2 *Global social movements and international non-governmental organizations (INGOs) in this book*

not on territorial branches, but on deterritorialized global networks. Some would only intermittently connect with the larger global issue of which they formed part. A sense of the coverage provided in this book can be seen in Table 1.2.

TOWARDS A COSMOPOLITAN POLITICS

What does the rise of GSMs and their ancillary and allied INGOs signify? We have hinted throughout this introductory chapter at a number of developing possibilities. These are best conceived around the idea of an emerging cosmopolitan politics.

As in the somewhat romanticized view of the birth of democracy in the Greek city state, politics needs a forum. Devetak and Higgott (1999: 491–2) suggest that a new 'embryonic global public sphere' is opening up, providing a new arena that allows space and voice to social movements, non-state actors, 'global citizens', international organizations and states. It is instructive that they include state actors in this global forum, even as they recognize that the state's legitimacy is weakening in the face of losing its near-monopoly on the loyalties of its citizenry. States, in effect, have to compete to stay in the game. The nation state is now increasingly one 'power-container' among many claiming primacy and fealty. This process of 'loyalty-bidding' and 'identity-claiming' may hopefully be seen as healthy competition that will empower citizens and force national political elites to earn their place in the global sun.

Vertovec and Cohen (1999) describe how the evolution of cosmopolitan politics requires not only a forum but also systems of relationships best described as 'networks'. This phenomenon is extensively analysed by Castells (1996) in his recent trilogy. The networks' component parts – connected by nodes and hubs – are both autonomous from, and dependent upon, their complex systems of relationships. Dense and highly active networks spanning vast spaces are transforming many kinds of social, cultural, economic and political relationships. Gupta and Ferguson (1992: 9) contend that

> Something like a transnational public sphere has certainly rendered any strictly bounded sense of community or locality obsolete. At the same time, it has enabled the creation of forms of solidarity and identity that do not rest on an appropriation of space where contiguity and face-to-face contact are paramount.

Further, Wakeman (1988: 86) suggests that the 'loosening of the bonds between people, wealth, and territories' which is concomitant with the rise of complex networks 'has altered the basis of many significant global interactions, while simultaneously calling into question the traditional definition of the state.'

In their path-breaking collection, Guarnizo and Smith (1998: 3–34) properly warn that we cannot automatically assume that transnationalism from below is something to celebrate. Political actors are generally not free-floating, deterritorialized subjects engaged in creative forms of social resistance through their writings, speeches, or perhaps through their very existence. Such a depiction is perhaps better understood as a rather fanciful self-projection of post-modernist writers. As Guarnizo and Smith insist, the 'discursive spaces through which transnational actors move are socially structured' (p 21). Even in transnational politics, they continue, we cannot forget the traditional axes of discrimination and disadvantage: patriarchal gender relations, racial hierarchies, class inequalities and differential access to the means of production, distribution, exchange and communication. It merely reinforces this point to refer to an instructive account of transnational activists by Keck and Sikkink (1998: 199–217). While centring their account on the cosmopolites themselves, they also are clear that individuals both are reliant on the density and power of particular advocacy networks and have to acknowledge the continuing political efficacy of states.

Despite these legitimate warnings, there is no doubt that place and localities have been fundamentally reconstituted by the emergence of cosmopolitan politics. The nationalist project was to make space and identity coincide. However, practices and meanings derived from old loyalties (religious, ethnic, regional, linguistic and specific geographical and historical points of origin) are increasingly transferred and regrounded outside national spaces. Today, a high degree of human mobility, together with telecommunications, films, video and satellite TV, and the Internet have created or regenerated trans-local understandings. Often these are still anchored in places, with a variety of legal, political and cultural ramifications, not only for the practices and meanings, but for the places as well. However, transnationalism has changed people's relations to space particularly by creating 'social fields' that connect and position some actors in more than one country. Appadurai (1995: 213) discerns that many people face increasing difficulties of relating to, or indeed producing, 'locality' ('as a structure of feeling, a property of life and an ideology of situated community'). This, he reckons, is due not least to a condition of transnationalism which is characterized by, among other things, 'the growing disjuncture between territory, subjectivity and collective social movement' and by 'the steady erosion of the relationship, principally due to the force and form of electronic mediation, between spatial and virtual neighbourhoods.' There have emerged, instead, what are described as new 'translocalities' (Appadurai, 1995; Smith, 1998).

Separating from their former subordination to the nation state are communities based on ethnicity, religion or occupation. The first have been described as 'global diasporas', designating the re-emergence of affinities that pre-date the nation state or new social formations that imitate and develop similar loyalties (Cohen, 1997). We have already mentioned the salience of global religious communities. But as a new programme of research of transnational communities demonstrates (see *www.transcomm.ox.ac.uk*), a wide range of new social formations are emerging that cross boundaries. International bureaucrats, gun runners, drug peddlers, sportspersons, musicians, seafarers or sex workers often share a specific occupational and class character that is not easily reduced to national categories. Alongside the TNCs, Sklair (1998) proposes that there has arisen a transnational capitalist class consisting of TNC

1650–1850	1850–1980	1980–2000+
Parochial and patronized	*National and autonomous*	*Transnational and solidaristic*
Food riots	Strikes	Band Aid concerts
Destruction of toll gates	Electoral rallies	Telethons
Machine sabotage	Public meetings	Earth/Women's summits
Expulsions of tax officials	Insurrections	International consumer boycotts

Table 1.3 *Three types of repertoire (with sample actions), after Tilly*

executives, globalizing state bureaucrats, politicians and professionals, and consumerist elites in merchandizing and the media. Together, Sklair claims, they constitute a new power elite whose interests are global, rather than exclusively local or national, and who thereby control most of the world economy. Virtual communities are developing in cyberspace, while elective communities of interest and political activism are developing around the global social movements that form the subject of this book.

With these shifts of loyalties, identities and senses of place and the development of transnational communities has emerged a new transnational political repertoire. The potent idea of 'repertoire' was developed particularly by Tilly (1978, 1981) who saw that the hoary debate as to whether agency or structure was predominant in human affairs was therefore easier to resolve. People make their own history, but only from a list of plays that have been designated by the company to which they belong. Precognition, ideology and action are united by the word 'repertoire'. In like manner social movements can develop their own ideas, agendas and forms of protest, but only from a range of possibilities and political opportunities that present themselves. However, we are not so much interested in the general advantages of the notion of a repertoire, as in Tilly's insight that it was possible to date, in rough terms, two phases of repertoire, signifying the movement from parochial to national forms of protest. He demonstrates his argument by reference to some typical forms of protest. We simply add a third, transnational column, with some illustrative examples (Table 1.3).[1]

CONCLUSION

Many social scientists have seen transnational corporations (TNCs) as the major institutional form of transnational practices and the key to understanding globalization (e.g. Sklair, 1995). This is due not least to the sheer scale of operations, since much of the world's economic system is dominated by the TNCs (Dicken, 1992). TNCs represent globe-spanning structures that are presumed to have largely jettisoned their national origins. Their systems of supply, production, marketing, investment, information transfer and management often create the paths along which much of the world's transnational activities flow (cf. Castells, 1996). The triumph of neo-liberalism, free trade and the agenda driven by the World Bank in the wake of the end of state communism would seem to have given a massive endorsement to this form of economic globalization.

For a number of commentators (e.g. Lynch, 1998) the principal task of the GSMs is to mount a discursive and practical challenge to economic global-ization as the principal force that adversely affects peoples' jobs, communities and the environment. 'Democracy, human rights, the "natural world" and peace, according to this logic, are threatened on a global scale' (p 156). The problem with such a defensive strategy is that proposals derived from a reactive agenda sound dangerously utopian and reactionary. A new protectionism mounted around relocalization, reinvestment and rediversification may generate consider-able rhetorical appeal, particularly to those who still are locked into the logic of local, participatory democracy. However, we are convinced, as our discussion of cosmopolitanism politics indicates, that the genie of transnationalism has largely escaped the exclusive confines of the local, parochial and national. Sometimes all levels can productively feed off each other. However, this did not happen until recently in the case of the international labour movement, which was severely weakened, then by-passed, by adopting protectionism in the face of the over-whelming global dynamic of capital. Other social movements need to learn the bitter lesson that they need to adapt.

Without a transnational framework – a global public space or forum – the possibilities for opposition and protest are seriously weakened. We need to think of the possible emergence of an alternative global civil society. The GSMs are part of this alternative vision and practice of globalization, one in marked conflict to the global offerings of the TNCs, the World Trade Organization and the World Bank. As our contributors show, their campaigns and protests are often popular and compelling. The need for a powerful global alternative, working with the grain of history rather than against it, will also force alliances between GSMs, a phenomenon that is still relatively under-explored in the literature. Some alliances have already taken institutional form – Greenpeace and Women Workers Worldwide provide two examples in their very names. This book provides suggestions though there remains room for much more discussion on the conditions, outcomes and possibilities of co-operation between GSMs and those organizations imbricated with them.

This thesis was given dramatic confirmation by the protests surrounding the meeting of the World Trade Organization in Seattle in December 1999. Even on the estimates of the conservative US newspapers (for example, *Newsweek* 13 December 1999) the numbers of protesters involved were 40,000. Activist groups claimed up to 20,000 more (*www.gatt.org* provides an alternative to the official WTO site). The protesters mounted a generalized attack on global consumerism and the domination of the transnational corporations. They also advanced specific causes like opposing the importation of US hormone-fed beef to France; demanding cheaper AIDS drugs for the developing countries; attempting to save turtles caught in shrimp nets; seeking to protect rain-forests and to ban genetically-modified food and demonstrating against local job losses by an apparently rejuvenated US labour movement. Partly through the incompetence of the negotiators, but also in response to the protests, the conference ground to an undignified halt amid accusations of mismanagement by the city authorities and police brutality. The chaotic, fluid, coalition street politics of the emerging GSMs confused and mystified US politicians and commentators but, as this book shows, conventional nationally-focused party politics will soon have to compete with the politics of an emerging global civil society.

2

ENMESHED IN THE WEB?

INDIGENOUS PEOPLES' RIGHTS IN THE NETWORK SOCIETY

Paul Havemann

Ethnocide, genocide and destruction of indigenous people's life chances have featured in all phases of globalization, while debates about – and, frequently, denial of – the human rights of indigenous people have dominated the official discourse of empires since Columbian times. Today indigenous peoples are becoming their own agents, and increasingly using the Internet, in campaigns to enforce their human rights. This chapter attempts to theorize these developments through the interrelated conceptual frameworks of 'reflexive modernization' (Giddens, 1990; 1991, and especially 1994), 'globalization' (Gray, 1998; Martin and Schumann, 1998), 'the risk society' (Beck *et al.*, 1994) and 'the network society' (Castells, 1996). These frameworks show the layered complexities that need to be addressed in evaluating problems and prospects for all social movements for advancing human rights in the present age. Specific dimensions of indigenous peoples' involvement in the politics of rights is examined in terms of the following themes:

- genocide, ethnocide, modernization and the network society;
- globalization, cultural singularity and reflexivity;
- agendas for survival: indigeneity and cosmopolitanism;
- implications for indigenous peoples' struggles of information and communication technologies (ICTs); and
- the politics of rights for a network society.

GENOCIDE, ETHNOCIDE AND MODERNIZATION

The process of 'simple' modernization (Giddens, 1994: 78–103) spanning the fifteenth to early twentieth centuries brought ethnocide and genocide of indigenous peoples at every phase and dimension of the imperial project. First, capitalism via colonization brought the coerced extraction of wealth and labour power and racialized social hierarchies based on class. Second, the unfettered quest for economic growth and the ruthless conquest of nature brought destruction of indigenous peoples' economies, until then grounded on preservation of the ecosystems upon which sustainable production for use depends. Third, coercive evangelical Christians used the Bible to legitimate racialized social hierarchies. Finally, supposed Enlightenment truths based on scientific rationality (e.g. in the form of eugenics) were also used to legitimate racialized social hierarchies and the geographical segregation of peoples and their cultures according to their ethnicity.

'Advanced' modernization has been accompanied by trends which have compounded and accelerated ethnocide and genocide, such as

- the radical restructuring of capitalism for the globalization of the new economic order;
- the polarization of the rich North and the poor South;
- the acute instability and flexibility of work and the individualization of labour;
- continuing global, local and interpersonal violence;
- the emergence of social reflexivity, hence reflexive modernization, leading to accelerated detraditionalization (coerced and voluntary);
- the emergence of the risk society, involving the unprecedented capacity to manufacture ecocidal harms; and
- the marginalization of indigenous peoples both by the majoritarian 'democracy' of elective dictatorships and by military–industrial totalitarianism.

Indigenous peoples' cultural survival has been multiply jeopardized by both simple and advanced (reflexive) modernization. Within the 'Fourth World' of indigenous peoples (Manuel and Posluns, 1974; Dyck, 1985), the pace and nature of societal change is peculiarly inimical to their survival as distinct traditional communities based on ascribed ethnic identities. The risk society continues the atrocities of the imperial past, exacerbated now by humankind's capacity for global ecocide. Innumerable environmental catastrophes are destroying the few places still under the control of the indigenous peoples who inhabit them. There continues to be widespread prohibition of, or denial of respect for, indigenous peoples' esoteric knowledge and the languages, which are intrinsic to their cultures. Every dimension of the present age has specific and interrelated negative consequences for indigenous peoples. The need to enhance their life chances through rebalancing of power towards greater symmetry of power for them as individuals and as peoples is unparalleled in urgency. Perhaps this urgency explains their eager embrace of the new ICTs that, on the face of it, seem more likely to be part of the problem than part of the solution.

Indigenous peoples are burdened by what David Held terms 'nautonomy' (Held, 1995: 163–72) – a lack of autonomy and structured disempowerment resulting from and in the asymmetrical production, distribution and enjoyment of life chances. At the heart of this condition is the absence of empowering possibilities for active participation in the political processes necessary for optimizing life chances. The degradation of life chances for indigenous people is directly linked to their systematic exclusion from political participation in dominant polities and their lack of access to control over land, capital and all other means whereby their cultural and material survival may be secured.

Even within relatively benign power hierarchies, indigenous peoples experience a grossly nautonomic predicament (examples include the Saami in Scandinavia, First Nations in Canada, the Maori in New Zealand, Aboriginal and Torres Strait Island peoples in Australia, and the Romany in Europe). In Latin America, Asia and Africa, genocidal conditions predominate (Moody, 1988).

With the advance of the network society, nautonomy, risk, reflexivity, life chances and choices and ICTs have all become symbiotically intertwined as key factors in the knowledge/power equation. In the absence of knowledge, people are powerless; without access to ICTs, knowledge and information are denied, and powerlessness results. Access to ICTs is necessary but not sufficient to empower indigenous peoples to participate in the political processes by which they can try to combat the ecocidal and genocidal risks they face.

Beck suggests that, in the age of reflexive modernization, all politics is ultimately risk politics. Risk politics concerns two types of power relations. The first, well understood since Marx, concerns conflicts for power over the 'relations of production'. The second concerns the 'relations of definition' (Beck, 1998) which are now, in the informational age of reflexive modernization, unfolding as another major site of contestation for power. The relations of definition 'include the rules, institutions and capacities that structure the identification and assessment of risks: they are the legal, epistemological and cultural matrix in which risk politics is conducted' (Beck, 1998: 18–19). Globalization driven by transnational capital and employing ICTs is concentrating power over relations of both production and definition into fewer and increasingly unaccountable centres of control. Invariably, indigenous peoples continue to occupy the black holes of both industrial and informational capitalism.

For violently and consistently excluded groups such as indigenous peoples, access to core knowledge as defined by the powerful and freedom to participate in negotiating the relations of definition are crucial to their survival. Indigenous peoples have known this for a long time and consequently had to become enmeshed in the 'White man's' laws, parliaments and courts to assert the right to their very existence. There seems to be a close analogy in this regard between using the liberal legal 'technology' of rights and the new ICTs as political means to survival. Critical analysts of the relevance of 'rights talk' for social movement strategists warn of the need to distinguish between the politics of rights and the myth of rights (Sheingold, 1974). The former may be a valuable form of the politics of embarrassment, whereas the latter is often a disempowering and resource-intensive diversion. Like the liberal rights 'technology', ICTs are also endowed with the dual capacity to mystify or to be used as a potent political resource.

The ICTs have certainly added to the potential of the politics of rights because they enable indigenous peoples and other social movements to go beyond state-controlled law-making bodies and political arenas to disseminate damning information to shame and confront the powerful. The world can be presented instantaneously with information (and disinformation) exposing gaps between the promises of the powerful and the realities of the powerless.

Since the Second World War a raft of international and national human rights provisions relevant to indigenous peoples has emerged which lends itself to an ICT-assisted politics of rights. It is no coincidence that in the network or 'informational society' (Castells, 1997: 21) indigenous peoples are investing massively in ICTs. These technologies enable them to build sites of counter-hegemonic power which give unprecedented exposure to their politics of naming and shaming to reclaim their traditions and lands through the assertion of rights.

GLOBALIZATION, CULTURAL SINGULARITY AND REFLEXIVITY

Castells (1997: 1) asserts that 'Our world, and our lives are being shaped by the conflicting trends of globalization and identity'. The ideal for would-be stake-holders in the New World economic order seems to be a globalized, homogenized and decultured 'Macworld' identity, which esteems the ideology of atomistic individualism and the capacity for material consumption. This synthetic identity clashes with traditional conceptions of self and identity founded on minimally renegotiable cultural conceptions of status or social position. Castells suggests that manifestations of ethnopolitics across the world reflect a 'surge of wide-spread expressions of collective identity that challenges globalization and cosmo-politanism on behalf of cultural singularity' (Castells, 1997: 1).

Such cultural singularity based on ethnicity, for instance, is perceived to be resilient against the corrosive power of globalization through time and space. Indigenous languages and cultural forms can be integrated into use of the ICTs, making them ideal for networking, movement building and political action. Even where discourse of struggle is dominated by the interpretive monopoly of rights, notions of individual and property rights can be juxtaposed with indigenous peoples' collectivist conceptions of identity which are bound up with stewardship obligations to things and places. Support for indigenous peoples can be garnered by ensuring increased understanding of and sympathy with their values and beliefs from segments of dominant cultures, notably postmaterialist social movements such as the Greens.

By the same token, in the conflict between globalization and identity, the globality of the ICT revolution provides sources of power that can undermine the work of movements to salvage traditional identities. Access to ICTs and accelerated social reflexivity threaten to erode traditional values and to facilitate the loss of control over language and sacred and esoteric knowledge (Smith,

1998). To secure protection for these treasures they often have to be translated into intellectual property rights or cultural rights to be comprehended and protected by laws of the powerful.

ICTs can help to accelerate fundamentally destabilizing processes of societal atomization and cultural assimilation, as well as help consolidate tradition. Social reflexivity (Giddens, 1994: 8–25) provides the individual and the collectivity with increased capacities for detraditionalization and re-traditionalization that can lead to either social cohesion or atomized individualism. The risk is especially high when hitherto naturalized cultural meanings are being called into question and a range of alternatives made easily accessible. Reflexivity inducing a myriad of ambiguities is increasingly evident in indigenous peoples' ethnopolitics. Indigenous communities and organizations are now continuously challenged with questions about their basic modes of organization and membership. Typically, the axes of cleavage and convergence reflect tensions between eight paired constructs:

- primary identities and cosmopolitanism;
- exclusivity and hybridity;
- tribalism and individualism;
- self-determination and voluntary assimilation;
- tradition and 'modernization';
- eco-indigeneity and capitalist productivism;
- patriarchal gerontocracy and egalitarianism; and
- remote and urban peoples.

Tradition has never been static; hence, de-traditionalization, which includes re-traditionalization involving processes of adapting and refurbishing old traditions and inventing new ones, has always occurred (Adam, 1996). However, for indigenous peoples, coerced de-traditionalization has been experienced in the form of church and state-sponsored ethnocide and assimilation. The ICTs perpetuate this process, yet are now essential media in the process of voluntary re-traditionalization. ICTs are involved in the building and salvage of indigenous peoples' primary identities as a basis for politics.

The enigmatic and Janus-like phenomenon of the ICTs is no more evident than in the context of indigenous peoples' struggles. ICTs create media for change, producing outcomes which are both virtuous and vicious, empowering and disempowering, as capable of subverting and destabilizing command and control hierarchies as they are of augmenting the capacity for surveillance. Paradoxically, by the very nature of the web, the identifiable centres of control are more diffused and obscured. In human terms globalized relational sterility now goes hand in glove with globalized transactional intensity (Hewitt, 1998).

In the context of reflexive modernization ICTs are intrinsic to many deeply ambiguous processes for indigenous peoples, enmeshed willy-nilly in the web. As much as ICTs are a medium for activities inimical to indigenous peoples' cultural survival, any strategy for cultural survival is now inconceivable without

ICTs. Paradoxically, while ICTs make the crisis of identity more acute by sparking fission within indigenous peoples' communities, at the same time they can aid in fusing such communities together around primary identities.

AGENDAS FOR SURVIVAL:
INDIGENEITY AND COSMOPOLITANISM

Conflict over agendas for survival arises within indigenous communities, with the forces of globalization and with new social movements (NSMs) promoting a cosmopolitan globalism. Some conceptions about which rights are most important are shared by indigenous peoples and their actual and potential allies, the cosmopolitan NSMs; though the latter are more comfortable with rights talk, loose political alliances have regularly been forged when promoting environmental causes and indigenous peoples' rights claims. Nevertheless, though their agendas sometimes converge, the two types of movement are predicated on different types of identity and are seen to be emerging as distinctive formations of the network society (Castells, 1997: 9–12). Castells highlights three categories of identity:

1. A *legitimating identity,* such as nationality, is conferred or withheld by dominant institutions such as the state, thereby rationalizing privilege, domination and assimilation into and exclusion from the nation. Indigenous peoples' experience has frequently been that they have been stigmatized with a delegitimated or illegitimate identity.
2. A *resistance identity* is adopted by communities of resistance made up of those devalued and stigmatized by the dominant order, for instance those people reacting against globalization. Indigenous peoples often form such communities of resistance: indigeneity is their primary identity, constructed by reinforcing the connectedness of kin with places, language and traditions over time.
3. A *project identity* is generated by cosmopolitan social movements attempting to build new identities by redefining their position in 'glocal' society to transform dominant structures such as patriarchy or capitalist productivism. Post-materialist movements like the Greens, human rights movements, the peace movement and women's movement fall into this third category. They often make up 'Rainbow' coalitions promoting radical democracy. Globalism (Albrow, 1996) rather than globalization is their goal. For indigenous peoples, however, it is possible that globalism may seem no less assimilationist than globalization.

Indigenous peoples' 'communes of resistance' aim to conserve and if need be redefine tradition to sustain their primary identity. The essence of their primary identity rests in their right to define and perpetuate their traditions, culture and languages, hierarchies, customs, modes of governance and mode of land use. Indigenous peoples base membership on birth.

Project identities, on the other hand, are typified by those individuals constituting cosmopolitan social movements that base membership on choice. These are 'communities of assent' and dissent in which identity is seldom, if ever, ascriptively defined and membership is negotiable. Their pluralist discourse often reflects liberal tenets such as 'tolerance' of 'minorities'. Any respect for difference is balanced against the quest for universalism and individualism. Ecumenicalism challenges denominationalism and fundamentalism. Women's rights feminism challenges patriarchalism. Ecologism and post-material understandings of the relationship between humankind and nature challenge newly asserted indigenous proprietary claims which tend to be based on territoriality and self-determination.

The essentializing tendencies upon which indigeneity stands also create dissonance for some indigenous people whose identity, after a process of diaspora through several generations, is hybrid – less rooted in tradition and place. Cosmopolitans proposing pluralist and universalist human rights and egalitarian modes of governance also question essentialism, since their project identity is constituted by social reflexivity, which is based on the assumption that self and identity may be constructed through the deliberate choice of narratives for understanding one's ascribed identity and reconstituting an achieved one. Progress in terms of emancipation is often understood as freedom from tradition and hence the ability to make a destiny of one's own choosing rather than passively submitting to one bestowed by lineage or biology, for instance.

Cosmopolitan movements are made up of individuals whose self-constituting narratives rely upon a process of de-traditionalization/re-traditionalization aimed at creating a reflexively modern civil society (Boggs, 1993: 145–80). De-traditionalization is seen as a necessary means to achieve the emancipatory goals of cosmopolitan social movements, which must challenge traditional hierarchies to secure social equality. Thus, de-traditionalization and re-traditionalization are the essence of counter-hegemonic struggles against hegemonic tradition.

Castells (1997: 356) suggests that political developments in the network society will feature disintegrating state apparatuses, increasingly dense global networks, self-centred individual stakeholders in the globalized market and a layer of communes formed around resistance identities. Indigeneity is just such a resistance identity based on 'communities of descent'. The rights claimed are for cultural survival, the right to exclude and the right of self-determination as peoples.

Cosmopolitan social movements generate human rights discourses constituting a vision of global and local social citizenship consisting of bundles of rights for accessing myriad sites of power. They are based on project identities formed by voluntary associations of citizens aimed at making a global 'civil society'. Castells further argues that project identities based on cosmopolitan social movements are today in the vanguard of re-inventing politics (Lloyd, 1998: 13) and may rival the increasingly powerless state in making the political case for decommodified social relations in local and global public spheres. The transformative project cosmopolitan social movements are often about the 'ethic of humanity'-grounded universalist human rights talk (Davidson, 1993; Heelas, 1996: 207–10). The politics of affinity and the need to reconcile this with respect for difference are stressed. Utopian ideas about 'local' concepts of universal, albeit differentiated, citizenship (Kymlicka, 1995) underlie the thinking of many cosmopolitan social movements. Their focus is outward and futuristic rather than inward and historical.

Thus project identities are concerned with the politicization of everyday life and demand an acute social reflexivity that often makes the automatic compatibility of their agendas with tradition-based indigenous peoples' movements improbable. Resistance identities frequently require what to cosmopolitans appear as the practice of an essentializing, exclusionary, often patriarchal ethnopolitics for constructing primary identity out of the myriad hybrid, self and diasporic identities found among their potential eligible membership.

The politicization of ecocide and the relations of definition bring cosmopolitan green social movements into potential conflict with some indigenous peoples. Indigenous peoples are among the most vulnerable of the world's populations to environmental change, so that they may be described as 'the miner's canary for humanity'. A highly visible dimension of their nautonomy is that they are grossly over-represented among people suffering the worst impacts of environmental devastation. Indigenous peoples are often presumed to be endowed with an ethic of stewardship of the ecosystem which will endure, as it has for millennia, regardless of the immediate pressures of the modern political economy. Today, however, indigenous leaders are frequently faced with the invidious choice of being co-opted into development or adding to their own nautonomy by refusing co-optation or joint venture partnerships. Should they choose development, the result is equally invidious, as they are likely to be accused by some of their own people and some green social movements of '"saving" the village by destroying it' and to find their claim to indigeneity is delegitimated.

ICTS IMPLICATIONS FOR INDIGENOUS PEOPLES' MOVEMENTS

The information technology revolution alters the transformation of the material foundations of life, space and time, through the constitution of a space of flows and of timeless time, as expressions of dominant modes of action determined by controlling elites:

- the polarization of 'infocrats' and cyber paupers;
- the increasing surveillance and information control by unaccountable publicly and privately controlled ICTs;
- the rise of the networking form of organization and social movements;
- the emergence of a culture of real virtuality constructed by a pervasive, interconnected, diversified media system

- the demise of national citizenship and the rise of supra-state citizenship claims;
- the rise of the contracting out of the state and the demise of the welfare state;
- the rise of supra-state forms of governance and of feral transnational corporations (TNCs); and
- the consolidation of hierarchies of power based on ethnicity, gender, region and class and access to the ICTs.

In theory, network society might seem to be quite hospitable to 'communes of resistance' and cosmopolitan social movements and the ICTs might seem to be offering new sites of power; in practice, however, the chasm between North and South, First and Fourth World over access to the ICTs is widening. All types of counter-hegemonic movements continue to face hostility from state and market élites. Increasingly, in network society, they may also be rendered docile virtual movements occupying a cyberspace black hole without any serious purchase on real sites of power. An inescapable and growing dimension of contemporary globalization is a lack of progress towards empowering peoples of the South, as well as all indigenous peoples, to enable them to overcome their nautonomy and achieve self-determination (Baxi, 1996).

Few indigenous peoples in Latin America are likely to be able to surf the web to discover that the International Labour Organization's home page fact sheet ranks as one of its key issues the fact that 'the Rights of Indigenous People have become central to the resolution of a long civil war in a Latin American country' (ILO, 1998). Few are also likely to discover that an organ of the World Bank, the International Finance Corporation, is currently using its web site to consult the infocracy about revising its environmental and social policies and procedures. Apparently this reform process was provoked by the in-house Hair Report, which was strongly critical of the weakness of the IFC's loan conditions relative to indigenous peoples in Chile. The IFC's current Environmental and Social Policies and Procedures, available on the web site, are revealing as to why this criticism arose. The manual lists, apparently as categories of the same type, 'involuntary resettlement' (seen to be normal practice without any self-consciousness that this is a code phrase for ethnocide), 'natural habitats', 'pest management' and 'indigenous peoples'! In fairness they do have one common theme: obstacles to the ecocidal and ethnocidal development practices of many of the IFC's borrowers.

One has to question whether the sort of easy access to information being made possible by the powerful represents evidence of a new transparency or mere window dressing. Are these informational sites signs of politicization of the relations of definition or merely symbolic distractions to enmesh the naive in the web? The increased ability of some individuals and groups to surf the web relatively cheaply and effortlessly into the databases of the powerful appears to offer considerable political possibilities; yet does access equate to power?

The information pie is most unevenly shared between North and South (Kisslinger, 1997; Panos Institute, 1998). Seventy per cent of host computers are located in the USA, and 80 per cent of the world's population lacks access to basic telecommunications. E-mail is still virtually the only form of access citizens outside state or market élites enjoy in eastern Europe, South America, south-eastern Asia, southern Asia, central Asia and Africa, adding to North/South polarization. Knox colourfully characterizes the new hierarchy consisting of infocrats on the top, cyber proletarians occupying Cyburbia and the lumpen-trash out in Cyberia (Knox, 1995). It both helps and hinders access that most of the ICTs use the English language as their medium: millions of non-English speaking people are excluded from using them even if they could access them. In some states even owning a modem is illegal, and nowhere do rights to access the ICTs appear to be entrenched in enforceable law (Logan, 1995).

Since the Cold War, ICTs have evolved to become new global vehicles for profit making controlled by Northern TNCs like Microsoft. New élites, the infocrats, within the ranks of old élites have emerged to control the new ICTs and the information they disseminate. Inevitably in the North a new proletariat almost dependent on the ICTs is emerging as well as a 'new' infor-mational poor in both the North and the South. To the poor's material impoverishment (Esping-Andersen, 1993) is now added their exclusion from access to information and participation in defining the relations of definition. Nautonomy has taken on further dimensions of meaning in the context of reflexive modernization.

Globalizing capital is successfully reorganizing itself into new forms of monopoly and oligopoly (e.g. airline and telecommunications 'alliances') as well as creating transnational institutional arrangements such as the World Trade Organization (WTO), Organization for Economic Co-operation and Devel-opment (OECD) and Asia–Pacific Economic Co-operation (APEC) conference and new normative arrangements based on business-friendly rights. Agreements such as that on Trade Related Intellectual Property Rights (TRIPs) and the Multilateral Agreement on Investment (MAI), for instance, are aimed at creat-ing a world without borders for the free movement of money and goods, together with the *apparatchiks* of globalization and some tourists; meanwhile, border fences are getting higher and higher to keep out workers and their families, and political and economic refugees.

The post-Fordist nation state has increasingly been decoupled from the market to become relatively powerless except, possibly, in the North when states are organized into supra-state political–economic blocs like the EU. Public telecommunications broadcasting media are being replaced by ICTs run for profit on contractualist lines. Citizens unable to access commercial user-pays systems will be barred from incorporation into the local, let alone global 'cyberproletariat'. (In New Zealand, the Labour Government, 1984–90, sold off Government Print to a private sector retailer with the result that The Knowledge Basket, a user-pays electronic database provider, now holds a licence to control access to the laws of New Zealand, which used to be freely available.) Informational and reflexive disenfranchisement will make such citizens the 'lumpentrash' and exile them to 'Cyberia' as powerless non-persons in an age where social reflexivity is the essence of identity.

A POLITICS OF RIGHTS FOR THE NETWORK SOCIETY?

The 'community' of nations shows little sign of being able to respond institutionally and normatively to regulate globalization and the network society in the interests of their citizens. The ineffectualness of US government attempts to rein in Microsoft frighteningly illustrates how the network society empowers old entities like TNCs with new and undreamt of power.

Little has yet been done by IGOs to develop normative human rights codes to guarantee access to the web, to regulate it or to decommodify it. Only limited intellectual property rights or censorship paradigms, with their conceptual framework based in earlier centuries, inform current debates about governance of the ICTs which are, as yet, primarily seen as a private technology for private gain.

Interestingly, there are signs that segments of the market itself are fighting back. Alternative new 'freeware' or 'shareware' operating systems (OSs), such as Linux OS, based on decommodifying principles, are entering into competition with the commercial Microsoft OS and Mac OS and being bankrolled by their competitors such as Netscape. This fascinating development may show the way for counter-hegemonic action initiated outside the state and by those on the fringe of the market.

The extent to which ICTs can serve an emancipatory purpose for social movements will depend upon how many free passes are allowed through the tollgates on to the ICT superhighway. Any hope that ICTs will enhance and universalize the capacity for social reflexivity and political action by social movements depends on radically new modes of governance of the ICTs and on free access. New markets, and NGO players concerned to promote the decommodification of the relations of definition, must emerge. Indigenous peoples' movements and cosmopolitan social movements should be able to ally on this project. A limited first step, albeit using the liberal legal technology of rights, would be to enact a new International Bill of Rights to Access to Information and to Communication. Rights would include free public access to information, and public supranational control over the ICTs. The Philippine Greens provided the only electronic resource (Verzola, 1998) I could find at the time of writing, outlining such a normative scheme.

The Greens' proposal argued that a human rights regime ought to be established to create a non-monopolistic information sector. The rights would include the right to know, the right to privacy, the freedom to share, and recognition of the moral rights of intellectuals.

A FORMATIVE CONCLUSION

From the mid-1990s cosmopolitan social movements and indigenous peoples' movements have utilised the ICTs to mobilize exposés of ethnocide, genocide and ecocide. Numerous battles are being waged via the web (e.g. *The Economist*, 1998a). There have been victories: for instance, in 1997–8 a most spectacular victory using the web against globalization has been the derailing of the MAI.

A Canadian NGO social movement released the hitherto secret text of the MAI over the web. Instantaneously the OECD's clandestine attempt to level the playing field by crushing obstacles to untrammelled foreign direct investment was exposed. It was discovered that vital matters such as nation state sovereignty rights, workers' rights, indigenous peoples' rights and environmental protection were targeted for elimination by OECD's draft MAI. The implications for sovereignty and possibly electoral viability of this plan to create a new world economic order by stealth seemed lost on some governments until the draft agreement was exposed on the web. This expose enabled social movements, notably OXFAM, and indigenous peoples to promote such effective media exposés and analyses that many governments have been embarrassed into re-evaluating their participation in the MAI in its present form for now.

A web-based campaign by the Canadian-based Aboriginal Roundtable against the globalization agenda of the APEC conference is at present being waged. The Aboriginal Roundtable's web site carries a detailed analysis of the disastrous impact on indigenous knowledges and intellectual property rights (IPRs) which globalization via the WTO and the TRIPs agreement are likely to have. The critique is radicalizing in the information it conveys and because the Roundtable highlights the fact that APEC apparently does not even give *locus standi* to NGO participants. This lack of standing denies indigenous peoples any opportunity for participation in APEC's far-reaching deliberations despite the fact there are an estimated 25 million indigenous people in the seventeen APEC countries (Aboriginal Policy Roundtable, 1997).

Since the development of the ICTs much more policy documentation and data can be accessed, promises made public and, sometimes, atrocities exposed. State and supra-state entities have been more susceptible to charges of hypocrisy. The reactions of IGOs, TNCs and states to indigenous peoples' human rights claims are increasingly visible, and they must now at least appear to devise remedial law and policy responses.

In the IGO arena, indigenous peoples' movements have staked a highly visible claim to recognition as subjects of international law and participants in law making and policy and programme standards setting. The collapse of time and space through use of ICTs has contributed to the effectiveness of this form of network politics. Indigenous peoples' movements now actively litigate, network and lobby in the UN context, such as in the Committee on Human Rights, and on the International Working Group on Indigenous Populations.

Many First Peoples have NGO status at the UN. Today they are probably as prominent as participants in international law making as environmental and women's rights groups, if not more so. A search of the UN (the *UNIONS site/unions/nph* yielded 40 hits in 30 seconds in the UNESCO file on indigenous peoples alone.

In First World settler states such as Canada and Australia, indigenous peoples' movements have a major network of web sites. In the courts and through the new technology they have been increasingly successful in asserting claims to the recognition of 'lifestyle' rights and modest forms of 'differentiated' citizenship. The official Government of Canada Indian and Northern Affairs Canada (INAC) web site is a rich one, as is the Australian Commonwealth's Aboriginal and Torres Strait Islander Commission (ATSIC) web site. Both sites offer access to daily updated data, enabling analysts and activists to read policy and to monitor events affecting indigenous peoples on a routine basis.

In authoritarian states in the South where development is often dependent on World Bank support, indigenous peoples' movements use ICTs to campaign against Bank-sponsored state and private sector development inimical to their welfare. One web site, for example, carried the desperate threat of mass suicide by the U'Wa indigenous peoples in Colombia if a proposed oilfield on their territory were to be opened up (*The Economist*, 1998b).

The ICT revolution clearly lies at the centre of the unprecedented pace and scale of transformation we now experience: 'Our technologies surround us, as they have for millennia but never before have they been so powerful. Never before have they brought so many benefits. Never before have they had so much potential for destruction' (Bijker and Law, 1997: 306).

Increasingly, by employing ICTs, tribal, pan-tribal, regional and global indigenous peoples' alliances have been formed which organize and act in a concerted fashion in supra-state and international fora that seem open to assisting their empowerment. Information concerning legal and political strategies, judicial decisions and human rights victories is now very easily disseminated via ICTs. Such information can be deployed in a localized politics of rights. Rights discourse has emerged as one of the most effective political devices for rendering visible manifold injustices to indigenous peoples and for providing a language for crystallizing and legitimating indigenous peoples' human rights. The transactional intensity of the web makes it an ideal amplifier for the politics of rights and embarrassment despite the apparent interpretative monopoly imposed by liberal rights talk and the alien cultural form represented by the relational sterility of the ICTs.

Human rights talk constitutes a basic though imperfect resource which indigenous peoples' movements must deploy to advance and defend their claims in the face of destructive ethnocidal and ecocidal forces. The ICTs can enhance their capacity to use this political resource. The cruel paradox, though, which indigenous peoples and all peoples living in network society must face is that the ICTs will make it both easier and harder to combat threats to our life chances. Identity, social citizenship, the decommodified public domain and ecosystems are all under severe threat. Collective and individual life chances are not, though, determined inexorably by technologies, networks or institutions. To render network society habitable for more than an élite infocracy, people enabled in the end by the new ICTs can and must act to tame the technology and make a destiny based on circumstances of their own choosing.

I conclude with three broad and tentative conclusions:

• The way indigenous peoples and movements appear to be mobilizing the ICTs to advocate their rights is more empowering than illusory.

- Some real gains of power are to be had, but access to the ICTs is not enough.
- ICTs concentrate power almost exclusively into the hands of those promoting the new World economic order, and so new modes of public governance and regulation and decommodified access to rights must be central platforms for all social movements concerned with challenging this source of power.

NOTE ON WEB RESOURCES

Most indigenous peoples in the North, all human rights intergovernmental organizations (IGOs), and most human rights non-governmental organizations (NGOs) – and some racist hate groups – have by now 'built' web sites. Indigenous peoples' sites include advocacy sites, news sites, information sites, personal home pages and business/marketing sites.

The USA-based Center for World Indigenous Studies's Fourth World Documentation (FWD) Project (at *http://www.halcyon.com/FWDP/cwisinfo. html*) lists 62 URLs and e-mail addresses for indigenous peoples' organizations in the USA, Canada and Australia, for Tibet (one) and for the Netherlands-based Unrepresented Nations and Peoples' Organization (one). The FWD Project has on-line 117 basic international documents relating to human rights struggles. Alastair Smith identifies up to 20 Maori-related and Maori-controlled sites (see his electronic paper 'Fishing with new nets: Maori internet information resources and the implications of the internet for indigenous peoples'); the University of Waikato Law School Library Indigenous Peoples link (at *http:// www2.waikato.c.z/lawlig/site/ip.html*) provides links to sites in the Americas, East Timor, Europe and the Pacific.

Among the very informationally rich sites are those of the James Bay Cree, Innu and Nisga'a (Canada); National Indigenous Working Group on Native Title (Australia); East Timor Internet Resource Sami People's site from Scandinavia; Hawaii Independent and Sovereign: New Zealand Maori Legal Resources. The situation of the Chiapas peoples of Mexico is now widely understood through web sites at Guelph University (at *http://www.tdg.uoguelph.ca/*); for activities of Sub Commandante Marcos, just key into Yahoo with this name for masses of material. See also *The Economist*, 7 March 1998, pp 130 and 133, and for a detailed analysis of the Zapatista Cyber Guerrilla movement see Castells (1997: 72–83).

Greenpeace used its web site to publicize the plight of the Ogoni and Ken Saro-Wiwa. Amnesty International's databases can make refugee reunification much simpler and have been used to correlate particular tours of duty by Salvadoran military with human rights specific violations.

The Human Rights Information Network carries a Reuters report 'Racism in Cyberspace' 11 November 98, identifying numerous USA hate sites with at least 200,000 users in the USA alone. According to *The Economist*, 28 March 1998, p 59, a Romany site has been developed in the USA to mobilize support for Romany in eastern Europe.

The Human Rights Information Network web site carries a Reuters article 'Rebel Movements Everywhere using the Web to Air their Views' citing the Bougainville Freedom Movement; Peru's Tupac Amaru Revolutionary Movement responsible for the Japanese Embassy siege in Lima; the Islamic Gateway, Kashmir, and the East Timor National Council for Maubere Resistance.

3

HUMAN RIGHTS

SUFFERING BETWEEN MOVEMENTS AND MARKETS

Upendra Baxi

It is not customary for social theory to refer to human rights movements as social movements. Nor does the human rights literature seem to learn much from social movements theorizing. This illustrates, yet again, the proposition of Georges Gurvitch (1973: 2) that too little sociology leads us away from the law and too much of it returns us to the law! What constitutes 'too much' and 'too little' is liable to contention. This apart, in an era of transdisciplinarity, the mutuality of lack provokes all kinds of questions concerning the construction of social reality of human rights: What are, or how one may construct, the material–semiotic spheres of human rights movements? Are these to be viewed as integral to social movements? Or are these to be viewed as relatively autonomous fields of study? How are the silences in movement theory concerning human rights movements to be grasped? Do these raise difficult issues concerning social suffering, a category that does not suffuse dominant traditions of social theory discourse? What fresh starting points may present themselves for the doing of human rights were this to be informed by the perspectives of social movement theory? In what ways do human rights movements get converted into human rights markets? Indeed, where do we, at a more general level, draw bright lines demarcating movements from markets? I explore, in this chapter, some of these questions in their bearing upon the future histories of human rights, assuming of course that human rights languages have an open future – an assumption liable to deep contention.

THE ABSENCE OF A SOCIAL THEORY OF RIGHTS

A striking feature of the latter half of the twentieth Christian century is the proliferation of endless enunciations of human rights norms and standards (hereafter 'normativity'), global and national. No preceding century has been witness to such an astonishing invention of a rapidly growing secular moral language seeking to supplant all other ethical discursive traditions. Indeed, it would be true to say that ours is the Age of Human Rights, where human rights become a 'common language of humanity,' a 'sociolect', a set of languages marked by distinctive patterns of reflexivity (Gouldner, 1976: 61–5). At the same time, the Age of Human Rights has also been the Age of Radical Evil. There appears to be a 'structural element in the realm of human affairs' in which human beings are 'unable to forgive what they cannot punish and unable to punish what has turned out to be unforgivable' (Arendt, 1958: 24). This moment of human rights in the face of radical evil has been insufficiently theorized in the social movement, and even human rights, literature (Baxi, 2000).

Neither the social reality of the restless and boundless production of human rights normativity, nor the varieties of experiences of radical evil, has yielded even a trace of comparative social theory of human rights. Thick and thin ethnographies of politics of cruelty have no doubt emerged, and these are even widely 'consumed'. Yet there is not yet in sight the emergence of the genealogies of human rights – sites where the politics of intergovernmental desire and NGO Will to Power contend and clash. Again, we cannot yet see the ways in which one may grasp the dialectics of human rights, marking zones of both 'regulation' and 'emancipation' (cf. Santos, 1995). Perhaps, if in terms of movement theory human rights emerge as too fluid a category to have a history or a future, in terms of the theory of practice of human rights the movement theory itself periclates (i.e. imperils) the futures of human rights.

Human rights appear to belong, at one and the same time, to institutionalized collective orders and to the spheres of social movements, 'old' as well as 'new'. If at one point of the spectrum they signify a grammar of governance, at another they register sites of insurrection. Rights emerge in several images:

> rights as boundary, and as access; rights as markers of power, and as masking lack; rights as claims and protection; rights as organization of social space, and as a defence against incursion; rights as articulation and mystification; rights as disciplinary and antidisciplinary; rights as marks of one's humanity and reduction of one's humanity; rights as expression of desire and foreclosure of desire (Wendy Brown, 1995: 96).

These different, and lived, embodied images of rights suggest heavily their dialectical character. 'Human rights' constitute different constellations of meaning, distinct cultural software in contemporary 'timeplace'. Diverse subject-positions and institutional structures are at play in the making and unmaking of human rights. Put another way, there is no underlying unity among human rights movements; indeed, these provide a startling variety of experience of cross-purposes and contradictions. In their sheer heterogeneity they share a feature of resistance to theory. With new social movements (NSMs) they resist narrative modes that essentialize or ontologize (Melucci, 1989: 18). However, a social theory of human rights ought at least to recognize the heterogeneity of forms of social action entailed in juridical production as well as social practice.

In terms of juridical production, at first sight the enunciation of human rights normativity seems overwhelmingly global. The registers of their birth are all too often sites of international organizations as the world, now weary of the recent Golden Jubilee of the Universal Declaration of Human Rights, knows well. Indeed, some social theorists of globalization regard the 'global institutionaliza-tion of human rights' as a defining feature of contemporary processes of globalization (Robertson, 1992). But these inter-sovereign auspices that generate clusters of events in human rights normativity entail countless renegotiations of global social organizations and collective behaviour of diverse social movements. Are these latter processes of coalitions of collective identity formations best viewed as products of contemporary globalization processes as suggested by Santos (1995) or Castells (1997)? Or as registers of resistance to it, as marking processes of de-globalization (Gibson-Graham, 1996)?

The timeplace of human rights movements is indeed difficult to theorize. Human rights performances, whether as policy or protest, social organization or collective behaviour, occur in a variety of moments of history and future. At one level, these take place as distinctly global happenings; at another level, the timeplace of attainment of human rights emerges as the local, the micro-sites of resistance to practices of power, often disarticulated with reference to the global. Human rights thus register 'critical events', both of power and resistance. That construction of 'criticality' of events depends, moreover, on the sense one makes of the newly-fangled notion of glocalization. If 'glocalization' is constructed hegemonically, the 'local' emerges, after all, as the ghetto of the global. But one may not thus reduce Daw Aung San Suu Kyi, and thousands of her followers in Myanmar, to no more than footnotes to a Derridian text. Differently construed, the glocal is the nested space marking the struggle for the innovation of the global by the local.

The heart of the matter, of course, lies in the choice of narrative and agency. How may we construct very different orders of reflexivity that emerge of the situated ways of knowing of the global-in-the-local and of the local-in-the-global in an era where the maxim 'think globally, act locally' has suffered many an inversion? Do we trace this in terms made available, for the study of NSMs, by the distinction between 'meta-' and 'sub-politics' (Beck, 1996) or between 'life politics' versus 'emancipatory politics' (Giddens, 1990: 157)? Prescinding here the dubious distinction between the 'old' and 'new' social movements in terms of orders of reflexivity (cf. Bagguley, 1999: 65), human rights movements seem to straddle these distinctions. These, often enough, seek social transfor-mation, which challenges sub- and meta-politics on the one hand (in the sense that these are concerned often with both changing the players as well as the rules of games of power/knowledge) and, on the other, the distinction between life- and emancipatory politics. The orders of reflexivity, or the nature of deliberation, also vary according to whether human rights movements are 'linear' or 'fluid' (Gusfield, 1981). Movements for global enunciation are more likely to be more linear, programmatic and goal-driven; human rights movements are fluid when they occur in less visible spheres of the local spaces or micro-arenas.

These features – the haunting ambiguities of the notions of human rights, their dialectical character, the differential global/local locations and orders of reflexivity – mark out human rights movements as social movements, as collective behaviour that (a) problematizes the existent formations of power in society and state; and (b) invests social praxis with the imagination of more just futures.

HUMAN RIGHTS AND 'NEW' SOCIAL MOVEMENTS

But I assume too much in equating human rights movements with social movements. That certainly is not a discernible trend of the movement theorizing.

The genre of literature on 'old' social movements (howsoever characterized) did little to focus on human rights movements as social movements. In so far as these were considered to be emancipatory movements, aimed at the redirection of human history through transformation of oppressive structures of ideology in dominance, social movements could hardly be conceptualized in terms of human rights. The figure of human rights occurs only in terms of critiques of extant models of rights, as was the case with Marx's classics *On the Jewish question* or the *Critique of the Gotha programme*. Although rights are conceived as necessities of class struggle (Baxi, 1993: 107–8) the notion of rights was, in the final analysis, a marker of a 'radically deficient' social order (Buchanan, 1982). In the within-the-Enlightenment utopian conception of emancipatory politics, human rights furnished a scaffold which needed to be discarded once the edifice of a just and authentic human future was constructed. Other, at times the radically Other forms of utopian thought such as those manifest in the life and work of Mohandas Gandhi, are impatient of the state-centric paradigms of human rights. On such perspectives, the extant regimes of human rights (of the colonizer to subjugate the colonized or of the right to property, both as *imperium* and as *dominium*) constituted a part of the problem, not of the solution. Social movements derived their historic potency in acts of transcendence from the received human rights paradigms.

At first sight, many of the 'new' social movements seem to be distinctly human rights oriented. It is, at first sight, difficult to grasp outside the frameworks of the contemporary human rights normativity, movements contesting patriarchy or environmental degradation, or those promoting self-determination, identity choice, sexual orientation or diversity. These movements are not just human rights *reinforcing*, in the sense that they revitalize through social action the texts of human rights norms and standards. They are also human rights *creating*. Many a development of new human rights is simply inconceivable outside the dynamic of NSMs.

And yet the literature on 'new' social movements is not concerned with ways in which these relate to the practices of human rights. Even the discourse on the demarcation between the 'old' and the 'new' does not seem to be concerned with the issue whether orientation towards human rights normativity might provide a specific point of departure between the 'old' and the 'new' movements. Rather, it is more centrally concerned with, *inter alia*, the social base of NSMs (ways that transcend their rootedness in class-specific locations), ways in which identities shaping collective behaviour are formed, the use of dramatic and disruptive modes of direct action and the emergence of agenda of radically pluralist identity politics (Touraine, 1981; Melucci, 1989; Castells, 1997). In saying this, I do not imply that the discourse is bereft of references to rights. Rather, I want to suggest that even when human rights do somehow seem to emerge as a constitutive feature of the distinction between the 'old' and the 'new' social movements the dimension of human rights movements as social movements seems not to receive its 'due' in the movement theory.

The 'new' movement theory is necessarily concerned, at least at the level of 'submerged networks', with social interactions, at face-to-face level, that translate histories of lived and embodied experiences of social harm into collective injustices. More generally, these processes entail conversion of individual biographies into social texts. The socialization of 'grievances' into causes of social praxis is a staple theme of the 'new' social movement theory. Yet, in my admittedly limited reading of this genre, 'grievances' stand seldom problematized as human rights violations, though these emerge as unconscionable human violations.

How does one understand this? It may turn out, at the level of empirical investigation, that some social movements do not contain or carry human rights referents. Or, their desired goals may not permit translation in the languages of human rights. On the other hand, it may also be the case that social science interpretive communities themselves may, even in this era of transdisciplinarity, remain strangers to logics and languages of human rights. If this is so, should it not be a cause for concern?

THE SILENCE OF SUFFERING

'Suffering' is not a category that suffuses the dominant traditions of social scientific thought. The study of social movements is no exception, although many of these arise out of an impulse to eradicate or limit sources of suffering, manifest or latent, in oppressive structures of the state, civil society and the market. The practice of social theory, overall, finds it difficult to give voice to human suffering even when it deals with the movements of the repressed.

Many reasons, of course, may be advanced to justify why this should be so. To cognize social suffering is to take a position towards it and this disturbs the canon of value-neutrality in social theory construction. Of course, human suffering may enter that practice as an assemblage of social facts, which need categories of description and explanation but the ideal of positivistic social theory is to look at facts of suffering as no more than raw materials for epistemic construction. Paradigmatically, Manuel Castells is able to write as late as 1997 (p 71):

Social movements may be socially conservative, socially revolutionary, or both or none. After all, we have now concluded (and I hope forever) that that there is no predetermined directionality in social evolution, that the only sense of history we have is the history we sense. Therefore, from an analytic standpoint, there are no 'bad' and ' good' social movements. They are all symptoms of our societies and all impact social structures, with variable intensities and outcomes that must be established by social research.

The 'analytic standpoint' is necessarily independent of consideration of social suffering, though not innocent of it. All social movements deserve equal theoretical attention. Movements that aggravate human suffering are then as much grist for the social theory mill as those that seek to combat structures of oppression. It is 'unscientific' to privilege the latter in doing social theory.

This epistemic egalitarianism would not be in itself so alarming but for the fact it exits from the dominant discourse any focus on human suffering. Violent social movements stand possessed with the potential of creating new forms of human suffering (Daniel, 1997). Obvious in the case of social movements based on violent practices of religious, ethnic and gender intolerance that create communities at risk and of misfortune, it is also often the case that ameliorative and even redemptive movements stand marked by a similar potential. The history of the Cold War when written will, for example, abundantly illustrate innovation in forms of imposition of human suffering that many social movements unleashed in pursuit of a 'democratic' and 'socialist' utopia. The 'analytic standpoint' fails to see the logic of social movements from the perspective of those violated.

Yet another reason is provided, reinforcing the first, by a whole range of assorted difficulties with the very notion of 'suffering'. Pain and suffering are egregious; some forms of suffering are considered 'necessary' and some 'unnecessary'. And different cultural traditions weigh social suffering as 'justified' and 'unjustified', making difficult the construction of suffering. Successful social movements for gender equality make patriarchs suffer everywhere. The overthrow of apartheid in the United States has made many a white supremacist suffer. Prison guards and officials suffer when their custodial sovereignty is assailed by prison reform favouring the rights of the inmates. People in high places suffer when movements against corruption achieve a modicum of success and we all get e-mail from Chilean groups that urge us to think of the suffering imposed on Pinochet by the extradition proceedings. The 'analytic standpoint' urges us to accord these forms of suffering with dignity of discourse which we extend to practices of politics of cruelty and catastrophic practices of power.

Even more important is the fact that social suffering is enclosed in the horizons of cultural pluralism. Thus, although Talal Asad does not reject the United Nations Convention on Torture, Cruel, Degrading and Inhuman Treatment and Punishment at the normative ethical level, he has recently argued that these notions remain 'unstable mainly because the aspirations and practices to which they are attached are themselves contradictory, ambiguous and changing' (1997: 285). 'Suffering' presents itself as a problematic notion not legible outside cultural scripts and afflicted by any transactional hierarchies that socially negotiate suffering (Das, 1995). Indeed, at times it constitutes phenomena that remain 'unnamable' (Das, 1997: 68). The dominant discourse has not much room for the languages of suffering. In this, the 'analytic standpoint' also plays a part (to borrow a phrase of bell hooks) in the 'effort to silence suffering coming to voice.' Taking human suffering seriously complicates the doing of social theory. Even so anthroposemiosis (as Daniel describes it) as 'silence that resists its own incorporation into semeiosis' is 'fundamentally threatening to humanity' (1997: 121). It is a hopeful sign that a minuscule emergent tradition still struggles against a theory-imposed disarticulation of social suffering.

A third, and less lofty for the neglect of suffering is that social research, towards the end of the Second Christian Millennium, has increasingly become a hi-tech, capital-intensive enterprise. This is an era of research 'bids' for funding that now need to be made for doing any serious social research. The investor rationality usually prevents focus on repressive structures that cause human suffering. This is different from the sponsorship of social science production of a narrative of suffering that commoditizes it by way of 'professional' appropriation of it (Kleinman and Kleinman, 1997) and production of suffering as a spectacle (Debord, 1970, 1990).

Finally (without being exhaustive) it is urged that studies of social movements gain authenticity when they take self-definition of the movement seriously: Castells, for example, observes: 'social movements must be understood in their own terms: namely, they are what they say they are. Their practices (and foremost their discursive practices) are their self-definition' (1997: 69–70). Is it necessary for movement theory to narrativize social suffering entailed in these definitions? If so, do contemporary human rights languages complicate the doing of movement theory by introducing ways of rendering problematic the very enterprise at self-definition? Is human rights discursivity that introduces notions concerning the illegitimacy of movements that forbid at all times certain forms of human violation[1] at all relevant to the 'analytic standpoint' measuring self-definitions of collective behaviour solely in terms the movements' 'foremost ... discursive practices?' To be sure, the quest for 'meaningful signs of new social conflicts, ... embryos of social resistance, and even ... social change' require an open-mindedness in the exploration of social movements through the 'shining paths, dark abysses, and muddled breakthroughs into the new society emerging from the current crises' (Castells, 1997: 70). But does this warrant a movement theorizing bereft of any, even a minimal, quotient of human rights reflexivity? Does this kind of reflexivity disable (to invert a fecund notion of Pierre Bourdieu) the practice of social theory?

These questions emerge only when human rights movements, in so far as they render human suffering problematic,[2] are regarded as social movements. It is true that not all social movements articulate responses to collective social suffering in terms of action oriented to the idiom or the language of human rights. People protesting against tyranny are not necessarily constructing a human right to tyrannicide or a right to revolution. Nor are moral crusades against corruption couched in terms of a human right to immunity against corruption in high places. While it may come to pass that some social movements may enhance, or even prefigure, human rights, it is also the case that others (those that promote ethnic cleansing, or xenophobia and other forms of intolerance and patriarchalism) are hostile to existing normative regimes of international human rights. For this latter, the very power of contemporary human rights to name orders of radical evil is in itself an evil that ought to be condemned and combated. And some social movements expose the complexity and contradiction in extant human rights normativity (as, for example, the right to life movements conflicting with the reproductive rights of women or the historic equality rights of the 'non-complicit' present generations confronting the logic of affirmative action programmes). And armed autonomy or secessionist movements in 'severely divided societies' (Horowitz, 1985; Kazanov, 1995; Hannum, 1996; Daniel, 1997) entail violation of human rights in the name of the exercise of the right to self-determination.

The problematic of self-definition is, at its roots, the problem of legitimacy. Discourse on legitimation addressed to the formations of state power is no less important for social movements. In part, the legitimacy of many social movements thrives, parasitically, on the pathologies of state power, often expressed more elegantly in terms of a 'legitimation crisis' or 'democratic deficit'. Different social and cultural logics are at play when social movements are thus state-formation oriented and when they are 'civil society' oriented. Principles of legitimation derive in the first case from the crises in the centralized unity of state power and in the second from mobilization of mass loyalty around causes that transcend structures of state power. In both forms of the quest for legitimacy, the rhetoric, logics and paralogics of contemporary human rights (Baxi, 1999) play a salient role in the social 'timeplace' (cf. Harvey, 1996) of law, both as an order of state and peoples' law (Baxi, 1982).

THE SOCIAL MOVEMENT FOR JUSTICE FOR THE VIOLATED OF BHOPAL

We are confronted, all over again, with the problematic of construction of social reality. How, for example, do we narrativize the now 15-year-old struggle of the victims of the Bhopal catastrophe? At different moments, the movement reveals distinct identities and agenda. It emerges as a spontaneous formation in the wake of the 'largest peacetime industrial disaster' (to borrow the description of Judge Keenan who first tried the suit against Union Carbide), one that released 47 tonnes of methyl isocyanate (MIC) on 2–3 December 1984, affecting at least 200,000 people in 36 municipal wards of the city of Bhopal. The conversion of a catastrophic community into a social movement for justice for Bhopal victims is a slow and turbulent process, whose history has yet to be fully traced. What follows is, more or less, a personal memoir of my ongoing engagement, now completing 15 years.

From the very first moment, the catastrophic community becomes available as a grand bazaar for international media and the contingency fee trial Bar of the

United States. The future collective behaviour of movements of victims carries this twin birthmark of conversion to the property of the media and the courts irreversible mediatization and juridicalization.[3] In this sense, the catastrophe itself becomes commoditized in global media and law markets, markets that shape decisively the response of governmental policy makers as well as of social and human rights activists. The movement of the victims in various moments of its emergence deploys the fora made available by these media and law markets; it also remains deeply wary of these.

The catastrophe as a global media commodity has a short shelf-life; intense in the production of spectacle of immense suffering in the first few weeks, the Bhopal stories become, more or less, annual rituals of memorializing around each anniversary of the event. In legal markets, for a brief while in the United States (Baxi, 1986) and for quite some time in India (Baxi and Dhandha, 1990) the shelf-life of juridicalized suffering is comparatively longer. It survives by the wayward attention of the Supreme Court of India when considering issues of disbursement of relief out of the settlement amount.

These markets shape many a feature of movements of Bhopal victims. The two major associations of 'gas-affected' peoples in Bhopal (and their activist supporters from the outside[4]) immediately feel constrained to provide an ideological orientation to the struggle of, and on behalf, of the victims. Is the struggle to be oriented towards an adversary defined in terms of an incarnation of global capital in the shape of the multinational corporation, Union Carbide? Or is it to be defined primarily in terms of the 'class enemy' within, manifest in terms of the state bourgeoisie (both in Bhopal and New Delhi) complicit with a multinational corporation? In other words, how was the violated and tormented collective self to be constructed?

The choice, either way, was problematic in terms of fashioning solidarities on the ground and national and global networks of influence and support.[5] No doubt, reflexivity supported a cleavage. And this is what came to pass in the very first year of the catastrophe. The 'socialist' oriented formation of victim groups found the 'liberal' formation both unprincipled and eclectic in identification of the adversary and strategy and tactics of using the law and the media markets to pursue Union Carbide by all means. The 'liberal' formation found little redemption in the strategy of locating the adversary primarily in the state bourgeoisie, whose support and sympathy, it felt, could be best mobilized for the benefit of the violated (at any rate for the time being). Neither fully trusted the Indian state and its law. But the 'liberal' formation found space for its contingent redemptive uses more compelling. If only the state and the law could be marshalled to pursue a perfidious multinational in all its sites, they felt the victims would be blessed with social and political space unique to their violation and the need for the reconstruction of their individual and collective futures. By contrast, the 'socialists' felt that a New Deal for the present and future victims lay in the relentless pursuit of the managers of the Indian state, a pursuit that, in the long and short run, would empower the people to constrain the state and the law to be more socially responsive in dealing with global capital.

In the event, what ensued was a bitter struggle among these ways of fashioning collective identity and solidarity, a struggle that was fierce and divisive. I recall to this day the street-play staged by the 'socialists', on the eve of the first anniversary of Bhopal, which denounced the 'liberals' as cohorts of Union Carbide! The fact that it took more than half an hour to light the effigy of CEO Warren Anderson (the only effigy-burning occasion that I took part in my whole activist life) furnished for the critics a symbolic demonstration of the 'collaborationist' nature of the 'liberal' enterprise!

In terms of political and legal strategies to be pursued, the 'liberals' favoured the enactment of the Bhopal Act, which aggregated all claims of victims in the Indian state. This was a jurisdictional necessity, as Union Carbide was not amenable to Indian judicial process. It may come as a minor surprise to students of NSMs but it is the case that movements that constitute a response to catastrophe-creation potential of contemporary global capital formations, need to anchor themselves (and their orders of reflexivity) into the complexity of the New Global Order Inc. The Bhopal Act, in empowering the Indian state to pursue the multinational corporation as the trustee of all the violated of Bhopal, assumed the role of *parens patriae*. It assumed that in dealing with the global capital its victims needed what the Indians (colonial and post-colonial) name as *maibap sarkar*.

But this created many a legitimation problem for the movement of the violated of Bhopal. How was one to accept the author of victimage as a champion for global justice for them? After all, was it not the state, which knowingly created the potential for this disaster?[6] And was it not also wholly unresponsive to the suffering that ensued in the catastrophe?[7]

These questions troubled the 'liberals' and 'socialists' alike by the proclamation of the Bhopal Ordinance (later to become an Act) neither of whom was consulted in the formulation of the policy. But each formation had to respond to this mode of juridicalization of the catastrophe. The 'liberals', given their logic of naming Carbide as the adversary, had little choice but to yield to this arrangement. They understood, hesitantly, that their hot pursuit of Carbide solely through the ambulance-chasing lawyers from the United States (who already held powers of attorney and had commenced 118 suits on their behalf) may be compromised by a settlement from which this Bar would benefit disproportionately. At least, the Union of India, they thought, could be trusted as a sovereign plaintiff to safeguard their interests; and the legal measure assured the creation of a political platform and a space within which the violated can pursue the here-and-now duties of redress by the state.

Needless to say, the 'socialists' responded to this juridicalization of the catastrophe as an act of mystification that needed a combat. The class character of the Indian state was the site of struggle for redressing the violated of Bhopal and assuring that there were no more Bhopals for the future. They did not feel assured that the Indian state bourgeoisie would act against definitions of development that served its interests pre-eminently by pursuing Union Carbide until the logical end of realizing the sum of US $3 billion that it quantified as damages. After all, was not the arrest and release (within 9 hours) of sojourning CEO Warren Anderson not indicative of what the state is capable of? Not merely will the victims be short-changed eventually but also the legal expropriation of their cause will progressively disempower peoples' movement. The 'socialists' were deeply offended by the state's assertion, before a New York court, that riddled with delays and inexperienced in fashioning remedies for mass torts, her own legal order was unable to accomplish justice to the violated in Bhopal. This forensic necessity, in a globalizing world, to bring a mighty multinational down appeared as evasive and offensive to the 'socialist' imagination of the ways to deal with the catastrophe.

Thus, the question of self-definition of legitimacy of social movements (which I raised earlier) returns. Castells's broad prescription does not quite help here. By practices of self-definition both 'liberals' and 'socialists' were movements for the violated of Bhopal. They differed not in their authentic concern for suffering but in their choice of strategy and tactic. They performed the role of internal critique of each other, making manifest distinctive orders of reflexivity amidst massive suffering. And despite the narrative symmetry I bring to these differences the movement of the violated marks the formation of collective behaviour and identity in terms of a quest for justice, not power. The struggle is characterized by a common quest for the translation of misfortune into injustice (cf. Shklar, 1990). Social movements are not always so readily characterized by a determined attempt by people, devastated by a catastrophe, to roll back a politically imposed fate into an event for a ceaseless quest for justice.

In this quest, also, the deeply conflicted ideological orientations also make space for solidarity. Each anniversary of Bhopal brings the 'liberals' and 'socialists' together in impressive acts of commemoration. Each of these pursue, variously, and from time to time, common tactics of activating judicial power and process, to catalyse the otherwise lackadaisical processes of disbursing compensation and for the provision of adequate health care and programmes of economic rehabilitation. There exists fluidity in patterns of social co-operation, which linearity in presentation of ideological differentials tends to obscure.

How then do we tell the Bhopal story? As a struggle for articulation of new human rights against that order of economic globalization which contests the perpetuation of a global risk society, symptomatized by (in the words of Beck, 1992) 'organized irresponsibility' and 'organized impunity' of global capital? Or in terms of construction of 'grievances', the multifarious narratives of neglect and hurt, leading to changing definitions and formations of fashioning of collective behaviour and identities? Or in the terms of the rise and fall of the emplotment of misfortune as injustice? Or in terms of providing a new pedagogy for the habits of adjudication?

This last mode of interrogation requires an additional narrative, if only for the reason that the Bhopal movement stands in an ambivalent relationship with activist adjudication.

TOWARDS A CONCLUSION

The struggle on behalf of the violated to convert Bhopal from a state of misfortune into a series of acts of planned injustice marks a singular accomplishment when the Indian state was constrained to pursue Union Carbide as legally responsible for the catastrophe. Harassed and harried by manifestations of activist solidarity, the state managers were forced to rupture the normally warm relations between global capital and the Indian state. The state assumed the guise of a sovereign plaintiff before an American court, in itself a most unusual occurrence; it also enunciated a daring principle of absolute multinational enterprise liability,[8] a principle that the Supreme Court of India swiftly translated as applicable to Indian industry and state-owned enterprises (Baxi and Paul, 1985). The state even sought to use its unreformed legal system (marred by high court fees and lack of legal-aid citizen pursuit of damages for torts) as a ground why a federal court in New York should try the Bhopal case![9] Even when the premature settlement by the Supreme Court of the Bhopal case precluded final vindication of this principle, its people-driven enunciation holds potential for conversion of communities of misfortune into movements for justice.

There were benign side effects as well. Not merely was interim relief granted pending judicial consideration of various matters, but it was enacted as a norm of no-fault public insurance liability. The early century Factories Act was substantially recast, providing greater public participation in location of hazardous industries. A brand-new and comprehensive Environmental Protection Act was passed, making state officials default in discharging their statutory duties into a criminal offence. In all this the colonial legacy of law reform finally came to its end. Unfortunately, the one-paragraph legislation that I proposed never came to pass! This was, heavily endorsed by the violated of Bhopal, a proposal that would have required all top management of hazardous enterprises to live with their families on the campus of the factories they proclaimed to be 'safe!' Despite this shortfall, the policy response that the violated of Bhopal generated renovates the Indian legal order. This bears reiteration: social movements are not usually considered (to transplant the notion of Cover (1975, 1987) in an altogether alien context) jurisgenerative, in the sense that these help annihilate an ancient regime of law and herald fresh human rights oriented practices of governance.

But all this stands accomplished by enormous cost of human suffering. The movement in law re-victimizes the victim communities in struggle. I have used throughout this essay the expression 'violated of Bhopal' because the language of victimage all through was the language of power. Indeed, in the long saga of Bhopal, everyone sought the status of being a victim! Union Carbide sought to portray itself as a victim of Bhopal activists, the Indian investigative journalism, the judicial process and the Indian government. The Supreme Court Justices publicly protested, through one of them, as themselves being victimized when I characterized their settlement orders as the Second Bhopal Catastrophe! And all sorts of people dressed in 'little brief authority' of the local and national state represented themselves as victims. Social activists, *inter se*, also complained of victimization! This discourse on victimage presented everyone as victims of Bhopal save those historically violated at Bhopal.

The policy, law and the media markets reified and commodified the multitudinous human suffering. In a cruel inversion, the idea of a victim became the victim. It was the injury to this idea that needed recompense through law, policy and administration. Human suffering was to be a calculable unit of injury under the rule of law regime, a regime under which, as Professor Dicey had sagely counselled early this century, one ought not weigh the butcher's meat in diamond scales. The suffering of the urban impoverished was, after all, the butcher's meat; the diamond scales of Indian justice were only made to weigh the claims of a mighty multinational with the gentle measures of due process.[10] Human suffering at Bhopal had to be measured grossly. The Bhopal victim-at-law had no age (neither young or old, neither infant or adolescent), no gender, no community, no sense of self (esteem, avocation, life projects) but was only a site of units of injury – simple, severe, temporary, permanent – which then could be quantified in terms of racism of contemporary law. (A Bhopal violated deserves intrinsically less recompense than the archetypal American lady scalded by a McDonald's styroform-cup coffee spill!)

The most moving event in the movement of the violated happened soon after the settlement. They, mostly women, staged a ritual purification by washing the magnificent steps and the marble edifice of the Supreme Court of India. It was their symbolic mode of cleansing the MIC-affected body of Indian jurisprudence. *Suddhikaran* (purification) is a sacred Hindu ritual; its secular adaptation marks a redemptive encounter between the globalizing Indian state and law and the resilience of popular notions of justice.[11] The fact that the purification was led by women signifies the cleansing of patriarchal sites of justice, which refuse to acknowledge that, of the violated of Bhopal, they suffered the most. It also marks the singularity of their leadership of the movement,[12] which reads the globalization script as a rape script (cf. Gibson-Graham, 1993: 120–41).

In a sense, yet to be archived, the violated at Bhopal through their movement prefigure a wider struggle against the catastrophic politics of cruelty encoded in the contemporary globalization. Their slogan is not for mere or more compensation in money terms. From the very first anniversary of Bhopal their battle cry has been *Union Carbide ko phansi do* (lit. Hang the Union Carbide by the neck until it is dead). Decapitation of Fortune 500 is a demand that becomes authentic when it becomes a roar from the 47 tonnes of MIC-impaired lungs of 200,000 human beings in Bhopal. One also understands, given the structures of production of social science knowledge, the reasons why it falls on many a social theory hearing-impaired ears. Karl Marx said more than a century and half ago that the future of humanity depends on the conjuncture of two conditions: when suffering people begin to reflect and those who think begin to suffer. The violated of Bhopal have been deeply reflexive. It is time, perhaps, for the theorists of the 'new' social movements to begin to respond.

4

THE WOMEN'S MOVEMENT

BOUNDARY-CROSSING ON TERRAINS OF CONFLICT

Cynthia Cockburn

It is often said, casually, that today there is a 'worldwide women's movement'. If we adopt the formula that a social movement is the non-powerful, non-wealthy and non-famous using both civil and confrontational means to transform the social world radically, to paraphrase Zirakzadeh (1997: 4), then, yes, the women's movement seems to fit. But what very often goes along with this kind of definition is a sense that a social movement is a political expression of a 'cultural singularity' (Castells, 1997: 2), the political project of an 'identity group'. But women, even when they identify as women, are as politically and culturally diverse as men, and the cohesion of 'women' in a worldwide movement cannot be taken for granted. Groups act together with a shared purpose only by means of conscious and careful processes of boundary-crossing, agenda-setting and alliance-building.

The action-research project, Women Building Bridges, which I describe in this chapter, was not designed to prove the existence of an international social movement. But it does bring to light some of the moves and motives involved in networking across borders. In particular it suggests some of the relational practices, the ways of identifying commonalities while taking account of difference and inequality, that may be necessary for broad-based movements to happen.

WOMEN WORKING CROSS-ETHNICALLY IN CONFLICT

Let me first introduce the three countries and the three project groups around which Women Building Bridges was built. The countries are all sites of wars involving ethno-national identifications. The groups are all crossing an internal border between collectivities, addressing and refusing or re-articulating the divisions created or exacerbated in the war. And, as will become clear, they have also been crossing state borders to reach each other, in a second phase of the project that we called Bridge Between Bridges. Each group encompasses women of varied backgrounds and varied politics. Each project does different things and manages its collective doings in a distinctive way. And the specificities are important, because it is precisely dealing with and transcending them that makes a movement, and failing to do so that breaks one.

NORTHERN IRELAND

The first is the Women's Support Network in Belfast. The conflict in and about Northern Ireland derives from the colonial period and indeed can be seen as a prolongation of it. The concession of 'home rule' to the Irish in 1921 involved the partition of the island to accommodate the refusal of the Protestant minority to accept inclusion in a Catholic state. The northeastern part of Ireland remained part of a 'United Kingdom of Great Britain and Northern Ireland'. But until 1972 it was governed, to the disadvantage of Catholics, by a local parliamentary assembly dominated by the Protestant ruling class.

Although there is a long history of conflict in Ireland, the present war dates from the emergence of a civil rights movement in Northern Ireland in the late 1960s. The British government responded to the resulting violence by imposing direct rule on Northern Ireland. A three-way conflict has ensued involving the British state, Republicans prepared to use force to unite the north with the Irish Republic (they are mainly Catholic) and Loyalists (mainly Protestant) prepared to use force to resist this. Resolving the problem of Northern Ireland thus involves among other things a renegotiation of the relations between the governments of Great Britain and the Republic of Ireland.

The 'troubles' as they are euphemistically called, have made of Belfast a violence-prone and impoverished city. It is a checkerboard of clearly demarcated neighbourhoods, either predominantly nationalist/Catholic or unionist/Protestant. The segregated communities, to a greater or lesser extent controlled by sectarian parties and paramilitary groups, have often been in fear of each other. The presence of the British military and frequent acts of violence, have maintained tensions at a high level. Social, and even economic, life has tended to be confined within community boundaries. Individuals living in mixed marriages must make a difficult choice about where to live. They and their offspring are likely to avoid a high profile when they live in areas where political feelings run high.

In the late 1980s there was a rapid growth of women's organizing at community level in working class Belfast. Given the high degree of territorial segregation, these new women's centres tended to be serving one ethno-political community or the other. The women's groups were strongly dependent on council funding. When in 1989 the Belfast City Council (controlled by strongly Protestant/Unionist political interests) threatened to cut selectively the funding of a centre in an area known for its Republican sympathies, other women's groups, even those located in areas of Protestant Loyalism, came out in support of them, protesting against political vetting.

From 1989 the contact and co-operation between women's centres in the various parts of Belfast was acknowledged and formalized in the Women's Support Network, which now has several workers and an office. The Network acts as 'a united voice of working class women' who, it points out, is 'the most excluded group in a viciously divided society' (Women's Support Network, 1996: 22). Through research and development, lobbying and advocacy, they aim to change policy, put equality on the official agenda, increase the flow of funding for women's projects and get women's voices heard in the political system and the peace process.

ISRAEL/PALESTINE

My second case study was situated in Israel/Palestine. The group involved was Bat Shalom in the area known as Megiddo, Nazareth and the Valleys, just south of Galilee in northern Israel. The name Bat Shalom is Hebrew and means Daughter of Peace. This is a local branch of a well-known project of the same name in Jerusalem, which in partnership with the East Jerusalem Women's Centre is known as The Jerusalem Link. The Megiddo group effects a similar 'link', between Israeli Jewish and Israeli Palestinian Arab communities in the north.

When international support for the Zionist project resulted in the creation of a state of Israel on Palestinian territory in 1947, the result was the uprooting of the Palestinian Arab people from their land. Three-quarters of a million were exiled to refugee camps in neighbouring Arab countries and to a worldwide diaspora. A minority remained, 'internal refugees' in the new state, where they and their descendants are now 18 per cent of the Israeli population. A high proportion of these Israeli Palestinians live in the north of the country. Their now landless towns and villages are physically adjacent to Jewish towns and housing settlements and the many collective moshavim and kibbutzim of this region. But they are socially quite separate. Many Arabs earn their living as manual labour in Jewish agriculture and manufacturing.

So the internal border crossed by the women of Bat Shalom is one between two ethno-national groups divided on the one hand by politics, on the other by culture. Politically, their relations are made difficult by the injustices inflicted both on Jews as an ethnic group, worldwide, and in the region by the Jewish Zionist movement and the Israeli state. Their alliance is put under further stress by the conflict between the state of Israel and the surrounding Arab countries, and the violent repression/resistance of the Palestinians in the Israeli-occupied West Bank and Gaza. The violence affects Israeli society in the form of permanent militarization and sporadic acts of 'terror' by extremists of both sides. Lack of democracy is felt acutely on both sides of the Green Line.

Unlike the Catholics and Protestants of Northern Ireland, who are not noticeably different in dress, language or lifestyle, Jews and Arabs in Israel are of sharply contrasted cultures. The Jewish women of Bat Shalom are, in the main, members of rural kibbutzim. They tend to be secular, collective and anti-consumerist. Bat Shalom's Palestinian Arab members are of both Christian and Muslim background. They and their families make their livelihood under very different conditions, in a competitive economy and discriminatory labour market. They live in under-resourced and densely populated villages and towns. Marriages between Jews and Arabs are very rare in Israel. Just seeking more than casual contact with 'the other' causes Bat Shalom members to be looked upon somewhat askance in their own communities.

The typical activity of Bat Shalom is to bring women of these two communities together to campaign and demonstrate in public places for the end of the occupation, for a just peace, the creation of a Palestinian state and the sharing of Jerusalem. They organize high-profile political and cultural events. Many members are active in left-wing political parties, and the group maintains close working links with women members of the Israeli parliament, the Knesset. At a local level Bat Shalom organizes, with minimal funding, cross-communal workshops raising consciousness on women's issues, and drama improvisations that bring humour to questions of bigotry, prejudice and discrimination.

BOSNIA-HERCEGOVINA

The third project group, Medica Women's Association in Bosnia-Hercegovina, differs substantially in focus from both Bat Shalom and the Network. It is a women's therapy centre that provides gynaecological and psycho-social care to women refugees and their children, and it began as a resource particularly for women who were raped in the Yugoslav wars.

When Yugoslavia broke up with the secession of Slovenia and Croatia in 1991/2, Bosnia-Hercegovina had little choice but to declare independence. But from that moment Bosnian Serb nationalist extremists began a military campaign of 'ethnic cleansing' to remove Muslims and Croats from areas of Bosnia-Hercegovina they planned to annexe to Serbia proper. In addition, for 18 months in 1993/4 Bosnian Croat extremists opportunistically attacked Muslims (and the few remaining Serbs) in other areas of Bosnia-Hercegovina that they wished to turn into an autonomous Croat region. Zenica, the home town of the Medica Women's Association, is a city that was successfully defended by the Bosnian government against both sets of aggressors. A city of 120,000 before the war, during the fighting it took in 70,000 – mainly Muslim –refugees.

The initial impetus and the funding for Medica came from the German women's movement. They have a gynaecology outpatients' clinic, a psycho-therapy unit, a creche and playschool, and residential accommodation for refugee women and their children. My research was carried out in the winter of 1995/6, by which time, in two and a half years of operation, they had provided 26,000 outpatient treatments, had helped 416 in-patients, and were currently sheltering about 80 women and children.

In the Yugoslav state consolidated under the Communist regime of Marshall Tito following the second world war there had been a purposeful attempt to diminish the salience of ethnic identities. There had been many mixed marriages, mixed parentage was consequently common, and many people had come to think of themselves not as members of a narod (constituent 'nation', such as Serb, Croat or Muslim), but as Yugoslavs. This was specially the case in Bosnia-Hercegovina in which no one narod had an overall majority.

But the wars that accompanied the break up of Yugoslavia created devastating forced population movements. Inevitably in 1995 the old mixture of central Bosnia was no longer in evidence. Even in Medica the great majority of the women staff were Bosnian Muslims. There were, however, still 10 per cent or so who were of Bosnian Serb, Croat or Slovenian background, and more who were of mixed parentage or in mixed marriages. These were women who had resisted the wave of nationalist fear and hatred, and had remained loyal to the idea of a democratic and mixed Bosnia.

There was an undoubted awareness of the value of this ethnic mixture in Medica, as the diversity in the local community around them declined. But here, in contrast to the Network and Bat Shalom, the different national 'names' that had been implicated in so much violence were not often invoked within the project. Rather, there was an ethic of simply living together, undifferentiated, 'the way we were', in the belief that the old Yugoslavism could be resuscitated in a mixed Bosnian identity. It was the way they sustained this residual mixture in Medica, while political parties organized on national lines hardened the territorial divisions around them, that was the focus of my study.

RESEARCH AIMS

The research aims were, first, to learn from the experience of the three projects how their internal 'cross-border' alliances are created and sustained. How and when do people work productively together across ethno-national lines used by others to divide them? Why and when do they fall apart? What is it that women, as women, bring to this work? Italian feminists have sometimes summed up their handling of difficult differences as doing 'transversal politics' (Yuval-Davis, 1995). By this they have meant a combination of what they term 'rooting' and 'shifting'. Each participant in the dialogue brings with her a rooting in her own acknowledged membership and identity (no false universalism). But at the same time she makes the imaginative shift that enables her to empathize and co-operate with women who have different membership (refusing essentialized identities).

The Women Building Bridges research, then, was directed towards finding out just what was the content of that container-term, 'transversal politics'. It involved thinking about nationalism in relation to feminism; and about identity in relation to, on the one hand, coercion and violence, and on the other the creation of sustainable democratic polities.

The research method combined three approaches to data gathering: participation, interviewing, and setting up action for observation. Phase 1 (1995–7) involved my participation in the life and work of the projects, gaining an understanding that was given depth by formal interviewing of project members. The study of the three projects as separate entities was effectively completed by the end of 1997 with the preparation of a photographic exhibit and writing of a book (Cockburn, 1998). Phase 2 (Bridge Between Bridges, 1998–9) was a development from the first. Learning of each others' existence through the research, the women of the three projects expressed interest in meeting each other to compare experiences and strategies. These encounters constituted the action phase of the research.

DOING TRANSVERSAL POLITICS AT LOCAL LEVEL

To begin at the beginning. ... A metaphor I found useful in thinking about the internal cross-border relationships of the three projects was the notion of relational 'space'. To achieve a sustainable harmony, whether as individuals in a loving partnership, as collectivities in a multicultural city, as nations sharing a world, or in projects like these three, a great deal of effort must be put into structuring a comfortable democratic space between us. The space has to afford an optimal distance between differences, small enough for mutual knowledge, for dispelling myths, but big enough for comfort. It needs to be criss-crossed with the webs of a structure and a process capable of conveying clear meanings from one side of it to the other, and sustaining stable relationships. It has to be strong enough to prevent a collapse of differences into silencing, rape or annihilation. But it also has to be flexible enough to permit differences to change their form and significance, and for increased interaction and intimacy as and when circumstances allow of it.

It is in such a dynamic field of love and hate, trust and fear, that the Women's Support Network, Medica and Bat Shalom have been trying to sustain their alliances. And the best resource they have in constructing their small democratic polities is a careful and conscious handling of identity processes.

Here I found it useful to draw on the work of Hall (1996) and others (e.g. Rutherford, 1990) who describe a 'self' that is not given at birth but is rather a production, involving a degree of agency. It is a view of the subject self as in problematic relation to discursive collective identities that bear upon it and bid for it to 'identify', to acknowledge 'belonging'. In times of war, nationalist discourses propagate national identities that are essentialized and fixed in antagonistic opposition to each other. Increasingly, as Connolly (1991: 65) puts it 'the voice of difference is heard ... as a symptom of sickness, inferiority, or evil'. To resist such compelling and divisive constructions, to continue to insist that one's sense of self depends precisely on remaining engaged with 'those others', takes courage and skill. The prize, however, is democracy itself.

Reflecting back, I can distil five principles from the identity work I observed them doing. At different times I saw the projects use these well and less well. First, at their best, the projects affirm difference. They resist the temptation of erasing it, of collapsing mixity into mere heterogeneity or, worse, a pretended homogeneity. In some circumstances they feel unable to acknowledge politicized difference very vocally (in the Bosnian situation in particular). In others (Israel is a case in point) the differences are so clear-cut that they structure the group uncomfortably into two halves. But it is an important principle in all three projects that difficult differences should not have to be 'left outside the door' in order for us to meet and work together.

Second, an important corollary, the projects are on the whole good at non-closure on identity. There is a certain tension evident here with the first principle of affirming difference. It is a question of acknowledging identities (whether gender or national identities) without essentializing them, without predicting what might flow from them. These women are unusually willing to wait and see, to believe there may be many ways of living, let us say, a Bosnian Muslim identity. You may be a Muslim by background, yes, but one in whom that identity is inflected towards secularism, socialism and internationalism. You may choose to live your Muslim-ness articulated tightly with 'woman', so that it is a little detached from the masculine interpretation. You may invest more in your woman-ness than in your Muslim-ness, and, what is more, choose to inflect it towards feminism. These things will shape a meaning for a Muslim very different from the stereotyped 'Turk' that some 'Serbs' like to hate. So, interrogating themselves, watching each other, the women in the projects seem to believe, with Jordan (1989: 114), that 'The final risk or final safety lies within each one of us attuned to the messy and intricate and unending challenge of self-determination'.

So the women take great care in the way they deal with identities in individual interaction and relationship. Most of the time, they avoid ascribing thoughts or motivations or qualities to others on the basis of their ethnic or national label. One woman will listen to the other's telling of history, her view of the event, idea of herself, reading of the situation, preference for action rather than making suppositions because she 'is' Catholic/Croat/Jew. Likewise she will avoid ascribing collective guilt. In Medica in particular I heard over and over again, 'we don't put everyone in one basket'. It is best to 'judge people by what they do, not what they are.' You are not to be held accountable for everything done in your name.

The third principle the projects show, one they feel important in alliance-building, is an acknowledgement of injustices done in the name of differentiated identities. In none of the three countries is ethnic difference the difference of equals. These regions are not just sites of war between peoples who harbour an ineradicable hatred of each other. They are societies that have seen terrible wrongs inflicted. Creating an alliance is therefore not just a matter of mutual opening. It involves a willingness to face ethical issues, to dig deep into layers of advantage, exploitation and oppression done to others in one's name. It is a painful process. There are factors in all the projects that inhibit the tabling of ethical issues of power and justice. But they operate best as alliances when they do recognize and make explicit ethical asymmetries. They cannot move any distance towards peace without facing up to it.

A fourth way the women put to use what they have learned about identity pain and identity work is in taking care in delineating the agenda of the projects. It is important to know on which matters it is safe to engage with each other, which should be avoided if the group is to hold together and, most importantly, to detect those that become more possible as peace approaches or cease to be possible as violence closes in.

The fifth principle, which can be seen as the guarantor of the other four, is an inclusive and transparent group process. A democratic polity has to ensure that all its voices are heard, that all are given equal weight and that decision-making is fully shared. At the level of the individual in a face-to-face group, the destructive 'othering' processes to which collectivities (such as ethno-national groups) are prone can be contradicted, and an alternative modelled. In a situation where everyone speaks, in a safe context where defensive masks can be set aside, each person can afford to be more 'herself'. Less projection occurs, and the group is more likely to cohere in such a way that energy is left over and above the management of relationships to commit to shared output, actual work.

ONE STEP FURTHER: THE MIJAS WORKSHOP

It will by now be clear that it was well within the logic of the projects' self-sense to engage in some networking with each other through our research co-operation. In this section of the chapter I shall discuss the networking we did by reference to the five main relational principles mentioned as having been in use within the projects.

The first step in Phase 2, Bridge Between Bridges, in effect began before Phase 1 was ended. We held a workshop for representatives of the three projects in Mijas, southern Spain, in late 1996. Among the criteria for selection of the participants it was stressed that the group of four should be ethnically representative. Thus, from Belfast, a balanced group of women of Protestant and Catholic backgrounds was implied; equal representation of Jewish and Palestinian Arab women from Israel; and the Bosnian team too was asked to think about ethnic representativeness. They nominated a Muslim religious counsellor, a woman of Bosnian Serb background, a Bosnian Slovenian and a Muslim woman married to a Bosnian Croat.

This request for a fair representation of ethno-national differences at the workshop, and the projects' response to it, immediately exposed the tension between the first two principles of their customary identity work: the affirming of difference and non-closure on identity. It is one thing to know and affirm the fact that 'we contain difficult differences in our project'. It is equally acceptable to attend a workshop to discuss 'negotiating difference'. But nominating participants to the workshop on the basis of ethno-national 'names' precisely calls for the kind of closure on identity the projects normally try hard to avoid. It means that actively categorizing individuals (or asking them to categorize themselves) in a way that distorts and misrepresents them, seems tasteless and seems in fact to play the game of the warmongers. Nonetheless, ethnic representativeness there was at Mijas.

This residential workshop, held in a secluded women's villa-hotel, powerfully affected the participants in several ways. At the simplest level, the retrospective evaluation suggested, it helped put local 'troubles' in perspective, both in the sense of showing that similarities exist in the sufferings of people in very different countries and finding a shared analysis of such troubles as having their origins in politics more than in prejudice, and as much outside the region as inside, as much in the international agency of big imperialist nations as in the domestic hatreds of little ones. It reinforced the sense already present in the projects that women have something to say to each other, not only about a shared positioning in conflict but about their potential contribution to community development, the restoration of justice, the reduction of violence and eventual peace.

Three facets of the Mijas workshop were particularly informative. First, the unforeseen effect it had within each project group; second, the issue of agenda making; and third, the significance of a group process.

As to the first, the project groups that came to Mijas were obliged, in a way quite unusual for them, to prepare an agreed presentation for the benefit of the women from other places about their history – as country, as conflict and as project. This involved them in detailed negotiation across ethnic difference, threw difference into unaccustomed relief, even before they set off from home. The outcome in each case was an account that had some common ground but was carefully and caringly devised to allow for differences in the 'facts' chosen for emphasis, and for multiple interpretations.

Second, as noted above, the three projects survive as alliances partly by careful delineation, and limitation, of the scope of the agendas on which they work together. At Mijas the groups were required to focus on divisive issues much more than they are accustomed to do in everyday life, which tends to be taken up with the project's ostensible work – caring for refugees, campaigning, demonstrating for peace. The risk was that those carefully limited agendas would suddenly explode when one group raised questions that another would normally tactfully leave unasked.

The agendas chosen by the participants for the last two days of the Mijas workshop will illustrate this point. They were themes that are vital to the life of each project. Yet, back at home, there is seldom the time or the safely managed space in which to open up to them. The first was 'Why are we women's groups? What are human commonalities?' Discussing this, of course, differences over 'feminism' became explicit. The second was 'What is nationalism? What is the relation between women and nationalism?' And here it quickly became clear there were women who felt themselves positively nationalist and other women for whom the concept was lethal. 'What is meant by tradition? ethnicity? culture? religion?' was the third theme, and this necessarily involved women negotiating divergences between them of belief/atheism, confession/secularism, deep enculturation versus a rejection of prevailing cultures. The final theme 'How can we build democracy out of differences – inside our projects and outside?'

among other things highlighted participants' affiliations to different political parties and differences in orientation to the political system.

The third facet was what we saw of 'process' at work. That the unusually taxing agenda in fact generated excellent, clear and succinct communication (and no more than survivable intra-project tensions) was, it was generally conceded, due partly to the relational skills already practised in each project, and partly to the carefully facilitated group process at Mijas. Difficult conversations had the result of strengthening rather than destroying group relationships. On the last day of the workshop, news reached us of an explosion of violence between the Israeli authorities and Palestinians in Jerusalem, involving many deaths. The event caused acute distress in the Bat Shalom group. But it did no more than increase the warmth and solidarity that had been generated between and within the projects in the preceding days.

One of the participants later described the Mijas experience this way:

> The space to listen and enjoy listening! I got to listen to myself too. Time to be still and think. Affirmation of our work, our ideas and processes and the beginning of a new process that is about 'linkage' across struggles and conflicts elsewhere. Renewal of my regard, love and value for the women I work with and the extension of the list of women I have such respect for.

STEPPING INTO INTERNATIONAL SPACE: THE EXCHANGE VISITS

What the workshop could not easily do (despite provision for 'reporting back') was enable the other project members, the ones who were not there with us in Spain, to benefit by the experience of the four who did come. It may even have given rise, on return, to a certain distance between the travellers (who talked animatedly about the experience) and those who had not been picked to go.

The exchange visits they now asked me to set up had the intention of deepening the contact between the projects. While in each others' countries the visiting groups would have time to get much more involved with the members of the host project as a whole, experience a deeper immersion in its work and problems, and also to visit other women's organizations in the political vicinity.

We arranged a programme that involved a group of four women travelling in each direction for visits of two weeks. The lynch-pin was the Northern Ireland project, the Women's Support Network, which exchanged visits firstly with Medica Women's Association, flying to and fro between Belfast and Sarajevo in June and July 1998; and secondly, in October and November 1998, with the Israeli project Bat Shalom. I accompanied all four visits as observer, studying the differences and commonalities revealed as the projects learned about each other, noting the relational practices through which communication was effected between the groups, and comparing them with the practices I knew by now to exist within the separate projects.

And this time the circumstances were far more challenging. First, language interpretation had already proved a problem in Mijas, where we had only one hard-pushed interpreter for Hebrew/Arabic/English and another for Bosnian/English. It became even more of a problem in the exchange visits, for which funding was very tight. Apart from an occasional input of professional interpretation, participants had to rely on their own language skills and interpret for each other. The limitations this placed on good and careful communication were all the time evident.

Second, facilitation was not nearly the controlled process it had been at Mijas. How could it be? The visiting participants were scattered in different homes. The programme of visits, workshops and parties was over-full, bringing us at moments to breaking point, especially in climates we were unused to too hot in Bosnia, too cold in Ireland. The distress of seeing injustice, fear and conflict first hand was also exhausting and exasperating. The Bosnian and Israeli visitors to Belfast could scarcely credit the degree of mistrust prevailing between the two communities, a 'peace process' notwithstanding. The Belfast women who went to Bosnia were gutted by the physical and human devastation remaining from the war. In Israel they were shaken by the explosive mix of repression and rebellion.

As in Mijas, the customary agenda of issues comfortably addressed within the projects had to be alarmingly extended in contact with each others' projects. But this time there was no possibility of carefully monitoring and democratically deciding on those extensions. Hard questions were thrown up daily by everything we saw and did.

Some of the questions bore precisely on those issues of 'how we do things': affirming but not essentializing difference; and acknowledging injustice. As to difference: the Bat Shalom women are never in doubt for a moment who among them, or in their environment, is 'Jewish' and who is 'Palestinian'. They are outspoken with each other and never hesitate to 'name names'. The women of the Women's Support Network, when visiting Israel, were sometimes startled by their roughness with each other. By contrast the Network women are adept at 'being appropriate'. They avoid using the terms Catholic and Protestant, which they feel are inaccurate and often abused both by ignorant onlookers and motivated parties to the conflict. Instead they talk about 'tradition', 'background' or 'community', or the area you live in or come from. They talk about beliefs rather than belonging: nationalist and Republican politics and Unionist or Loyalist convictions. But outsiders coming to Belfast cannot tell by looking or listening who is who in Northern Ireland, and they do not know the codes, euphemisms and synonyms in the Northern Ireland political thesaurus. So this exemplary 'non-closure', learned by the Network women to avoid the destructive stereotyping that is so prevalent in the Belfast political environment, sometimes seemed to them like a coyness, an evasion of difference running contrary to the principle of affirming difference. 'Why did you not tell us' the Bat Shalom women asked, 'whether the groups we were visiting, or the women we were meeting, were Catholic or Protestant?'

The boot was on the other foot in the exchange between the Network and Medica. Medica sent four women of Muslim background to Belfast. The Network women said nothing at the time, but wondered about the absence of Medica's non-Muslim minority. And when they made the return visit to Bosnia what they learned of Medica confirmed their feeling that the Bosnian women, despite or because of the horrors of a war waged between groups dressed as ethnies or nations, were too reluctant to distinguish women at all by narod. Surely it mattered, now if not before, what 'name' your parents had, what 'name' you carried, 'who' you were married to? This is precisely what people had killed and been killed for. Were not hurts tied up in these supposed identities that needed openly addressing and healing? The Medica women however, in the main, felt that with political parties throughout the region asserting division and separation in the name of narod, the creative thing to do was to find commonality in a survival of the old 'Yugoslav' spirit while waiting and hoping for better times. The Network women perhaps felt, as the Bat Shalom women had felt in Belfast, that this was carrying non-closure to the point of failing to acknowledge variants of pain embodied in variants of ethnic identity.

'Acknowledging injustice' became an issue in the exchange between the Network and Bat Shalom. It was hard for the Belfast women not to feel overwhelmed by the plight of the Palestinian people, and for their anger with the Israeli state not to spill over to become an anger with Jews. Could the injustice of the fact that Israel's celebrated Independence Day is the Palestinians' 'tragedy', their Nakhba, be sufficiently addressed in a project of co-operation and co-existence like this? But their stay included a visit to the Holocaust Museum, a reminder of the wrongs underlying the wrongs. And in the course of two weeks they met Jews of a range of different political beliefs, so that the complexity of the alliance that Bat Shalom is, and the courage of all the women participating in it, were in the end inescapable.

The other side of this coin is, of course, the distribution of privilege in Northern Ireland and in the Women's Support Network. In Northern Ireland the ethno-political injustice is compounded with class: the Protestant ruling class governed from 1921 to 1972 in a way that was unjust to Catholics but was also expressive of class divisions among Protestants. The Women's Support Network is an alliance of women from impoverished working class areas. Its Protestant women are those who gained least by the Protestant monopoly of power and been least implicated in oppressing others. So the issue, within the Network, of 'acknowledging injustice', while not entirely absent, is more muted than in Bat Shalom.

These and other tensions did not in any way invalidate the exchange programme. The travellers felt the experience had been positive. As one of the Network women said, in Bosnia, 'in trying to make sense of your situation, we're really making sense of our own'. It was a challenge, of course, to transmit the value of the experience to those who remained at home, something we tried to address by making videos to use in reporting back. The exchange between the

Network and Medica led to a new awareness in the Belfast women of the extent to which their own situation has been not merely 'troubles', but war; their suffering not a case of 'nerves' but of 'trauma'. The Bosnian women thought more about their relative lack of experience in community development, campaigning, engaging with the political system. The visits ended with a plan of co-operation between the two projects. The exchange between the Network and Bat Shalom did not generate such concrete plans but led to a new alertness to each others' situation and focused attention on new features of their own.

STRENGTH THROUGH WIDER NETWORKS

The Bridge Between Bridges project, at Mijas and in the exchange programme, was thus a stepping stone from inter-ethnic alliance building to transnational networking across nation state borders. It may be useful, further, to map the particular women's networks, part of the putative global women's movement, from which our contact with each other sprang in the first place, and into which we moved deeper as our work together progressed.

The awakening of a 'new' feminism, as noted earlier, began in the USA and Western European countries in the late 1960s and by the 1970s woman-identified groups and activities were developing fast in many countries of the world, in part inspired by the Western example but more importantly responding to local changes in women's circumstances.

It may be that designating this proliferation of local organization and action a 'global social movement' appears the more plausible for the increasing involvement from the mid-1970s of the UN and other official international agencies though it may conversely be argued that these agencies jumped on the bandwagon of a global social movement women were autonomously creating. Be that as it may, the UN declared a Decade of Women in 1975. At first, few feminists saw much significance in this hype. But this had begun to change by the mid-decade conference in Copenhagen in 1980, had shifted considerably by the Nairobi conference in 1985, and yet further by the time of the Fourth World Conference on Women in Beijing in 1996. What had happened in the interval was that myriad separate women's local and single-issue groups and women's national organizations had formed links, ranging from personal friendships to powerfully structured alliances, which enabled them to make mileage out of these occasions in massive 'alternative summits' alongside the official events. The Forward Looking Strategies of Nairobi, and the Platform for Action resulting from the Beijing conference, became important organizing tools for women's groups worldwide (Ashworth, 1995).

Women in Development (WID) was one of the first themes to take off in this contemporary internationalization of feminism. Kathleen Newland has described how the WID movement stepped from being a transnational to an international phenomenon in the early 1970s precisely through the intergovernmental machinery of the UN (Newland, 1991). But mobilization spread from one issue to the next as one dimension of women's disadvantage could be seen to underpin another. Women's international fora accompanied the World Conference on the Environment and Development in Rio de Janeiro in 1992 (Peterson and Runyan, 1993), that on Human Rights in Vienna in 1993 and the International Conference on Population and Development, where the focus was reproductive rights, in Cairo in 1994 (Yuval-Davis, 1995). Women's organizations from different member states also work together to sustain a permanent lobby at such bodies as the UN Commission on the Status of Women and the UN Commission on Human Rights, in New York. The EU also has its Women's Lobby in Brussels (Hoskyns, 1996).

One of the more autonomous, because more politically contentious and confrontational, strands in the global women's movement has been that which concerns itself with opposing militarism and war. Women's peace groups and networks take many different names Vrouwen voor Vrieden, Dones Antimilitaristes, Frauen für den Frieden, the Women's International League for Peace and Freedom. They also choose different styles and strategies. The Greenham Peace Camp, for instance, was noted for its effective use of local, grassroots non-violent direct action. But Greenham women also internationalized their protest by networking widely with women opposed to the siting of cruise missiles at various European sites, at Pine Gap in Australia and Seneca Falls in the USA (Roseneil, 1995). An example that contrasts in style is that of the NATO Alerts Network, which mobilized women Members of Parliament and other notable women and undertook daring 'alternative diplomacy', forming alliances with women of the Warsaw Pact countries and addressing leading statesmen and military leaders (Paula Rose, 1995).

One name given to women's anti-war actions in many countries today is Women in Black (WIB) (Mujeres en Negro, Femmes en Noir, Zene u Crnom). And the trope of WIB recurs at different moments in the stories of Bat Shalom, Medica, the Women's Support Network and their Women Building Bridges project. It has been one theme in their international connectedness, and it exemplifies the cross-fertilizations that characterize the worldwide women's movement.

The name WIB was first used in Israel in the mid-1980 by women demonstrating against the Israeli occupation of the West Bank. They established a certain style for WIB actions – women standing in silent vigil, wearing black, carrying banners and placards, boldly positioned in public places such as busy cross-roads.

I first made contact not only with the Bat Shalom women but also with the Bosnian women at a WIB conference organized by the Israeli women in Jerusalem in 1994. Most of the women who are members of Bat Shalom today were previously active in WIB groups.

Women of the Italian peace movement, particularly the Donne Associazione per la Pace, had been actively networking with the Israeli/Palestinian women. They carried the WIB theme back to Italy, so that WIB groups now exist in many cities there. At the outbreak of the Yugoslav wars in the early 1990s the

Italian women went to Belgrade to lend solidarity to anti-nationalist feminist groups. The WIB group that formed there has held weekly vigils in Republic Square ever since, withstanding abuse and sometimes with violence for their witness against the Milosevic regime. WIB Belgrade organizes annual WIB international encounters at Novi Sad, drawing together women from many parts of the world who by now identify with this name. They are also the source of international information flows via e-mail about developments in the Yugoslav region.

In 1991 with other women I began co-ordinating a WIB group in London in opposition to Britain's involvement in the Gulf War. During the Yugoslav wars in 1993–5 we organized vigils in Trafalgar Square in support of WIB Belgrade and in solidarity with women suffering ethnic aggression and rape in Bosnia. WIB vigils have been held since then in many UK cities, including Belfast where women of the Women's Support Network were instrumental.

WIB Belgrade has been an important ally of Medica. In Bosnia-Hercegovina, in the first war-torn years of the new state, there was no Bosnian postal service. There were no postage stamps printed until the war was over. But the international telephone lines, though often interrupted, survived during the war. But WIB ensured contact with Medica through telephone, fax and e-mail. Linked by the 'zamir' (it means 'peace') e-mail server both groups were also in touch throughout the war with women activists in Zagreb. They were also getting news by e-mail to and from women's organizations in Germany, other European countries and in the USA, some of whom helped to fund the project. No sooner had the Dayton Line been drawn to separate the Republika Srpska from the Bosnian–Croat Federation than women of WIB Belgrade, together with Zagreb activists, facilitated a meeting in Banja Luka between women of the two halves of Bosnia.

The result of this networking was that, ironically, there was more of a 'Yugoslav' feminist movement after the war than there was before Yugoslavia disintegrated. This was very clear at the conference organized by women in Zagreb in 1996, under the title Women and the Politics of Peace (Centre for Women's Studies, 1997). Women attended from all the former Yugoslav countries, undeterred by the new state boundaries set up purposely to divide Serbs, Croats and Muslims. Other women came from much further afield. At this conference Marie Mulholland, then co-ordinator of the Women's Support Network, and I gave a talk about the Women Building Bridges project. A member of Bat Shalom was also there.

Like Medica, Bat Shalom has made good use of telephone, fax and e-mail. It has put out almost daily bulletins to women's organizations around the world about abuses of human rights and the vagaries of the peace process in Israel/Palestine. Bat Shalom's own political practice is in turn sustained by inward information flows both from supporters and from other women in areas of conflict.

The Women's Support Network, until its involvement in Women Building Bridges, had fewer international contacts than the other two projects. They had, however, co-ordinated or co-operated in broader women's alliances in Northern

Ireland, such as Women Working for Change which focused on equality proof-
ing the Peace and Reconciliation funding programme, involving contact with the
EU in Brussels. They had also been developing cross-border links with organiza-
tions in the Republic of Ireland, particularly the National Council of Women of
Ireland. Since the exchange visits the Network have continued their contact with
Medica, including participating with them in a conference on War, Gender and
Traumatization in Bonn in October 1998.

An interesting and potentially effective link between feminist peace
researchers, and increasingly between researchers and activists, is the Women
and Conflict Zones Network (WICZNET), based in York University, Toronto.
WICZNET uses e-mail to exchange information about women caught up in
war, to report women's anti-war action and to share research and analysis.
Through my membership of WICZNET the Women Building Bridges project
has been presented and discussed by women from many other conflict zones.
And Medica woman attended a WICZNET seminar in Sri Lanka and will be
involved in hosting one in Bosnia in 1999.

The process of international feminist networking described here is of benefit
to women in two ways. First, within the projects, being able to emphasize other
unaccustomed differences, differences between one country and another, one
conflict and another, one women's group and another, can be a helpful way of
putting in perspective your home-grown bitter ethno-national tensions and so
reducing polarization inside the project. It becomes possible to look beyond the
divided community, putting communal boundaries into softer focus by
stepping outside and looking back at them from an international vantage point.

Conversely, the skills required for the detailed, intimate and sustained
practice of cross-national working across differences, necessarily developed by
projects like the Women's Support Network, Bat Shalom or Medica to handle
internal ethno-national difference, are a valuable resource when it comes to
relating across state boundaries. And they have relevance beyond the anti-war
movement. The same skills and sensitivity to difference and inequality, the tools
of transversal politics, are needed in encounters between women of the rich
North and those of the poor South, or in co-operation between women of the
capitalist West and the ex-communist East.

Deploying the skills of transversal politics, 'feminists, despite and because of
their diversity and pluralism, have become a new force in international politics.
It is a force of ideas, invention and commitment rather than economic resources,
of courage, morality and justice instead of technology and tanks' (Ashworth,
1995: 2). Even a sustainable global women's movement cannot of itself eradicate
women's disadvantage, but it can ensure that when new abuses come to light,
when women's wellbeing and rights are further attacked, as in Bosnia yesterday
and Afghanistan or Algeria today, women are quicker to support each other in
exposing and resisting this.

5

MAKING GLOBAL CONNECTIONS AMONG WOMEN, 1970–99

Deborah Stienstra

As I suggested in an earlier account, up to 1991, very little had been written about women's movements

> which organize specifically at the international level or deal with global issues related to women. A different approach could be taken that identifies indigenous or national women's movements in different countries of the world and how they have formed bonds across national borders. The approach I have taken could be called top-down, while the second approach could be called bottom-up (Stienstra, 1994: xvi).

Since 1991, many others have written on women's global organizing from different perspectives. Amrita Basu's marvellous collection, *The challenge of local feminisms: women's movements in global perspective*, takes the bottom-up approach, emphasizing the 'local origins, character and concerns' (Basu, 1995: 19) of women's movements across the globe. Inderpal Grewal and Caren Kaplan's *Scattered hegemonies: postmodernity and transnational feminist practices* (1994) uses post-modernism to unsettle our understandings of how women's organizing is shaped by local and global discursive practices. Others have sought to find ways to understand and explain specifically how women in the South organize globally (Afshar, 1998), how specific groups of women, like Muslim women, organize (Afkhami and Friedl, 1997), or how particular global networks contribute to an understanding of global feminism (Moghadam, 1996). Still others have approached women's organizing from the context of their contributions to public policy (Lycklama à Nijeholt *et al.*, 1998).

I earlier argued that when women's groups organize, they use a range of political practices especially in relation to international organizations from disengagement to mainstreaming:

> Disengagement is an attempt by groups to remain separate from existing society institutions and provide critiques of and alternatives to these

institutions. Mainstreaming refers to the practices of those groups that work for change within the context of existing institutions and propose adaptations that would allow for change without transformation (Stienstra, 1994: 32).

This remains a useful distinction, although there is more blurring of the line between the two even within groups, and the forces of globalization (or neoliberalism) have created greater constraints for action by groups, states and international organizations as I shall argue in my update to the original piece at the end.

WOMEN'S INTERNATIONAL ORGANIZING, 1970–90

The two decades from 1970 to 1990 were the most dynamic in the history of international women's movements. More women than ever before organized at the international level and in the context of global issues such as the debt crisis, prostitution and the international sexual division of labour. The international groups established during the earlier periods continued their work, using their status within the United Nations (UN) to work for alternative spaces for women within that system. Many of the new groups defined themselves as feminist and worked inside and outside the existing international system. Their goals were to bring women together to share information, resources and strategies and as a result to create alternative spaces for women at the global level outside of the UN framework.

These two patterns of women's organizing complemented and reinforced each other throughout this period. While the established groups had access to more resources, especially money, organizational strength and the links to the UN system, the newer groups had vitality, creativity and links to grassroots networks of women.

The traditional groups were able to spearhead the campaigns for an International Women's Year and co-ordinated the organization of the UN Decade for Women non-governmental conferences which were the major focus for women's international activity between 1975 and 1985.

The newer groups were often organized in response to the activities around the UN Decade for Women conferences or in response to changes in the situation of women resulting from changes in the international political economy. While activities such as the International Tribunal on Crimes Against Women in 1976 were organized in conscious opposition to the International Women's Year Conference, other groups, such as Women's Studies International and the network 'Women, Environment and Sustainable Development' came directly from the non-governmental fora held parallel to the official UN Decade for Women conferences. Other groups have organized around the increased poverty and hardship caused by changes in the global political economic order. Development Alternatives for Women for a New Era (DAWN) is a network of third-world scholars and activists who seek to provide alternatives strategies, based on women's experiences, to the existing process of economic development in the regions of the South. Another network was formed in 1990 to develop 'gender-focused' alternatives to structural adjustment policies.

ESTABLISHED GROUPS

Many of the already established international women's groups, including International Alliance of Women (IAW), Women's International Democratic Federation and International Federation of Business and Professional Women, continued their activities for international co-operation among women during this period, especially under the umbrella of the UN. Much of their activity inside the UN could be described as interest-group activity, such as providing information about the opinion of their constituencies to the UN and member states; providing information about the activities of the UN to their membership; and lobbying representatives of member states and members of the UN Secretariat to ensure their positions were taken into account (Judge and Skjelbaek, 1975; Steele-Orsini and Wuthrich, 1984). Established women's groups failed to provide expert advice or technical expertise to the UN. While specific individuals within these groups did provide technical expertise as consultants, the groups themselves did not provide the support that some human rights groups such as Amnesty International provide to the Commission on Human Rights.

Those established groups working within the context of the UN system, for the most part, had consultative status with the Economic and Social Council (ECOSOC) or one of the other specialized agencies. Consultative status with ECOSOC allows groups to make or submit statements and attend intergovernmental meetings as observers.[1] Seven of the established women's groups have ECOSOC status I; eighteen have ECOSOC status II and six are on the Roster. These groups have also obtained consultative status in a number of the specialized agencies, but in almost every case their participation is limited to agencies which focus on traditional areas related to women including education, food, children, labour and health. Other organizations formed links with other intergovernmental organizations outside the UN system including the Commonwealth, the Council of Europe and the Organization of American States.

The activities of established groups with UN consultative status are the most important for our discussions here, since they provided much of the framework and support for the UN Decade for Women. Once the decade was declared, thanks in large part to the work of these groups, many groups used their consultative status to press for specific research and funding institutions for women and mechanisms to monitor the status of women within the UN system as well as for action around specific issues.

The groups with consultative status used their statements to the Commission on the Status of Women (CSW) and their participation in other fora as the basis for lobbying governments for action on the establishment of the International

Women's Year, and for bringing forward new issues of concern to women. Members of the UN Secretariat credit the groups with putting the issue of vulnerable women, and especially women with disabilities and elderly women, on the agenda for the CSW during the Decade for Women (Mathiason, 1990).

But the groups with status also co-ordinated non-governmental activities around women within the context of the UN. Within the Coordinating Body of Non-Governmental Organizations (CONGO), three separate committees on women exist in New York, Geneva and Vienna. All three were established during the UN Decade for Women and facilitated the discussion of women's concerns among interested international non-governmental organizations (INGOs), including mixed-gender groups. These committees not only provided for discussion on the advancement of women, but they also allowed for research on specific topics and presentation of specific resolutions or actions to inter-governmental bodies. The Geneva committee established a working group on unhealthy traditional practices, did research on the subject, and eventually provided the Commission on Human Rights with a resolution on this topic (Herdt, 1990). The three non-governmental committees on women also provided the organizational support for the three non-governmental women's conferences during the Decade and for a number of non-governmental consultations held prior to sessions of the CSW since 1985.[2]

A third type of action by international women's groups with consultative status were co-operative ventures with the UN agencies or the UN Secretariat. The most long-standing has been the development, together with the Joint UN Information Committee, of development education kits on different issues of concern to women. This venture was initiated following the 1980 Copenhagen Conference and was seen as an opportunity to provide groups with educational and reference material for further exploration on these issues.[3] Other groups were contracted by agencies of the UN to deliver services or programmes in different countries. This is only beginning to happen among international women's groups and it is due in large part to the increasing emphasis of the UN Development Program for Women (UNIFEM) on creating links with non-governmental organizations. The International Women's Tribune Centre delivered a series of workshops for UNIFEM in 1990 (Walker, 1991).

A final area where international women's groups with consultative status were active was through the development of joint NGO initiatives. While the NGO committees on women in New York, Geneva and Vienna collaborated to develop positions to bring to UN bodies, several NGOs also joined forces to develop new initiatives for women. This was a relatively new and very limited approach within the women's community at the UN. It was rare for the leadership of the different organizations to meet together, apart from signing each others' statements to the UN (Haslegrave, 1990). At the 1990 NGO Consultation, the presidents of the different women's NGOs met for the first time to discuss the possibilities for common action.

One long-standing collaborative venture between four of the INGOs is Project Five-O. When it was first conceived in 1975, five INGOs were involved –

Soroptimist International, International Federation of Business and Professional Women, International Federation of University Women, International Council of Women and the Associated Country Women of the World. Its project was to establish projects to assist women in the Third World, especially in the areas of literacy, health and agriculture (Project Five-O, 1990). Despite limited funds and the small number of projects started, the participants consider this a successful co-operative venture. Another example of a joint NGO venture is the group Advocates for African Food Security: Lessening the Burden for Women, although from its beginning in 1986 it has included both women's and mixed-gender groups and has more recently been joined by UN and governmental agencies.

Between 1970 and 1990 the established international women's groups brought both strengths and weaknesses to their work within the UN. The continuing presence of INGOs with consultative status at meetings on the advancement of women, as well as in areas not traditionally associated with women, sustained the pressure to incorporate an analysis of women's situations from a non-governmental perspective within the context of the UN. The NGOs were persistent in advocating an international conference on women in 1972 and were able to get an international year for women adopted. The International Women's Year in 1975 and the UN Decade for Women were major catalysts in international activities related to women at the governmental and non-governmental levels. In the context of these events, INGOs were able to encourage governments to continue to address issues related to the advancement of women in the UN context. These groups were also, as a result of their many volunteers and institutional resources, able to organize major non-governmental conferences on women in 1975, 1980 and 1985 which have given women who had little or no contact with the UN an opportunity to meet and exchange ideas and strategies. More generally, the strengths of the established groups during this period were their constancy and persistence, as well as the volunteer labour and institutional and organizational resources they have brought to international organizing.

But their work remains extremely limited for a variety of reasons. The historical structures of their own organizations as well as their access to resources constrain their work. By opting to work within the framework of the consultative status of the UN they remain bit players in the overall production of intergovernmental activities on women.

The primary purpose of most established groups was to promote international cooperation among women or to organize women who shared a similar identity. Only the IAW organized in order to work for change in the situation of women, and the means to do this for the IAW was equal rights. Thus, none of the groups, except the IAW, define themselves as feminist, and most remain reluctant to do so. The result of this is that most of their memberships have remained separate from the developing feminist consciousness around the world and the feminist organizing at the grassroots. Rather, these established groups continued to pursue issues as they came up, either through their memberships, the interests of an individual or leader within the group or as a response to activities of other groups or agencies. Their relatively broad mandates gave the international representatives the opportunity to comment on a wide variety of issues, but the broad mandates also meant that the goals or strategies for change in women's lives pursued by these groups remained vague. This limited their ability to act effectively and with the full support of their memberships.

The established groups were also constrained to act because of the structure of their organizations, memberships and funding.[4] Many of the established groups retained a very bureaucratic and hierarchical organizational structure, with local chapters, national bodies and an international federation. The impetus for action at the international level came from international meetings every three, four or five years that gave policy direction. Yet the implementation of these directions as well as the response to immediate situations came from the international executive, the secretariat and the representative to the UN. Most of the organizations had a difficult time maintaining the links between their memberships at the local level and their leadership (Bloomer, 1990; Haslegrave, 1990; Mlango, 1990). While some organizations allocated at least one seat on the executive for a woman from the Third World, white, middle-class women from First World countries filled most of the executive positions. Most of the presidential and international representative positions in these groups remained volunteer unpaid jobs located in cities in the First World. These features prevented from participating in these decision-making positions many women from Third World countries, except for those who had some external financial support, as well as many women who were otherwise employed or without a partner to support them biannually. What this created was an élite of increasingly elderly, married and middle- or upper-class women who represented their organizations at the international level and provided direction to NGO activities around women in the UN. When combined with the vague mandates, these organizations remained unable to provide the vitality and feminist direction that was needed at the international level. One sardonic comment made about the issues brought forward by these groups is that as their leadership aged, the issue of women and ageing became the priority area for the established groups. While clearly somewhat facetious, there is a kernel of truth that illustrates the privileged position of many among the international women's leadership in bringing forward issues to the UN.

The established groups also remained constrained at the international level by the sources of their funding. For most, the funding they received came from their membership, which were disproportionately located in the North and especially in North America and Europe. The Women's International Democratic Federation, in contrast, received much of its support from individuals and governments in Eastern Europe as well as from socialist movements in the South. As well, many of the established groups received project and conference funding from international aid agencies. In all cases, the funding received shaped the type of participation of these groups. Membership funding remained modest and was used to maintain an international secretariat and fund the regular international conferences. Governmental funding, especially that from the East European countries, had often been suspect and seen to link groups to promoting an official line (Mathiason, 1990). Funding from international aid agencies was usually used for travel for women from the Third World or for specific development project work. In all cases, the established international women's groups were ineffective in raising large sums of money for their work (Haslegrave, 1990) and this further constrained their ability to work at the international level.

A final constraint on the effectiveness of the established international women's groups was the structure of the UN consultative arrangements. While the ECOSOC consultative arrangements gave minimal access for NGOs to the decision-making processes, they required a certain level of organizational development to produce the necessary documentation. To do this with volunteer labour was a fairly demanding requirement. But more importantly, international NGOs with consultative status remained at the margins of decision-making, left to perform lobbying and information-exchange functions. Their work also had to be tailored to the agenda of the intergovernmental agencies and it was difficult to encourage the discussion of new issues or different approaches within the intergovernmental arenas, especially if access to the process was limited to written or oral statements and corridor lobbying.

NEWLY EMERGING GROUPS

A large number of international women's groups that focused on specific issues and organized around feminist principles were newly organized between 1970 and 1990. Their issues included communications, health, reproductive rights, peace, prostitution and the exploitation of women, and the environment. Of these groups well over half considered their work to be networking. While earlier established groups had practised networking among those women active at the international level, their organizational structures did not facilitate networking outside of this élite. The groups that emerged during the 1970s and 1980s made it their priority to mobilize women and co-ordinate local and national activities through networking. As Karl (1986: 10), one of the founders of the International Women's Information and Communication Service (known as ISIS), the earliest network during this period, notes, many of the networks 'have rejected rigid and heavy bureaucratic structures in favor of informal, non-hierarchical and open structures and ways of operating. This gives networks a flexibility and possibility to respond and take action quickly when necessary'.

Often these networks organized around specific issues or actions. For example, the International Feminist Network was established in 1976 to provide support for and action on behalf of women around the world who were being persecuted because of their sex. Another network, and one of the strongest during this period, is the international network on women and health issues, which has been at the forefront of identifying women's health concerns since 1977.[5] A network, formed in 1984, that links women in Africa, Asia and other parts of the world is

Women under Muslim Laws, which supports the struggles of women who live where Islam is the basis for the state structure.

But the international activities of women between 1970 and 1990 were not limited to forming organizations or networks. A significant part of women's organizing took place through international and regional conferences, tribunals and workshops. While the international women's organizations held regular meetings at the international level, there were many international gatherings of women not linked to the maintenance of one specific organization. These ranged in scope from the 1985 Nairobi NGO Forum, with its 15,000 participants from 150 countries and 2,000 workshops, to the 1979 Bangkok workshop on Feminist Ideology and Structures in the First Half of the Decade with its 15 participants from 11 countries (Bunch and Castley, 1980: 23–44). These two gatherings also reflected some of the changes in international women's organizing through these two decades. The Nairobi meeting was held at the culmination of the UN Decade for Women. Women from all over the world travelled to Kenya to celebrate the work, share strategies and information, and create new networks for further collaboration. But the Nairobi meeting could not have happened without the diligent work of those 15 women in Bangkok struggling with the definition of feminism, or without the other organizing efforts of women before and since 1970.

THE ROLE OF COMMUNICATIONS

In the first half of the 1970s, at a time when women, especially in North America and Europe, were reforming their feminist movements, women began to develop a foundation for international communications among women. At least four different organizations responded to the need to promote communication among women and information about women across the world. All were initially based in the North, and while all developed communications systems, their goals and approaches to feminism were quite different.

The first feminist communications network was the ISIS, which was explicitly feminist in orientation and organized by a group of women in the North and the South. These women, who were working with women at local and international levels, felt the urgent need to share experiences and information among the many new women's groups that were springing up all over the world. We felt, and still feel, that information and communication are basic elements for empowerment and development, for women to become aware of their situations and do something to change it (Karl, 1986: 12).

ISIS began its work by publishing the proceedings of the 1976 International Tribunal on Crimes against Women in Brussels. This gathering of 2,000 women was developed as an opportunity for the legitimate concerns of women to be raised on their own terms rather than in response to the intergovernmental agenda of International Women's Year in 1975.

From its initial publication onward ISIS voiced the words of women's movements and maintained a documentation centre for information about women. It was based initially in Rome and Geneva. In addition, after the 1976 Tribunal, ISIS co-ordinated the International Feminist Network. The vision of the founders of ISIS was of an organization in many ways antithetical to the earlier international women's groups. As Cottingham (1989: 244) notes:

> The essence of ISIS is that it is small and autonomous. It was conceived as a channel of communication for women and women's movements internationally. Its very philosophy excluded the building up of a heavy institutionalized structure with member associations all over the world. We wanted to work directly with groups in their own context, responding to their need for information, and helping to put them in touch with others doing similar work.

In 1984, ISIS split into two separate and independent organizations: ISIS International, based in Rome, and ISIS-WICCE (Women's International Cross-Cultural Exchange) based in Geneva. ISIS International has continued to maintain resource centres and publish information in conjunction with women's groups all around the world and to co-ordinate, through an office in Santiago, the Latin American and Caribbean Women's Health Network. In 1990, ISIS International moved its office in Rome to Manila. ISIS-WICCE has taken a very innovative and successful approach to sharing information among women. Each year it facilitates a cross-cultural exchange programme on a different theme between women who work in different regions of the world. Several of the themes have been women and health; women living under Muslim laws; documentation and information exchange; and prostitution and poverty. Each of the 10 or so women involved in the exchange spend about three months working with their receiving group in a culture different from their own. This type of interaction has created new links among women at the local level and enabled many women who would not otherwise be able to travel a chance to work and learn about women's situations in another culture.[6]

Another communications network begun during the mid-1970s was the Women's International Network (WIN) and its newsletter, *WIN News*. This one-woman show, based in the United States, provides a wealth of information on women's international activities and opportunities for women in international organizations. Fran Hoskens, the co-ordinator of this network, has been at the forefront of several issues of concern to women, such as genital mutilation. But for some *WIN News* also epitomized the patronizing attitudes of Western feminists on the issue of genital mutilation. While it was filled with interesting and accurate information on the subject, *WIN News* was written by someone from outside the cultures affected and could be seen as a criticism of traditional practices. Hoskens has been criticized for failing to recognize that most cultures have traditional practices that oppress women and that change of these practices must come through the women within the cultures, not from outsiders (Hoskens, 1978/9).

In 1975, following the International Women's Year Conference and NGO Tribune in Mexico City, the International Women's Tribune Centre (IWTC) was established. Its purpose was initially to maintain communications between the 6,000 participants at the tribune. Since that time, the IWTC has developed as a network of networks, providing technical assistance to women's groups and sharing information through a newsletter and publications. At the 1980 and 1985 NGO Forums, IWTC sponsored a special exhibit; in 1980 entitled Vivencia, which provided an ongoing support and information service for participants who wanted to create workshops and activities at the forum (IWTC, 1984: 27); and in 1985, entitled Tech and Tools, which provided information and hands-on displays related to appropriate technology for women. The IWTC's special contribution to international women's communications is that its publications are available in several languages, are easy to read, and are accessible to those who are illiterate or only partially literate. Thus, the publications, and they are free to women from the South, can be used not only by the leadership of groups, but also by those at the grassroots level.

The final corner of the foundation of international women's communications came with the development of international press services focused exclusively on women. In the late 1970s women's feature services were established in the Caribbean (the Caribbean Women's Feature Syndicate), Asia (Depthnews Asian Women's Feature Service) and Africa (African Women's Features Service) (Rush and Ogan, 1989: 268–73). When funding became a problem in 1986, the Women's Feature Service was established within the Inter Press Service of Rome to provide features written by women journalists from the Third World for the news media. In addition, between 1980 and 1985 women journalists organized their own international news service called the Women's International News Service through the Women's Institute for Freedom of the Press (Kassell and Kaufman, 1989).

These four corners provide only the basis from which international feminist communications has developed. Other women's news agencies have been developed in France, Germany and Chile. As well, an international conference of women's documentation and information centres took place in 1989 to discuss new communications technologies and strategies to co-ordinate the collection of information. These activities all reflect the relatively strong communications links that have developed between women's movements around the world.[7]

FEMINISM AS A BASIS

In the 1970s a conscious attempt was made by many women's organizations to develop a conceptual framework relating feminism to other structures or forces in the world. Initially, the attempts came through the link between women and development and dealt with the relationships between feminism and socialism, but by 1979–80 some women were attempting to define feminism and to outline the specific relationships among women and their relationship to global structures. These discussions and the follow-up work provided a conceptual basis for international women's organizing.

At the 1975 Mexico City non-governmental Tribune the initial debates about feminism began. A number of the participants assumed that the feminism they knew provided a common framework to describe women's concerns. In one instance, a number of predominantly Western women – as part of a 'feminist' caucus led by Gloria Steinhem, a prominent US feminist – prepared a feminist manifesto that put forward a picture of women's situation that lacked input from Third World women (Greer, 1975: 4). The differences around the importance or priority given to feminism between women from First and Third world countries were significant. Many Latin American women rejected the primacy of 'women's issues' put forward by US feminists. As one commentator notes:

> there [was] a subtle but significant resistance to feminism as a new form of cultural imperialism. Gloria Steinhem's speech left a number of women distrustful of the clean sweep of her logic. 'She claims that she does not want to choose for us,' they said, 'but she has it so well figured out that it seems to leave no alternatives; her speech is coercive' (Whitaker, 1975: 178).

Similar tensions around the place of feminism in women's organizing and the primacy attached to it by many Western feminists, were also evident at an international conference on women and development held at Wellesley College in the United States in 1976. This was in part a follow-up conference to the Seminar on Women in Development held just prior to the Mexico City Tribune, and which attempted to define how development programmes had ignored women's contributions to society (Tinker, 1976: 1). In 1976, 500 participants, most of them with academic backgrounds, came together to discuss the issues that women in the Third World had to face in response to the changes in their economies, societies and cultures as a result of development processes (Wellesley Editorial Committee, 1977: ix). While the conference represented a unique attempt to bring academic women together from the South and the North, in the eyes of some of the women from the Third World it continued to assume a singular vision of feminism based on white Western women's conceptions. An open letter from three of the participants, Nawal El Saadawi from Egypt, Fatima Mernissi from Morocco and Mallica Vajrathon from Thailand, was published in a number of international women's magazines (El Saadawi, 1978). In it they voiced as their goal 'to destroy the myth that the mere fact of being women will unite us and that women are not political beings; that political discussions at women's meetings mean "diverting from women's issues." ' Their efforts were aimed at encouraging discussions, at international gatherings, on the impact of economics, multinational corporations and trade on women's lives and exposing the links between women's oppression and these aspects of the global political economic order.[8]

Women, mainly from Europe, came together to discuss these relationships in May and June 1977 at two conferences on feminism and socialism. In Paris between 3,000 and 5,000 women met in May to discuss what links the women's movement has and how it can create links to other movements of the left.

In Amsterdam women came with the commitment that 'no feminism without socialism, no socialism without feminism' to develop an analysis of reproduction, housework and the family to broaden socialist analysis. These two meetings provided a strong basis for socialist–feminist organizing especially in Europe.

In 1979 the issue of whether or not one could describe feminism as the goal and conceptual basis of women's organizing at the international level was addressed in a systematic fashion, and for the first time a definition of the goals of feminism was given. Through an international workshop in Bangkok, sponsored by the Asian and Pacific Centre for Women and Development (APCWD) of the UN Economic and Social Commission for Asia and Pacific, 15 women from 11 countries were brought together to discuss Feminist Ideology and Structures. The participants at this workshop described two long-term goals of feminism:

> First the freedom from oppression for women involves not only equity, but also the right of women to freedom of choice, and the power to control their own lives within and outside of the home. Having control over our lives and our bodies is essential to ensure a sense of dignity and autonomy for every woman. . . . The second goal of feminism is therefore the removal of all forms of inequity and oppression through the creation of a more just social and economic order, nationally and internationally. This means the involvement of women in national liberation struggles, in plans for national development, and in local and global strategies for change (Bunch and Castley, 1980: 27).

These goals, and development in the workshop report of the links between the goals and structures such as the state, socialism, political parties and the women's movements, provided a firm conceptual basis upon which women's international organizing could build. The type of feminism that was advocated was a transformational politics (Bunch *et al.*, 1985: 244), one which was involved in bringing about changes in women's lives by creating movements and challenging structures through strategies of mainstreaming and disengagement, or as the participants called them, reformist and revolutionary strategies.

As a follow-up to the Bangkok workshop, a second workshop was held in April 1980 in Stony Point, New York, entitled Developing Strategies for the Future: Feminist Perspectives. Its goal was to bring women from the South and the North together to discuss whether common strategies for change could be developed in the specific areas of women and development; the role of the women's movement; and networking, alliances and linkages (Bunch and Castley, 1980: 4–18). With a videotape of this workshop, the report was used as a tool to continue discussions around these subjects and strategies among women's groups around the world.

Together these two workshops gave a written framework for discussions around feminism during the 1980s. Charlotte Bunch suggests that these conferences 'were seen as manifestos for the 1980 Mid-Decade Conference in

Copenhagen. They aimed at mobilizing women and calling attention to the global implications of feminism in general as well as in relation to development' (Bunch and Carrillo, 1990: 78). At the Copenhagen non-governmental Forum, ISIS, the IWTC and several feminist publications, facilitated workshops on the subject of the global nature of feminism and the implications of working with women at the global level.

During the 1980s, women in the Third World, increasingly organized around and defined feminism for themselves. In 1981 in Bogotá, the first Latin American Feminist Meeting was held with 270 women from 11 Latin American countries (Portugal, 1990: 19). These women chose to call themselves feminists and created space for an autonomous feminist movement in their region. Latin American and Caribbean feminist meetings have continued and grown in strength: meetings were held in Lima in 1983, Bertioga in 1985, Taxco in 1987 and San Bernardo in 1990 with 3,000 women.

In 1982 in Senegal some 40 women from the South and the North again chose the starting point of feminism and developed an analysis of the links between women's situations and the direction of development in what is known as the 'Dakar Declaration on another development with women'. Their work complemented the earlier work of the Bangkok and Stony Point groups because most of the participants were from francophone or continental European countries (Bunch and Carrillo, 1990: 78). The Dakar declaration described both what unified and diversified feminists around the world:

> Feminism is international in defining as its aim the liberation of women from all types of oppression and in providing solidarity among women of all countries; it is national in stating its priorities and strategies in accordance with particular cultural and socio-economic conditions (Bunch and Carrillo, 1990: 80).

These articulations of feminism in the global context remain at the foundation of much of contemporary feminist organizing at the international level. Two examples illustrate this. In 1984 women from different regions of the South came together in Bangalore, India, to examine development policies and the economic and environmental crises from the vantage point of poor women in the Third World (Sen and Grown, 1987). From this initial meeting came the network DAWN which brings together women from the South to do research and initiate action based on women's experiences and links feminist analysis with other types of analysis, such as socialism.

A second example of women's organizing that more explicitly used the analysis of feminism developed around 1980 was the series of workshops on feminist perspectives held at the Second International Interdisciplinary Congress on Women in Groningen, the Netherlands, in 1984. These workshops were held in order to allow women to explore their own understandings of feminism, but also to use feminist perspectives on the issues of power, strategies and diversity to evaluate the many sessions of the congress and the workings of the congress itself (Bunch *et al.*, 1985). The congress had over 600 women in attendance, although the majority was from Europe and North America. The recommendations of the participants of the feminist-perspectives workshops were for a more focused, truly international and diversified conference in the future. The organizers of the Nairobi Forum used many of these recommendations in 1985.

ORGANIZING AROUND EMERGING ISSUES

During the Decade for Women, the importance of different themes changed partly in response to the rise of leadership from women in the Third World, but also in response to the changing situation of women around the world. In Mexico City in 1975 the largest number of workshops related to issues of women's equality in areas like equal rights, discrimination and political participation. Development issues were discussed in the context of the discussions around a new international economic order, and the absence of any mention of women's role in this. Sessions were focused on identifying the ways that women participated in the development process as agricultural or craft producers, and the way that development policies have negatively affected the lives of women in the Third World.

By 1980 and the Copenhagen Forum, the concentration of issues had shifted into a broader range of issues. Development, at the Copenhagen meetings, was wider in scope than in Mexico City, covering issues such as income generation for women, how to use international development networks, critiques of women in development ideologies, women and credit and the use of appropriate technology. Many of these were co-ordinated through a project sponsored by the African–American Institute called the Exchange, concerned especially with the effects of development on women in the Third World. As Peggy Antrobus from the Barbados and the chairperson of the advisory committee for the Exchange noted:

At Mexico City, the issues [around women and development] seemed very clear to me, and maybe to many of us. We were talking then of integrating women into the process of development, both as agents and beneficiaries. After five years and a lot of thought and a lot of action on my part, I am not so certain. The problem seems much more complex. Some of us are beginning to wonder whether women *do* want to be integrated into what are essentially patriarchal structures (Exchange, 1980: 5).

The Exchange workshops also acted as a lightning rod for many criticisms about the lack of participation from women in the Third World, and some commented that the presenters were 'from either developed countries with "developed" ideas or from developing countries adapted to the "developed" world's thinking.' (Exchange, 1980: 1.)

In the 1985 Nairobi Forum development issues were the predominant issue. But as women's situations had changed in the previous five years with the debt crisis in the Third World and famine in Africa, so had the themes of the workshops at the 1985 forum. A large percentage of the development sessions were held on the world development crises, grassroots organizing, food security and women and energy and environment (Forum '85, 1985: 62). An increasing number of workshops were held on the themes of refugees and migrants, a topic initially discussed at Copenhagen. Finally, as at Copenhagen, a large number of sessions dealt with networking, although those involved were different than in 1980. Asia–Pacific women, Black American and African–American women, and African women (Lewis, 1988) were among the major groups to organize at Forum '85. Lesbians were also much higher in profile than they had been at the previous conferences. These workshops illustrated the growing strength of organizing among women in the South as well as among women who have often been marginalized in the women's movements in the North.

One of the clearest examples of women's organizing at the international level in response to changes in their situation is the development of DAWN. DAWN was initiated in 1984, but the measure of its support was first seen in the number of women who attended DAWN workshops at the Nairobi Forum. The 2,000 participants who attended these workshops outlined the effects of a growth-oriented development, the effects of the economic and political crises on women's lives, the movements women have been organizing in response to these, and the relationships between socialism and feminism. The analysis upon which these workshops were built is developed further in the book *Development, crises, and alternative visions: Third World women's perspectives* (Sen and Grown, 1987). DAWN has continued to research the effects of the economic and political crises on women and the alternative movements formed in response throughout the South (ISIS and DAWN, 1988). In the years since it was established, DAWN has developed a fairly strong network among researchers in different regions of the South. Several of the members of DAWN, however, comment that making the links between these researchers and women working at the grassroots is a weakness of DAWN's actions thus far (DAWN, 1990; Rodney, 1990; Viezzer, 1990; Nzomo, 1991).

Other groups, based in the North, have also organized in response to issues related to the global political economy. The Women's Network on Global Corporations was formed in 1979 to share information on the effect that multinational corporations have had on the lives of women, especially in the areas of electronics and textiles. Its initial work was with women electronics workers in California, and textile workers in Texas. Much more recently, the network on Gender-focused Alternatives to Structural Adjustment was established in 1990 to provide research and solidarity based on women's experiences as a response to government structural adjustment programmes (UNNGLS, 1990).[9]

Several groups, including the Third World Movement Against the Exploitation of Women (TWMAEW) and the International Feminist Network Against Forced Prostitution and other forms of Female Sexual Slavery, were organized in response to the globalization of prostitution caused in part by the increasing military presence in Asia, the globalization of production and the increase in sex tourism throughout the 1970s and 1980s.[10]

In a different area, and yet also reflecting technological changes in biomedical research and practice, has been the group FINRRAGE (Feminist International Network of Resistance to Reproductive and Genetic Engineering). FINRRAGE was organized in 1984[11] at the Second International Interdisciplinary Congress on Women in the Netherlands. Its goals are to monitor and raise public awareness of the development of reproductive technologies such as contraceptives, *in vitro* fertilization, sex predetermination and genetic screening, and to create an international resistance movement among women to these types of engineering. In 1989, FINRRAGE, together with the Bangladeshi research group UBINIG (acronym of their Bengali name which means Policy Research for Development Alternatives), brought women from the North and the South together in Bangladesh, the first time such a meeting was held in a Third World country, for an international conference on these issues. At that time, the Declaration of Comilla was agreed to by the 145 participants from 30 countries. This declaration traces the links between reproductive and genetic engineering and the ideology of eugenics, which reduces women to reproductive objects and experimental subjects and maintains discrimination on the basis of gender, race, class, caste, religion and disability.

Women have also organized themselves around issues related to the international military order and the effects this has had on women's lives. Women have been organizing around peace and against specific international conflicts for many years. With the 1970s this organizing took on a new form, even though it involved several of the earlier established groups such as Women's International League for Peace and Freedom (WILPF). The primary type of organization, especially in the early 1980s, was the women's peace camp, such as the best-known Greenham Common, and less known camps such as Seneca. These camps were organized initially in opposition to cruise missiles on military bases in Great Britain and the United States, but since then have become a network of women's peace groups and a movement around feminist non-violent action. This method of women's organizing has been limited primarily to first-world countries, as with many peace-related activities.

In 1985, an international conference brought 350 women from 33 countries to Halifax, Canada, around the theme The Urgency for True Security: Women's Alternatives for Negotiating Peace (Runyan, 1988; MacPhee, 1990). This conference, held just before the Nairobi Forum, was one attempt to let women from all parts of the world redefine the ways to negotiate peace in the world. Their ideas were all-encompassing: linking a rejection of militarism to feminism; analysing the ways that military spending reduces the funds available for development; identifying the need for international solidarity among women; and describing the need to provide education on ways to live in peace.

Several of the women went from Halifax to Nairobi, joining the unique efforts to establish a peace tent at the Nairobi Forum. This peace tent provided a space for women to speak about their differences in a safe place. Israeli and Palestinian women talked about the conflicts in their own homes, and women from the United States and the Soviet Union discussed how to bring about peace between their countries. (Forum '85, 1985; Berhane-Selassie, n.d.)

The activist work of women in response to military issues has been complemented by some academic research on women and the military system. In 1987 an international symposium was held in Helsinki with 120 women and 10 men from 17 countries to discuss women's place in the military economy, liberation struggles and the liberation of women, the militarization of women and women and the peace movement (Feminist Forum, 1987; Prudtatorn, 1987; Isaksson, 1988).

Finally, women have organized around the superpower summits of the late 1980s through the network, Women for Mutual Security (WMS). WMS was initiated in 1986 as a response to workshops at the Nairobi Forum in 1985 led by Margarita Papendreou. In response to her call for women to become involved in international negotiations, a number of American women went to the first Reagan–Gorbachev summit in 1985. The network, together with World Women Parliamentarians for Peace, organized a women's presence, from NATO and Warsaw Pact countries, at most of the superpower summits during the latter part of the 1980s. WMS activity is targeted at the élite level – the leaders of the countries, their foreign ministers or the wives of the leaders – and correspondingly many of the WMS representatives, from the East and the West, are high-profile or élite women such as politicians or journalists.

One of the most recent areas in which women have organized in response to changes in the global order has been the environment. While the group WorldWIDE, World Women in the Environment, was established in 1982, it remained a limited international network on women and the environment until after the Nairobi Forum. At the Forum, discussions were held on women and the environment and sustainable development. These evolved into the Women's Environment and Development Organization (WEDO) in 1989 (Union of International Associations, 1990/91: 1455). Women's organizing around the environment was evident at the 1991 World Women's Congress for a Healthy Planet in Miami and participation of many women's groups in the 1992 non-governmental forum accompanying the Earth Summit.

WOMEN'S GLOBAL ORGANIZING AND THE 1990s

The decade of the 1990s saw women's movements move from being bit players on the world stage to main stage actors. Women's groups gained respectability and expertise that extends well outside the traditional women's areas of the UN. Women's movements across the world also developed stronger and more constructive ways of working together at the global level and have used new technologies to strengthen their networks and be more effective in their work. Yet the challenges of globalization and neo-liberal economics continue to challenge women's, and especially feminist, organizing. This section will explore the further development of global women's organizing over the decade, examine successful strategies for affecting the UN, and identify some of the major challenges to global women's organizing.

Women who are organizing transnationally have first and foremost become much more engaged with the UN system. Many more groups have consultative status with the Economic and Social Council, although most of the newer groups have more limited access than do the established ones. An increasing number of these groups are national or local in their scope rather than international. The participation of these groups in the UN is both a cause and effect of increased flexibility in the UN's relationships with NGOs. The UN held a series of global conferences on specific topics including the environment, women, population, human rights, social development and food throughout the 1990s to set a new framework for international actions. NGOs became important players in these meetings and women's groups were among the most active NGOs. At the Earth Summit in 1992 the UN allowed 'competent and relevant' NGOs to receive accreditation to the conference even though they did not have consultative status (Donini, 1996: 84). Approximately 1,400 NGOs were accredited to the conference and thereafter many of these continued to participate in UN proceedings. This more open model of participation was used in most of the other world conferences and many more NGOs participated in the UN as a result. The height of women's groups involvement was in the Beijing Women's Conference where approximately 4,000 representatives of NGOs participated in the intergovernmental conference. Many have continued to attend meetings of the Commission on the Status of Women and are planning for the Women 2000 follow-up conference.

Beyond the work within the UN structures, the face of women's global organizing has moulded in response to the growing strength of women's organizing in the South and an increased capacity to work co-operatively. Women in the South have taken increased leadership in women's groups and an increasing number of international headquarters are located outside of Europe or North America. The best example of the shift to leadership from the South can be seen in the devolution of ISIS International from an organization based in Geneva to multiple organizations based in Manila, Kampala and Santiago. *Women in Action*, which comes from ISIS International in Manila, is an excellent information tool with its roots in the experiences of women in the South. DAWN has continued to play a leadership role among women of the South as well as in coalition with women in the North, especially in providing research by women in the South of the experiences of women in the South. DAWN has been at the forefront of signalling the harmful effects of structural adjustment on women. In fact, DAWN alerted women in the North that this was not simply a Southern woman's problem, but one that would also reshape the lives of women in the North. Canadian activists, such as the president of the National Action Committee on the Status of Women (NAC), Joan Grant-Cummings, credit DAWN for cautioning them about the pending restructuring and the negative effects and identifying possible strategies for working against restructuring (Stienstra, 1999b). This concern about the effects of the global economy led, especially since the Beijing Women's conference, to a coalition of international, regional and national women's groups working together for economic and social justice. The coalition, called Alianza or the Women's Global Alliance for Economic Justice, includes Women in Development Europe (WIDE), DAWN, WEDO, the Centre for Women's Global Leadership, European Solidarity towards Equal Participation of People (EUROSTEP – Gender Working group, an advocacy network in 15 European countries), Alternative Women in Development (Alt-WID, a catalyst group of ad hoc women from different organizations in the USA), and the Society for International Development – gender working group.[12]

Working in coalition has been an effective strategy for women's groups especially in relation to the UN. Within a coalition they can jointly strategize about action around a specific issue while not having to work together around other issue where directions or perspectives may diverge. At this point in the development of global women's movements, there is a strong enough base of women's groups in different countries as well in relation to a wide variety of issues and this makes coalition more possible. Discussions within the movements around issues of diversity or what some call identity politics have also pushed for action strategies that are more fluid and issue based. The advent of more readily available information and communications technologies such as e-mail have also made organizing quickly across distances much more possible. The Women's Net at the Association for Progressive Communications (APC) has been especially important in providing Internet access, training and support for women's groups, especially in the South (Stienstra, 1999a).

Women's groups have also used the organizing strategy of caucusing at major international events. Caucuses have long existed at international meetings, but it was not until the Earth Summit the caucuses became a place where participants were moved to political action especially lobbying around specific joint demands (Chen, 1996; Stienstra, forthcoming). Caucuses allow open spaces for mobilizing for action and sharing information but are not effective as places for making strategic decisions. As a result they create privileged positions of insiders/outsiders – those who make decisions and those who do not. Often the insider positions are taken by representatives of NGOs with the greatest access to knowledge, usually those based in New York.

These New York-based groups, including WEDO, the IWTC and the Centre for Women's Global Leadership, are first and foremost international groups. Their goals and constituencies are global, but they have little direct accountability to community-based groups. Thus, the strategies they propose are often directed most at what will work at the international level without addressing the complexities of the community-based work around the world. This tension raises problems within both caucus and coalition work. The leadership by the New York-based groups has been very effective at ensuring that there is a feminist presence at the major UN conferences in the 1990s and that gender equality is addressed within the resulting commitments. Yet in many ways some of the power relations between North and South, between white women and women of colour and between women on the front lines and those with UN expertise have replicated the unequal power relations within women's movements in the 1980s. Those groups which lead discussion, have the greatest access to the UN and the greatest visibility are Northern-based groups whose work is primarily directed at mainstreaming women's concerns within the UN. There is a much broader basis of knowledge across the world of what is happening around women in the UN, but there remains an unsettling problem of leadership within the movements.

Many groups have chosen to keep their involvement in the UN process to a minimum because they identify the major problems of women as outside the UN's control. For many, one of the overarching, or framing, issues for women's lives is the global economy. The increased push by countries to join the 'free trade' economy has shaped the agenda of the UN on women as Runyan (1999) argues. The effects of an increasingly global economy have been significant for women and women's groups. The policies governments pursue to address the demands of being part of the global economy have meant fewer resources for individual women who receive less pay, have to move to part-time work, or lose their jobs as a part of restructuring (Bakker, 1996). Groups who may have received funding from governments have seen their funding levels drop or be eliminated. But there has been a more strategic result of globalization as well for groups. The effects of globalization in communities have been quite severe and many women's groups have wanted to keep their attention at the local level. They often have limited time and resources as well as willingness to consider undertaking global action. In many cases, there is also a sense of victimization as a result of global economic policies. Global economic issues are framed outside of the control of local citizens and many women's groups feel that there is no point trying to change it because they do not have the power to make this level of change. Finally, globalization has fragmented the interests of non-governmental communities. Labour, environmental and women's groups have different interests they are trying to protect and strategies for action often come into conflict when working at the global level (Lynch, 1998).

Movement to a neo-liberal or 'free trade' economy has also framed the capacities of women to organize at the international level (Marchand and Runyan, forthcoming). For example, for some women's groups, globalization has meant groups have shifted their action focus to the fora where free trade is being negotiated. This includes Asia–Pacific Economic Cooperation (APEC), the World Trade Organization (WTO) or the discussions around the Free Trade Agreement of the Americas. For others, the strategy has been to reduce the sense of victimization and increase women's capacities for addressing issues in the global economy. For example, WIDE prepared a 'gender mapping' of European trade policy which highlights the key players and strategies taken by governments in relation to trade policy. WEDO prepared primers on different institutions in the global economy such as the WTO. Others have placed all of their focus on mobilizing women at the community-level to action on the effects of globalization. March 2000 is a global campaign for local actions on ending poverty and violence against women, co-ordinated in Quebec but supported by over 1,400 groups around the world. The strategy of March 2000 is to have local communities undertake appropriate local activity as well as have national, regional and international marches on a set of global demands.

Women's groups have undertaken increasingly complex strategies to address global issues and arenas. They have begun to work more in coalitions and caucuses using information and communications technologies. They have become better lobbyists and advocates within the UN. They have begun to recognize and address the challenges of an increasingly global economy. Neither the strategies of mainstreaming or disengagement have proven successful in themselves and most groups pursue some mix of both. For the coming millennium, women will have to become increasingly attentive to the ways in which their global practices are affected by and affect globalization. International groups will especially have to be more responsive to the need to do their work from the community level up rather than from the international level down.

6

LABOUR IN THE GLOBAL

CHALLENGES AND PROSPECTS

Ronaldo Munck

In one of his recent wide-ranging and ambitious three volumes on the new capitalism, Castells (1997: 354) suggests that labour's prospects in the global arena are bleak indeed: 'Torn by internationalization of finance and production, unable to adapt to networking of firms and individualization of work, and challenged by the degendering of employment, the labour movement fades away as a major source of social cohesion and workers' representation'. This negative prognosis is a powerful and persuasive one but I would argue one that is already dated. Labour has been written off in the past as a social force and a political actor only to come back on the scene in some form. It is interesting in this regard to find the Danish General Workers' Union organizing a 'global labour summit' at the same time Castells' book appeared, which declared that: 'The time has come for the trade unions to use the positive sides of globalization to the advantage of workers and poor people all over the world' (Global Labour Summit, 1997). It is the apparent contradiction between these two statements that we need to explore.

GLOBALIZATION: NEW TERRAIN?

When the International Congress of Free Trade Unions (ICFTU) met at its 16th World Congress in 1996, the key document before delegates was aptly entitled 'Globalization – the greatest challenge for unions in the 21st Century'. The ICFTU, as the major transnational representative of labour understands well that: 'The position of workers has changed as a result of the globalization of the economy and changes in the organization of production' (ICFTU, 1997: 4). The huge structural transformations of the labour market and labour process over the last 20 years have had a dramatic impact on labour worldwide. Globalization, a convoluted discursive terrain to be sure, now sets the parameters for labour activity across the globe. It would also appear to act as the spearhead of an ideological offensive against autonomous labour and, indeed, other social practices. Yet these are processes that are fluid, perhaps even contradictory and they certainly need to be deconstructed. We cannot work on the basis of a simple determinism whereby labour's role in the new global arena is always already determined. After all, even the remote ICFTU now declares that 'one of the main purposes of the international trade union movement is the international solidarity of workers . . .' (ICFTU, 1997: 5).

It is certainly possible to draw a direct unilinear correlation between the process of globalization and decreasing labour rights across the world. Thus, Tilly argues that globalization has undermined the nation state which in turn means that the state cannot now fulfil its historical role in guaranteeing workers' rights. For Tilly (1995: 21): 'No individual state will have the power to enforce workers' rights in the fluid world that is emerging'. All rights embedded in nation states are necessarily under threat by economic globalization. Tilly (p 1) argues bluntly that: 'As states decline, so do workers' rights'. While not wishing to deny a certain reality to this scenario it does seem too deterministic and 'necessitarian'. Tilly's (welcome) call for workers' organization to develop new strategies at international level then seems purely voluntaristic. The logic of his position is actually to call for a defence and strengthening of the nation state if that is seen as the only way for workers' across the globe to retain or gain social, economic and political rights.

Indeed, we now find the 'Monthly Review school' arguing precisely this in a recent collection examining labour's 'Rising from the Ashes' (Monthly Review, 1997). The logic here is that globalization is but the latest of noxious ideologies, from 'Western Marxism', through post-Marxism to postmodernism designed to subvert the historical agency role of 'the working class'. They reject any appeals to an 'abstract internationalism', in favour of focusing on the state 'as a target in an anti-capitalist struggle', 'the focus of local and national struggles' and 'a unifying force . . . within the working class' (Monthly Review, 1977: 16). From this perspective, internationalism can only mean solidarity between different national struggles and no credence is given to such notions as international civil society. What is noticeable is the parallel with Tilly's determinism, even if on the assumption that globalization is basically a myth. To advocate an unreconstructed nation-statist workerism seems an inadequate riposte to the admitted excesses of the globalization discourse. As with Tilly we find globalization treated as a homogeneous, irreversible, all-encompassing process and labour seen simply as victim, 'done to' by the powerful, abstract, economic forces it unleashes.

It now seems clear that globalization is a term which has undergone a conceptual inflation in recent years and has now been devalued. It can mean anything, everything or nothing. It has, as Louise Amoure and co-authors point out, become firmly established as the key to the 'brave new world' we are entering whether from a Panglossian or a demonization perspective but its guiding principles are being accepted across the board as the new common sense for the era. Globalization is seen as obvious, inexorable and, at the end of the day, simply 'out there'. Yet the concept can be understood as both amorphous and labile in the extreme. For example, as Kim Moody (1997: 37) puts it, it is 'an all-encompassing analytical device that frequently concealed more than it explained'. The temptation to abandon the whole terrain of the globalization debate is there, but I think we should resist it.

For the ICFTU (1997: 4) globalization is quite simply 'the biggest challenge to the free trade union movement in its long struggle on behalf of working women and men around the world'. That is because of the cumulative effects of neo-liberal economic policies, structural adjustment programmes and privatization, financial deregulation and the growing mobility of the transnational corporations. The end of the Cold War is seen to offer a unique opportunity for the once divided international trade union movement to develop common objectives and joint action faced with a hostile climate for labour worldwide. One of the largest ITSs (International Trade Secretariats), now working more closely with the ICFTU, the ICEM (International Federation of Chemical, Energy, Mine and General Workers' Unions), has also launched a new global strategy, declaring that 'Action has to be planned on an international basis right from the start' (ICEM, 1996: 55). The dramatically increased level of internationalization over the last decade has created the conditions and the need for a new international labour strategy. As Doreen Massey (1995: 58) has suggested, a new 'global sense of place' has brought home the very real points of interconnection between people across the globe. This goes far beyond the communications revolution – e-mail making contact between labour leaders and activists easier for example – to create a new objective and subjective sense of commonality amongst workers worldwide and, at least, the possibility of a global strategy for labour. Exploring its current contours and possible prospects is the main purpose of this chapter.

There has now been a backlash against the early globalization theories and now most talk is about its 'limits' (e.g. Boyer and Drache, 1995). In some cases this revisionist case has led to a 'business as usual' attitude prevailing. Hirst and Thompson (1996) have articulated this case most clearly and with the explicit political intent of countering the idea that 'there is no alternative' to globalization. Their attempt to relativize the dominating role of the transnational corporations (TNCs) is well taken but there is a danger of quantitative reasoning obscuring the qualitative changes which have undoubtedly occurred in the world economy over recent decades. David Held has quite rightly, to my mind, reminded us that

> there is a fundamental difference between ... the development of particular trade routes ... or even the global reach of nineteenth-century empires, and, ... an international order involving ... dense networks of regional and global economic relations which stretch beyond the control of any single state ... (Held, 1995: 20).

There is, furthermore, a view of globalization in Hirst and Thompson which is somewhat reductionist and economistic and, seemingly, with little awareness, for example, of the burgeoning literature on cultural globalization (e.g.

Featherstone, 1995; Friedman, 1994). At times it seems that globalization acts as simple surrogate for neo-liberalism in relation to which many of their analytical points and political 'line' make more sense. Ultimately, however useful it may be to reject the Manichean view of globalization as a *deus ex machina*, the implicit political message of 'business as usual' in the nation state leaves social groups such as labour ill-prepared to consider how the local, the national and the global are today interrelated.

While maintaining all the caution that is due, it is still possible to detect something different or distinct in this new phase of world history we are calling 'globalization'. Jan Scholte (1997: 3–4) takes up the sensible (to me) stance that globalization can 'when developed with care, precision, consistency and suitable qualifications – be more than intellectual gimmick'. That is arguably now being done across a range of disciplines and applied to a host of specific topics in a more concrete manner than the first-generation literature on globalization. We do not need to become either propagandists for globalization or demonize it, a binary opposition if ever there was one. Nor is dismissing it as simply a new-fangled way of describing internationalization really adequate. One of the simplifications to overcome is the early idea of the global as dynamic and fluid as against the local as embedded, static and tradition bound. We could do worse than follow Ash Amin (1997: 133) in interpreting globalization 'in *relational* terms as the inter-dependence and intermingling of global, distant and local logics, resulting in the greater hybridization and perforation of social, economic and political life'. There does seem to be a growing convergence in various disciplines around the notion of hybridity and the blurring of traditional boundaries. This would, logically point us in the direction of hybrid, open, fluid and multi-polar solutions to the old/new social issues arising in the era of globalization.

A stronger case for the positive potential of globalization comes from James Agnew and Stuart Corbridge (1995: 219) who argue, but do not really sustain, the case that: 'Globalization is not only a synonym of disempowerment: it creates certain conditions for democratization, decentralization and empowerment as well as for centralization and standardization. Globalization opens as many doors as it shuts'. This last phrase deserves exploring further to take it beyond its allegorical status. The end of the master-narrative, problematic for the orthodox Marxist, is liberating also in questioning the capitalist story. This is a story which Marxists have done much to propagate, conceiving of capitalism as a unified and totalizing entity. Capitalist hegemony has thus been assumed rather than problematized. The 'economy' is reified rather than being conceived as a hetero-geneous and fragmented formation which cannot be subsumed under a single logic (Gibson-Graham, 1996). The discourse on globalization has suffered from a similar operation with its 'normalization', in Foucaultian terms, foreclosing the possibility of effective resistance or transformative strategies. In a suggestive parallel with rape, Gibson-Graham calls for

> rewriting the globalization script from within, denying the inevitability and 'reality' of MNC (multi-national corporation) power over workers and

communities and exploring ways in which the hard and penetrating body of the MNC can be seen as soft, fragile and vulnerable (Gibson-Graham, 1996: 146).

The myth of an omnipotent unidirectional globalization process, led by the all-powerful transnational corporations, needs to be exploded if labour and other social groups are to have a strategy.

GLOBALIZATION AND LABOUR

With regard to the effect of globalization on labour we could do worse than begin with the World Bank's (1995) authoritative 1995 report *Workers in an integrating world*. The World Bank notes, with undisguised glee, that by the year 2000 less than 10 per cent of the world's workers will not be fully integrated into the global capitalist economy, compared to the one-third of the global workforce which 20 years ago was told it was building socialism. The driving forces of global integration are seen as unstoppable by the Bank and the world's workers have no option but to submit. Or, in the Bank's own words 'Globalization is unavoidable – the welfare of Joe, Maria and Xiao Zhin is now more closely linked than ever before' (World Bank, 1995: 54). These 'representative' workers are seen to face risks but deeper international integration (globalization) is seen to hold positive prospects 'for those countries and groups of workers with the capacity to respond' (World Bank, 1995: 188). Of course, the Bank acknowledges that increasing international competition and 'free-wheeling' capital will not only cut jobs and wages but will, effectively, wipe whole nations and regions off the economic map. It understands that the scenario of workers' fortunes worldwide converging is less likely than growing divergence. In brief, according to the World Bank (1995: 124), 'Globalization offers opportunities but also exacerbates risks'. This may well serve as a watchword (and possibly epitaph) for a new era of global capitalist expansion. The World Bank makes optimistic noises about workers' fortunes but, at the end of the day, holds out few prospects.

In his sweeping review of the new network society we are living in, Castells (1996: 474) argues that under global capitalism: 'Workers do not disappear in the space of flows, and down to earth, work is plentiful'. Against apocalyptic prophecies about the 'end of work' and the dire effects of the new information technology, we actually see a massive incorporation of people into the global workforce. But while work, workers and the working class expands, the relationship between capital and labour is transformed radically. For Castells (1996: 475) 'networks converge towards a meta-network of capital that integrates capitalist interests at the global level and across sectors and realms of activity . . .'. Meanwhile, 'Labor is disaggregated in its performance, fragmented in its organization, diversified in its existence, divided in its collective action' (Castells, 1996: 475). The overarching image in the brave new world of Castells' network society is that capital and labour live in different places and times. Capital is

global and it exists in the space of flows and lives in the instant time of computerized networks. Labour is, on the whole, local, exists in the space of places
and lives the clock time of everyday life. In brief, capital lives in hyperspace
while labour still has its feet on the ground. This is a very powerful image and,
undoubtedly, reflects part of what is going on. It certainly reflects the fluidity
and dynamic nature of the current epoch. Yet it is perhaps only part of the
picture, because uneven development means much of the world is still living an
'old' capitalism and non-capitalist relations are far from dead.

The globalization debates, if they have done nothing else, have forced the
social sciences to take on board the spatial dimension. If space is where capital is
constructing its brave new world it is in place that labour lives and constructs its
social relations. As Jamie Peck (1996: 233) argues there is a growing move
towards reducing place to space: 'Places to live seem increasingly to be reduced to
spaces in which to earn, or strive to earn a wage'. Global competition, neo-
liberalism and structural adjustment programmes are constantly eroding labour's
bargaining strength. Deregulation, in all its multiple facets, is exposing labour to
this new capitalist onslaught. The point, however, as Peck stresses, is that:

> This does not mean that place − as a theoretical category or as a political
> site − somehow matters less, but is rather to insist on an appreciation of the
> local in the context of (and in relation to) the global' (Peck, 1996: 233).

Workers still live in Buenos Aires, Bombay and Birmingham, they work in these
places and their aspirations are in relation to these places. Globalization is not
just 'out there' in cyberspace but exists, operates and is contested in these local
places. Globalization has prompted new identities, and new interests within
local, political processes. Local politics in the global era has not been shut down,
rather that it has been transformed and in many ways reinvigorated by the
multiple identities and fluid processes of the current era.

The problem with most of the literature on labour and globalization is that it
tends to conceive of labour as passive victim of the new trends, the malleable
material from which globalization will construct its New World Order. Capital
is seen as an active, mobile, forward-looking player in the globalization game
while labour is seen as static, passive and basically reactive. The game has
changed and labour is seen to have few cards. Only rarely will someone point
out, as Andrew Herod (1998: 40) does, that 'workers and unions have been
actively involved in shaping the processes of globalization . . . both by modifying
the impacts of capital's activities and by shaping internationally the very
possibilities for these activities'. The invisibility of labour seems most marked in
radical political economy writings keen to demonize globalization. The reality is
that labour has been back centre-stage since the mid-1990s at least. General
strikes have occurred in many parts of Europe, in Latin America, in Canada, in
South Africa and, most crucially, in South Korea. The disorienting changes
within the labour movement in the first decade of globalization seem, at least
in part, to have been overcome. Change was a slow but organic process, often

initiated by the middle ranks. As Moody (1997: 14) recounts, 'The unions took on new roles: as champions of the interests of the working class as a whole, not just as representatives of their members, and as political surrogates for failed parties of the left'. I am not suggesting that this process is universal – it is clearly uneven – nor that it is irreversible. However, we need to view the new-found interest of the ICFTU in international labour solidarity in this light and not just assume that it is a cynical exercise in political correctness.

The world of global capital is not unaware of the dangers that labour poses to the ultimate success of the globalization project, if that is what it is. *Foreign Affairs*, an influential organ of the US foreign affairs establishment, carried in 1996 a rare article on Workers and the World Economy (Kapstein, 1996). It began with the basic statement that 'The global economy is leaving millions of disaffected workers in its train' and ends by warning policy makers that if 'like the German elite in Weimar, they dismiss mounting worker dissatisfaction ... and the plight of the unemployed and working poor as marginal' (Kapstein, 1996: 14, 37) they do so at their peril. Kapstein was telling the readers of *Foreign Affairs* that labour could not be seen as infinitely pliable and that the official ideology of neo-liberal globalization was wearing a bit thin. That this was not a call in the wilderness can be attested by the sober yet dramatic warning by Klaus Schwab, founder and president of the World Economic Forum at Davos that present trends are 'multiplying the human and social costs of the globalization process to a level that tests the social fabric of the democracies in an unprecedented way' (cited by Martin and Schumann, 1998: 231). Concerned that we are now entering a critical phase of the globalization process and that a 'disruptive backlash' is emerging, Schwab calls for the global economic and political leaders to show that the 'new global capitalism' can function 'to the benefit of the majority and not only for corporate managers and investors' (p 231). At once revealing of the true nature of globalization and pipe-dream about its reforming potential, this statement does at least show that all is not well in the capitalist garden.

LABOUR AS SOCIAL MOVEMENT

'Trade unionism was, at a given time, a social movement; it is now a political force that is necessarily subordinated to political parties and to governments ... Gone is the link between unions and alternative images of a reconstructed society' (Touraine, 1986: 173). It has been a commonplace for over a decade now to refer to the 'end' of the working class and the 'death' of the labour movement as a social movement. It might seem now that these reports are somewhat exaggerated. Touraine (1986: 153) operates with an organic image of the labour movement to diagnose its demise: 'Movements such as unionism have a life history: infancy, youth, maturity, old age and death'. Whatever provisos are put on this scheme to avoid the charge of evolutionism, it does appear to be a misplaced biological analogy. It would be more productive to examine certain cycles of the labour movement in relation to economic and political processes in society at large than to take this lifecycle view of the labour movement. It also suffers from the good past/bad present syndrome, positing a mythologized golden era where labour was heroic against which the present seems lacklustre and labour pedestrian. As with capitalism, labour would seem to have a great ability to regenerate and transform itself, adapting to new situations, mutating organizational forms and strategies, and living to fight another day.

Another more recent dismissal of the labour movement comes in Castells' (1997) broad overview of contemporary society. In a sweeping review of contemporary social movements from the Zapatistas to the American Militia and from the women's movement to Aum Shinrikyo, Castells finds no room for labour. He makes the rather apocalyptic statement that 'the labor movement seems to be historically superseded' (Castells, 1997: 360). Structural transformations of the world of work – globalization, neo-liberalism, flexibilization, etc. – are seen to foreclose any possibility of labour generating a transformative project identity ever again. As with Touraine, Castells seems to reduce trade unions to more or less influential political actors but denies them any legitimacy as a site for social movements. What is extraordinary is that such a dismissal of the labour movement occurs in a sparse couple of paragraphs in a book that is over 450 pages long. Certainly labour is facing a huge challenge, but these peremptory statements by Touraine, Castells and others neglect any attempt to seek out what is changing in the global labour movement, which is ironic in authors who seem mesmerized by the 'newness' of the social movements. Indeed, we find that in the past labour's low points have also been periods of reorientation and renewal. This is not to advocate a naive optimism but to return the question of agency to the centre of our social research.

From the workerless world of the globalization and (some) NSMs' discourses we can turn to very definite signs of renewed labour activity across the globe. Nor is all this activity confined to desperate rearguard actions against neo-liberalism as was, in the main the case a decade ago. The first reaction of fear and insecurity in the face of the forces unleashed by globalization has given way to a new more settled and even confident mood. While still weakened by the ravages of the last 20 years, the international labour movement has begun a process of recomposition in most of its key sectors. Giovanni Arrighi makes the useful point that there has always been a considerable time lag in terms of labour's response to capital restructuring (Arrighi, 1996). Looking back to the previous period of global financial expansion in the late nineteenth century, Arrighi finds that there were 25 years of organizational instability with more defeats than victories, and then it took another 25 years 'before the ideological and organizational contours of the world labour movement began to crystallize and be discernible, and yet another 25 before the movement became powerful enough to impose some of its objectives on world capitalism' (Arrighi, 1996: 348). Now, we can expect that, due to the current condition of 'time–space compression', the labour revival this time round will not take 50 years to materialize. Indeed, the signs of this revival are there to be seen; it is more a question of when and how, not whether it will take place. What is also clear is that this new labour movement will be much influenced by the example of the 'new' social movements that have come to the fore over the last 20 years.

The main set of theoretical principles, explaining the strategies and nature of the 'new' social movements can be traced to the work of, amongst others, Laclau and Mouffe (1985). This work helps us understand the open and contingent nature of political identities and political struggles. Against the privileged status of workers in traditional labour/socialist discourse, they examine the plural nature of society and the autonomy of the various oppressed groups. Radical politics, for them, should abandon a narrow, productivist logic, and adopt a broader strategy aimed at articulating new democratic political identities across society. Society is seen as open, unstable and contingent, being discursively constituted through a process of articulation and negotiation. Once the traditional idea of the working class, as a central unifying feature in the socialist strategies, is abandoned, the doors are opened on a new radical democratic politics more attuned to the needs of the next century. This, more pluralist, politics clearly entails an engagement with the multiple identities and diverse struggles of the NSMs. Faced with uncertainty, fluidity and even chaos it is not surprising to see radical thought and new approaches. The post-modern (or, more precisely, post-structuralist) approach bids us reject the broad interpretative schemes or meta-narratives of Marx and the socialist/labour icons which seek to provide us with the 'truth' of how everything under the sun is connected and why things are the way they are. Instead of a 'totalizing' account we are directed, rather, towards a 'deconstruction' of narratives and an understanding of the radical contingency of structures and events.

NEW SOCIAL MOVEMENT?

If the traditional labour/socialist projects of transformation are now in crisis, we should perhaps turn to the 'new' social movements and their associated politics of reconstruction. These movements, conventionally contrasted to the 'old' movements of labour or nationalism, are taken to include the women's, peace and human rights movements, as well as, in some conceptions, a diversity of regional, local or community associations. These are seen to represent a qualitatively different form of transformative politics and, in embryo, a new societal paradigm. These movements stress their autonomy from party politics and prioritize civil society over the state. In social movement politics, power itself is redefined, no longer being seen as something out there ready to be seized, but as a diffused and plural quality woven into the very fabric of society. These social movements have, arguably, helped to create a new political space where new identities have been developed, new demands have been articulated and the dividing line between the public and private domains has lost much of its meaning. The very notion of power is, hereby, redefined, the limits of state politics exposed, and a challenge laid down to the atomization and alienation characteristic of contemporary capitalism.

Sometimes, however, there is too stark a counterposition drawn between the 'old' labour movement and the 'new' social movements around gender, race, ecological or peace issues. Alan Scott (1991) has usefully summarized these assumed differences in terms of the distinct location, aims, organization and medium of action of the workers' movement and the NSMs respectively. Whereas the struggles of labour have increasingly been located within the polity, the NSMs are usually assumed to operate within civil society. As to the aims of labour they have usually focused around securing economic rights for workers and the political integration of labour within the dominant system. Conversely, the NSMs stress the autonomy of civil society and often seek changes in social values or life-styles. The organizational mode of labour has traditionally been formal and has adopted a hierarchical aspect (the famous 'iron law of oligarchy' of Michels). For their part, the NSMs tend, at least during their inception and in theory anyway, towards a networking and/or grass roots type of organization. Finally, whereas the worker's movement has usually stressed political mobilization, the NSMs often go for direct action and/or daring attempts at cultural innovations (witness the dramatic tactics of Greenpeace). The above represents only two ideal types, which are not always reflected in practice, but we can see in this general picture, albeit tempered by empirical counter-examples, the challenge posed by the NSMs to the old, or at least traditional, labour movements.

I think we need to take seriously the warning by Allen Hunter (1995: 6) that 'the harsh juxtaposition between the (bad) old politics and the (good) New Social Movements is self-deceptive, misleading, and can inhibit the kind of critical interrogation of current prospects for radical change that is needed'. For one thing, the international labour movement has, in recent decades, explored innovative forms of actions. From the 'social movement unionism' of Brazil, South Africa or South Korea to the 'new realism' of Western Europe and elsewhere, labour has been seeking ways out of the apparent impasse of the old tactics, organizational modes and even objectives. Union leaders, as much as workers themselves, increasingly realize that unions are no longer 'representative' in the old way. Contemporary trade union discourse is well attuned to the need to go beyond the traditional demand for 'more and more', to address the quality of life of workers today. It is important to acknowledge, following Marino Regini (1992: 102), that 'some trade unions have undertaken a search for new, less defensive responses to the current challenges'. The growing heterogeneity of the labour force and the increasing impact of 'flexible specialization' can be, and has been, seen as an opportunity for labour even while it is a constraint on traditional strategies. As against a homogeneous working class we now have a heterogeneous labour force. Union leaders presume less to speak 'on behalf' of a mythical working class, instead diverse identities find their own voices and articulate their own strategies. Interest representation in a simple one-to-one model gives way to the pluralism of identity politics.

As the old paradigms of labour structuring and organization dissolve, so new forms are developed. Women working worldwide have thrown up novel and effective forms of struggle. Whether in the Free Trade Zones on the Mexican border, homeworkers in India or African township traders, women are imagining ways of resisting the neo-liberal capitalist onslaught. In introducing a collection describing new forms of economic organizing among poor women in the Third World and the First, Sheila Rowbotham and Swasti Mitter (1994: 6) point out that 'The experience gained by Third World poor women, in developing forms of survival and resistance, are becoming increasingly relevant to women of the First World'. Organizing outside the trade unions in various ways linked into the community, these women are often developing a synthesis of old and new forms of organization of great relevance. In a parallel move, some commentators are now pointing to the potential of the 'third sector' or social economy. Thus, Rifkin (1995: 283) refers to how:

> The third sector is emerging in every region of the world. Its meteoric rise is attributable in part to the increasing need to fill a political vacuum left by the retreat of both the private and public sectors from the affairs of local communities.

We increasingly find trade unions worldwide moving beyond the factory gates and breaking with a narrow, economistic conception of trade unionism. As De Martino (1991: 116) argues, in relation to the USA, there was once a powerful left workerist orthodoxy which 'grants privileged status to workers in an enterprise, they alone are empowered to determine when and how to struggle, and for what'. The broader community could express its 'solidarity' when called upon, but could not interfere with union 'autonomy'. Today it is widely recognized in labour circles that unions are not simply about defending workers rights at the place of work, and the artificial barriers between workplace and community are not so impregnable. After all, workers are gendered, they are citizens and they are consumers too. Often unions become 'populist' campaigning organizations, from South Africa, to Poland to the USA, with a fluid view of how to pursue their struggle under contemporary capitalism.

It is heartening to see Moody's (1997) recent comprehensive study of current labour relations worldwide renewing the call for a 'social movement unionism' first mooted some ten years ago by Waterman (1993) and myself (Munck, 1988). This approach rejects equally the economism of 'business unionism' and the 'political bargaining' approach. It has been manifest in the working class struggles of the 1980s in Brazil and South Africa (see Seidman, 1994) and, more recently, in South Korea. It is also, perhaps surprisingly, emerging in some struggles in the USA. Social movement unionism is an active, community oriented, strategy which works with a broad conception of who the working people are. It breaks down the binary oppositions between workplace and community, economic and political struggles , and between formal sector workers and the working poor. When workers adopt this orientation they often find allies amongst the 'new' social movements and, in particular, with NGOs. The ICFTU campaign against child labour with its broad alliance strategy including active collaboration with relevant NGOs, is in its own way a reflection of the growing power of social movement unionism in the trade union imaginary. The clearly perceived diminishing returns on 'business as usual' strategies leads even sectarian and bureaucratic trade union leaderships in the direction of social movement unionism. It is no magic wand, but in the words of Sam Gindin of the Canadian Auto Workers 'it means making the union into a vehicle through which its members can not only address their bargaining demands but actively lead the fight for everything that affects working people in their communities and the country' (Gindin, 1995: 268).

Reconsidering now whether labour does, or can, constitute a social movement we need to clarify some points. In the first instance, the 'newness' of the 'new' social movements to which labour is counterposed is a dubious proposition. There is none better to demonstrate this than Alberto Melucci (1994) who did so much to popularize the term in sociological debates. This newness can only be relative and its useful function just one of counterposing as ideal types two forms of social phenomena as we did above. But, as Melucci (1996: 5) points out, 'if analysis and research fail to specify the distinctive features of the "new movements", we are trapped in an arid debate between the supporters and critics of "newness"'. The labour movement has, to some extent, acted as a negative other to those keen to stress the 'newness' of whatever social movement they were examining. Thus, the conservative, bureaucratic, ritualized and reactive nature of trade unions has been stressed and their capacity to adapt to new circumstances or their inherently contradictory nature (within and against the labour relation at the same time) denied or downplayed. With the gendering and greening of many trade unions and some labour movements it seems increasingly anachronistic to counterpose the labour movement to its 'new' relations. Perhaps no social movement can, or should, articulate a project identity 'by itself and from itself' (Castells, 1997: 360), a failing which Castells uses to dismiss trade unions as a transformative force in the new (post-capitalist?) Information Age.

Another point of clarification is in relation to the counterposed analysis of social movements in terms of resource mobilization theory and the 'European' identity politics approach. Again labour is seen as a mechanical aggregation of material interests whereas the 'new' movements are seen to articulate essential identities. Yet as Melucci (1996: 190) points out 'a radical form of "identity politics" is not only dangerous for society in its intolerant fundamentalism, it is self-defeating'. Collective action for transformative change can only occur in our complex societies through establishing common ground and forging a new democratic imagination. In terms of analysis, it seems wrong to counterpose resource mobilization issues to identity politics when most social movements engage in both. In terms of politics we should consider carefully Harvey's (1996: 100) argument that 'in part this romantic turn to the marginalized "other" for political salvation derives from a certain frustration at the inability of traditional movements (such as those of the working class) to foment radical change'. If our hypothesis that working class organization and militancy cycles are part of the 'long waves' of capitalism is correct then this frustration is possibly premature. Anyway, as previous searches for 'alternative' revolutionary subjects have shown this is not a particularly fruitful endeavour. An anti-modernist movement or orientation will not take working people into a 'post-modern' future but, probably inevitably, into a *cul-de-sac* which leaves the capitalist juggernaut free to carry on down the highway.

INTERNATIONALISM: IMAGINED COMMUNITY?

'International solidarity must become a natural reflex throughout the union movement', said Bill Jordan, General Secretary of the ICFTU (1997). When the new leader of the ICFTU, the cautious ex-leader of the British engineering workers' union, proclaims that international labour solidarity must now be the order of the day something new is happening. The International Federation of Chemical, Energy and Mine Workers' Union (ICEM) now advocates to its 20 million members that 'Action has to be planned on an international basis from the start' (ICEM, 1996: 55). Fire-fighting, or wheeling in the international dimension when local action has failed, is no longer seen as good enough. This line represents a sea change in attitudes amongst trade union leaders. International labour activity is now becoming quite normal as it were. Forty-five years ago Lewis Lorwin (1953: 334) in his history of the international labour movement, wrote that 'the inner logic of trade unions is to concern themselves more and more with questions of national policy, since these impinge directly or indirectly on the basic trade union function of improving working and living conditions'. If we substitute Lorwin's 'national policy' with 'international policy' this phrase would make perfect sense today. It is a measure of the great transformation that has taken place in the international labour movement that such a radical shift could be possible.

However, not so long ago the consensus was that labour did not have much of a future as an international, let alone global, social actor or movement, After a considered review of the relationship between workers and MNEs (multinational enterprises) Peter Enderwick (1985: 170) concluded that 'effective labour responses to the MNE are unlikely to develop in the near future, at an international level'. Not only has the internationalization of capital severely weakened labour, but workers were simply not playing by the same rules as capital. One was mobile, footloose and fancy-free, the other was fixed in place with the only sanction at its disposal being absence (the strike). Stress was placed on the asymmetry of capital and labour and on the fact that there was no reason why the internationalization of one would have similar effects on the other (Haworth and Ramsay, 1984). Carolyn Vogler (1985: xiii), in a study of British trade union's foreign policy, also concluded in a negative vein that 'so far at least, there are no indications of the proletariat emerging as a transnational class actor'. Rather, all the evidence seemed to point towards British (by extension metropolitan) trade unions becoming increasingly national and sectional in their outlook and in their actions. Even when this type of union did project itself on to the international scene it only tended to reproduce its national characteristics leading to at best a syndicalist internationalism and, at worst, an international business unionism at the service of the nation state, the infamous trade union imperialism (see Thompson and Larson, 1978).

The question now arises as to whether things have changed so dramatically over the last decade or so or whether this negative stance was unjustified. A careful reconstruction of the debate around labour and the NIDL (new international division of labour) would show its many problems from its economism to its tendency to generalize from specific areas (see Schoenberger, 1989). Arguments against glib, voluntaristic views on the 'objective' tendencies towards a new internationalism were probably justified. However, I believe we can argue that we are now in a qualitatively new situation and that many of these old arguments are not quite so relevant. It is interesting to note a discussion by Zsuzsa Hegedus on the NSMs, and how analysis fell behind changing reality. Hegedus (1989: 19) notes that:

> No period in the post-war era has witnessed such a massive and unexpected emergence of new movements on a global scale as has the eighties. And rarely has the discrepancy between the practices and analysis of New Social Movements been so acute.

It would seem that this undue 'pessimism of the will' was due to applying 1970s paradigms (and moods) to 1980s phenomena. I think it would be important to note this problem of analysis having to 'catch up' with changing reality and not seek to examine the international labour movement of the 1990s through the grey-tinted spectacles of the 1980s. The 'old' labour movement is catching up with the 'new' which in the 1980s began to 'directly address planetary issues and challenge the dominant problem-solving process at a global level' (Hegedus, 1989: 33).

The very nature of international labour 'solidarity' (a labile term if ever there was one) has changed significantly over the last decade. Dan Gallin, General Secretary of the International Union of Food and Allied Workers (IUF) argued recently that 'there can no longer be any effective trade union policy, even at a national level, that is not global in concept and international in organization' (Gallin, 1994: 124). More interestingly he provided an insider's account of what passed previously as internationalism: 'For many [trade union leaders], international activity was recreational and diplomatic, at best, charitable and declarative' (Gallin, 1994: 125). Denis McShane (1993: 203) has referred, in a similar vein, to the need 'to go beyond the rhetoric of labour internationalism, fraternal tourism, or neocolonial sponsorships'. It would certainly be naive to think that these labour practices are all now a thing of the past. However, there is at least a paradigm of a new labour internationalism that can act as an alternative. Waterman (1998: 72–3) has amalgamated some of its characteristics into something of an ideal type of a new labour internationalism:

● a move from leadership contacts to grass-roots relations between workers;
● a move from bureaucratic organizational models to decentralized flexible forms;

- a move from an 'aid' model to a 'solidarity' model;
- a generalized solidarity ethic embracing national, gender, racial and religious discrimination;
- a move from workerism to a broader conception of democratic internationalism;
- a recognition that solidarity is not a one-way process but involves workers from the South as well as the North.

Whether this idealized notion of the new labour internationalism materializes in this form is by no means certain. However, it does seem to point towards a transcending of earlier an categorization of trade unions as always simply 'sectional economic groups' (Willetts, 1982: 2) in terms of the types of international pressure groups which exist. Labour could just as well be seen as an NGO campaigning, lobbying and networking along with the best of them at international fora. In reducing its sights the international trade union movement has probably become more effective. A good example is in relation to the campaign against child labour where the ICFTU campaigned effectively alongside various more activist-type organizations (see White, 1996). Finally, it would be worth drawing attention to the distinction drawn by Rebecca Johns in her research on the efforts by US trade unionists to develop international solidarity activity with workers in Central America (Johns, 1994). Johns distinguishes between an 'accommodative solidarity' where workers in economically developed countries seek to prevent capital flight to other locations where wages are lower and a 'transformative solidarity' in which workers unite across space jointly to challenge the power of capital and seek to transform the prevailing relation of production and consumption. While in practice the distinction may be blurred it is a useful conceptual marker to frame our discussion of some examples of international labour solidarity.

LABOUR IN THE GLOBAL

There are various levels at which labour has responded to, adapted to or contested globalization. The 'highest' level has been around the increasingly important movement to get the WTO to accept a 'social clause'. There is a growing momentum behind the ICFTU campaign to establish some social control over globalization through this mechanism. Though modest in appearance – a commitment to respect the main ILO (International Labour Organization) conventions such as freedom of association and the abolition of forced labour – its implementation would have far-reaching effects. The campaign even pays lip service to neo-liberalism and rejects the label of protectionism. Yet it is still novel even to discuss the relationship between free trade and internationally recognized core labour standards. I believe this issue reflects the dictum of Bob Deacon *et al.* (1979: 3) that 'the other side of the coin of the globalization of social policy is the socialization of global politics'. The ICFTU would thus be absolutely correct in perceiving a growing tendency of international capitalist organizations to acknowledge the crucial social component of their interventions. Of course, it is not surprising that many NGOs and non-advanced industrial society unions opposed the core standards campaign as yet another anti-South move. The interesting point of this complex of issues is, as Robert O'Brien (1997: 43) maintains, that:

> In northern labour's attempt to respond to globalization of neoliberal industrial relations, their own strategy may undergo radicalization. Although northern workers organizations are still financially superior to those in the South, their need for Southern cooperation is far greater than in the past.

Labour has also reacted to globalization at the regional level, a good example being the North American trade union campaign around and against NAFTA (North American Free Trade Association). The conflictual but ultimately productive interaction between US, Mexican and Canadian trade unions over NAFTA may yet prove to be a watershed in terms of international labour solidarity or, to be more precise, labour transnationalism. Nationalist responses by the three labour movements moved, albeit partially and hesitantly, towards a common position in relation to this major move towards capitalist rationalization. Establishing a community of interests amongst the workers of North America is not easy and it did not do away with particular national interests. The US union orientation towards 'upward harmonization' of labour rights and standards in the region was by no means unambiguously welcome in Mexico where different priorities might prevail. However, it is also noticeable that the Canadian unions, which previously knew little about labour conditions in Mexico, developed a remarkably sophisticated and sensitive policy towards transnational co-operation with Mexican workers and unions. Careful study of this whole experience can help move us beyond the sterile counterposition between the globalization blues and an abstract internationalism. Some of the ambiguity (and hopefulness) of the new transnational labour discourse can be discerned in the statement by the American Federation of Labour–Council of Industrial Organization (AFL–CIO) President Lane Kirkland that:

> You can't be a trade unionist unless you are an internationalist. You can't be a real trade unionist unless you think of workers wherever they happen to be, and unless you realise that substandard conditions and poverty anywhere in the world is a threat to good conditions and comparatively good standards anywhere in the world (cited in French et al., 1994: 1).

Finally, labour has increasingly projected local struggles to the global level, a good example being the long-running struggle of the Liverpool dockers. A quite distinctive aspect of the 1995–6 Liverpool docks dispute has been its international projection. This began, as so often before, because the national terrain was not too fertile for labour. As the account of the dispute by Michael Lavalette and Jane Kennedy (1996: 113) recalls:

> The creation of an international strategy was seen by the shop stewards committee as essential for the success of the dispute. As the months have progressed it has taken centre stage in their pursuit of victory and has been the major focus of the dockers' energies and activities.

Small delegations were dispatched to friendly ports where previous contacts existed such as Bilbao in Spain, and to uncharted territory such as Canada. This international activity was undoubtedly successful in, for example, forcing a major US user of Liverpool (American Container Line) to leave the port under threat of 'blacking' of their ships by US longshoremen. Just as significantly their global outreach tactics took the Liverpool dockers through new experiences and created a new internationalist consciousness. The depth and intensity of the solidarity displayed towards what was considered as a 'lost' dispute at home was remarkable. The conclusion of the Liverpool dockers is of more global significance:

> With so many things in common between workers such as the jobs we perform ... common employers such as the big shipping companies ... [and] ... the global problems of casualisation and privatisation, international solidarity between dock workers of the world, should really be our first course of action and not our last' (cited in Lavalette and Kennedy, 1996: 115).

As labour's new global role is a recent one our conclusions can only be partial and provisional. One issue that emerges is that the national and international actions of labour are not incompatible. Labour has always had a national base/role/orientation (see, e.g. Wils, 1996) and it still does. Labour needs to have an international orientation and practice too. It would be wrong, however, to establish a hierarchy between these two levels or see them as good/bad. Nor do trade unions have the option to turn their backs on their national base or simply move towards 'international social movement unionism' as though it was simply a matter of choice. While unions need to confront these issues to survive in the new global labour market they cannot be expected just to shift their scarce resources to organizing the unorganized while reflecting their present base (Borgers, 1996: 70). Another related conclusion is that 'rank and file' action can sometimes be elevated to a principle that becomes divisive. Thus, some commentators complained that the Liverpool dockers' international work sometimes passed through the dreaded 'trade union officials'. This abstract critique (based on spurious notions of their 'social position') ignores the fact that for most social movements the key layer for organizing/mobilizing is precisely 'middle management'. Whether it is within the labour movement, or in linking the global level and local struggles, it is crucial to develop the mediating structures, thinking and personnel to link up and energize the base/local with the leadership/global.

If there was one final point I would like to make it is that it is now time to invert the 'old' slogan 'Think globally, act locally'. The Liverpool dockers were, it would seem thinking quite explicitly, in terms of 'Think locally, act globally', and that will increasingly be the case. This does not mean a move towards an abstract internationalism as though there was a pure global ether far removed from the hurly-burly of local places. Globalization only exists through the concrete and complex socio-economic–cultural processes in specific localities. Unfortunately in the past, as Harvey (1996: 314) argues, 'internationalist working-class politics often abstracted from the material world of experience in particular places'. What we are witnessing now is a revalorization of the local understood fully as part of globalization and not 'a place apart'. In the local/ international responses to the social and spatial effects of globalization we see how 'local efforts to accommodate the work of globalization are contributing to political practices ... that challenge our current theoretical approaches' (Clarke and Gaile, 1997: 40). In breaking down the old local/global dualist thinking these new (theoretical) practices are renewing the possibility of international solidarity. John Dunn's (1985) categorical rejection of internationalism as an 'unimagined (unimaginable?) community' just over ten years ago looks less persuasive now, especially his argument that 'in the absence of a plausible medium for fair exchange or any clear and rational basis for mutual trust to expect [human beings] to appreciate this enforced [international] fellowship is wholly unreasonable' (Dunn, 1985: 115–16). Is it?

It is well to remember that globalization is not just an economic affair but is also, crucially, about culture. In this regard many previous barriers in international labour communication have been broken down. All social struggles are now more clearly than ever also struggles over interpretation at the discursive level. Labour movements are now much more attuned to the crucial power of interpretation and the potential inventiveness of language. The new solidarity is not based on a simple identity but recognizes difference. It understands reciprocity to be a better basis for solidarity than charity. The global neo-liberal consensus seems to have broken down and options are emerging for labour beyond the narrow confines of business unionism. Dominant cultural paradigms can be unsettled, subverted and countered. The Danish General Workers' Union in its New Global Agenda refers ambitiously, but in a grounded way, to the 'need to make our voices heard for a new global social development, for democracy and human rights and for the improvement of workers' rights everywhere in the world' (SID Global Labour Summit, 1997). International labour organizations are bound to play a role in the discursive construction of this new common sense. There is a role for labour in the global.

INTERNATIONAL LABOUR SOLIDARITY AFTER THE COLD WAR

Sarah Ashwin

Throughout the world, most people spend most of their lives working. . . .
It is mainly through their work that most households are swept up in the
profound changes that are interweaving their national and regional
economies into a single global economy (World Bank, 1995).

Unions at a national level are seeing much of what they have achieved
being undermined by global financial and industrial decisions. The need
for an effective national, regional and international trade union response is
greater than ever before. . . . International solidarity in the 21st century will
have to be more than a rhetorical slogan (ICFTU, 1996a).

Globalization has many dimensions, but its most dramatic implications are
in the sphere of employment. The erosion of national economic boundaries
through the liberalization of trade and capital markets is transforming both local
and national labour markets as well as the organizations for which people work.
It might therefore be expected that the international trade union movement
would be at the centre of the new global stage as prominent defenders of the
weaker members of global society. As it is, however, while organizations such as
OXFAM and Amnesty International are household names, few have heard of
the world's largest international trade union organization, the International
Confederation of Free Trade Unions (ICFTU) or even the more prominent
international trade secretariats (ITSs). This is not simply a matter of the relative
effectiveness of the organizations' press officers or the amount of money available
for publicity. It reflects the fact that in the post-Second World War era the
international trade union community was embroiled in an ideological battle
which was remote from the concerns of most of the world's workers. The politics
of international trade union assistance in this era were structured by the divisions
of the Cold War, the struggles between the two main wings of the international

labour movement, the Soviet-dominated World Federation of Trade Unions (WFTU) and the Western-dominated ICFTU, reflecting those of the opposed armed camps.

This chapter looks at the implications of the end of the Cold War for the international labour movement, in particular focusing on ICFTU politics in the former Eastern Bloc as an example of wider trends.[1] I argue that the ICFTU took some time to adapt to the collapse of communism, with the struggle between the WFTU and ICFTU initially being reproduced within the ICFTU itself. As reform in the former Soviet bloc progressed, however, this form of politics became increasingly redundant, and the debate within the international trade union community refocused on the common problems faced by all forms of trade unions in responding to the challenges of the global market. In effect, the ICFTU was forced to find a new role now that the enemies against which it had defined itself were either collapsing or clamouring for ICFTU affiliation. These developments in the trade union sphere coincided with an attack of uncharacteristic self-doubt among some of the international financial and government institutions, which has opened up the possibility of trade union contributions being taken more seriously within international economic debates. The final sections of the chapter will review new initiatives and thinking which are emerging in the international trade union community.[2]

THE STRUCTURE OF THE INTERNATIONAL LABOUR MOVEMENT[3]

In the immediate post-1945 era the international labour movement — which had previously been fragmented into three international federations — was united in one all-encompassing labour organization, the WFTU. The principal initiators of this development were the British TUC, the Soviet All Union Central Council of Trade Unions (VTsSPS) and the American Council of Industrial Organizations (CIO). The American Federation of Labour (AFL) declined to join because of the presence of communist organizations in the federation, while a small number of organizations remained within the Christian international labour federation which adopted the name World Confederation of Labour (WCL) in 1968.[4] The unity of the WFTU was of short duration: unions from Western countries severed their ties with the organization in 1949 after disagreements over the Marshall Plan and the independence of the ITSs. The ICFTU was established the same year. The international trade union movement was thus divided along ideological lines, with the ICFTU uniting the main Western trade union national centres (with the exception of a 12-year absence from the AFL–CIO ending in 1981), and the WFTU drawing its main affiliates from the Soviet bloc. In addition to this division in the international confederations, there was also competition between international sectoral groupings. The Soviet equivalents of the ITSs were the Trade Union Internationals (TUIs) which grouped unions from individual economic sectors such as mining.

Although 'solidarity' was not entirely absent from international trade union politics in the Cold War era, the wider goal of both the ICFTU and WFTU was to promote their own political positions within the trade unions to which they provided assistance. This chapter will not examine the murky history of trade union assistance in the developing world, but it is certainly the case that the major driving force of action in these countries was related to the Cold War.[5] Instead, the next section of the chapter will focus on developments within post-communist Eastern Europe, which amply illustrate the way in which Cold War politics in the trade union movement undermined any effective international solidarity.

AFTER COMMUNISM: FIGHTING THE SPECTRE IN EASTERN EUROPE

After the collapse of communism the WFTU began to crumble from within in a fashion which recalled the implosion of the satellite states in Eastern Europe. This obviously had implications for the ICFTU, a significant part of the activity of which had been devoted to countering the influence of the WFTU in the world labour movement. The 'free' labour movement took some time to adjust to the new situation, and initially divisions between the WFTU and ICFTU were reproduced within the ICFTU itself, with the AFL–CIO championing the anti-communist cause in the former Eastern bloc while the European unions, in particular the Scandinavians, co-operated with the former communist unions. This section begins with an examination of the predicament of the ICFTU in the aftermath of the collapse of communism, followed by an analysis of the political problems involved in providing international trade union assistance to the former Eastern Bloc. This analysis constitutes a case study of the negative effects of Cold War politics on international trade union assistance, highlighting problems which were by no means confined to post-communist Eastern Europe, but occurred wherever the ideological battles of East and West were fought out on trade union terrain.

The most significant member organizations of the WFTU were the Soviet bloc trade unions. These unions were subject to a dual subordination to the ruling communist parties of the respective states, and to managers at an enterprise level (Clarke *et al.*, 1993; Ashwin, 1994). Given this strong association with the communist 'old guard', after the collapse of communism these unions were identified by both liberal observers and some international trade unionists, in particular those connected with the AFL–CIO, as potential centres of restorationist activity. Such fears were only reinforced by the role of the former General Secretary of the VTsSPS, the Soviet Union's trade union centre, Gennadi Yanaev, as one of the leaders of the August 1991 putsch against the reforming regime of Mikhail Gorbachev. But, in general, leaders of the former communist trade union confederations across the region showed themselves to be eminently adaptable and highly sensitive to fluctuations in the political fortunes of potential sponsors. It quickly became clear that the collapse of communism implied the end of the global role of the WFTU, and the former Soviet bloc trade unions were equally swift in dissociating themselves from a dying organization. With the exception of the All-Poland Trade Union Alliance (OPZZ), all the East European successor organizations to former WFTU affiliates left the organization between 1989 and 1992. In the aftermath of the failed coup in the Soviet Union even the successor to the VTsSPS, the renamed General Confederation of Trade Unions (VKP), froze its membership of the WFTU giving as its reason the tardy response of the WFTU to the challenge to democracy presented by the putsch. In April 1992 the VKP transformed itself into a regional organization for CIS countries and announced that it would not be affiliated to any existing world body. Given that, on the 1986 figures, the VTsSPS accounted for over half the 200–50 million members of the WFTU, this exit effectively sounded the death knell of the organization (Windmuller and Pursey, 1998).

Meanwhile, within their respective domestic contexts the former communist unions claimed to have reformed, to have become independent from their former communist masters, and to be redefining their role as 'normal' trade unions. In all cases, the official trade unions held conferences in late 1989 or during the course of 1990 at which they changed their names, often with the judicious addition of 'independent' or 'free' to their titles, and declared their independence of all political parties (Ashwin, 1995: 142).[6] In implementing such changes, these unions wanted nothing more than to be admitted to the free trade union family. Their political survival was at issue: in a situation in which all institutions from the communist past were perceived as tainted and all that appeared to glister was Western, gaining support in the West was a means of the unions gaining legitimacy at home. Thus, after the effective demise of the WFTU as a serious contender in the international trade union arena, the ICFTU was faced with a somewhat bizarre victor's dilemma: its vanquished trade union opponents, the supposed last bastions of communism, were all interested in developing relations with the ICFTU, its affiliates and the ITSs which were once seen as the competitors of the TUIs.

The political difficulties for the ICFTU associated with the attentions of its new former-communist suitors were compounded by the emergence of new independent trade unions in the former Soviet bloc.[7] The prototype of such unions was the Polish trade union Solidarnosc, which had played a key role in the collapse of the Soviet bloc and was admitted as an ICFTU affiliate in 1986. The experience of Poland was different from that of other East European countries, since Solidarnosc was the main force behind the defeat of communism, whereas elsewhere independent trade unions developed later, played a less significant role during the 1989 revolutions and had substantially fewer members. But the independent trade unions which developed nonetheless had strong political similarities with Solidarnosc: they saw themselves as part of the reformist opposition to communism; they sought to promote both political and economic reform; to develop trade union organizations which genuinely defended workers' interests, and they were implacably hostile to the official trade unions, which they saw as remnants of the past which would have no place in the bright capitalist future.[8] These then were 'free' trade unions *par excellence,* precisely the sort of anti-communist champions of democracy and workers' rights which the ICFTU could have been relied on to support in the past. And to these new trade unions, which did unite many sincere activists who had taken great personal risks in opposing communism, it was anathema that the international trade union movement should have cordial relations with organizations they perceived to be one of the most dangerous existing remnants of the old communist élite.[9]

The ICFTU thus had two distinct and opposed types of organization clamouring for its support. But ICFTU affiliates in the main donor countries were far from united in how to respond to the challenge presented by the collapse of communism. At the one extreme, the AFL–CIO and its European operation, the Free Trade Union Institute (FTUI), gave unquestioning support to the new independent unions and strongly concurred with the latter's analysis of the political threat posed by the former communist unions. (Except in the case of former Czechoslovakia, where the communist trade unions were incongruously deemed to be reformed – partly because no Czech or Slovak independent alternatives existed.) Meanwhile, European trade unions, in particular those from Scandinavia, were loath to support the independent trade unions: while they were prepared to acknowledge that these organizations were no doubt made up of very worthy individuals, they posed a threat to the unity of the official trade unions. With millions of workers, as they perceived it, on their doorstep, the priority of European unions was to have stable and numerically strong counterparts with whom they could work to prevent what they termed 'social dumping'. Moreover, in some cases the unions concerned had established bilateral relations with their communist counterparts before 1989: this was true of the Scandinavian and Russian and Baltic unions, and the Austrian and Hungarian trade unions, for example. Thus, the collapse of communism did not immediately spell an end to Cold War divisions, which were transposed into ICFTU ranks, albeit in a modified form.

The division between pragmatists and committed anti-communists did not express itself in violent verbal or even written confrontations within the ICFTU Co-ordinating Committee on Central and Eastern Europe or within the Executive Board of the organization. Instead, the major protagonists committed their resources to the pursuit of bilateral activities with their chosen partners. Although the ICFTU tried to assert a co-ordinating role, there was in fact very little co-ordination in the activities of its affiliates who were supporting opposing sides in bitter inter-trade union conflicts. Meanwhile, the ITSs generally took a pragmatic line, tending to affiliate branch organizations from both types of union without paying too much heed to, or initially having much knowledge of, the sharp political conflicts in which the unions were involved.[10]

The results of this bilateral activity highlight the destructiveness of the international trade union movements' obsession with Cold War ideological struggles. First, the question of who was to receive trade union assistance was often decided by the criteria of Cold War politics. Correspondingly, crucial questions such as the representativity and internal democracy of the unions concerned were neglected. Meanwhile, the form of assistance provided was frequently inappropriate and unhelpful. This could again often be traced back to the old ideological divides. For example, because of its strong anti-communist traditions, the AFL–CIO saw it as important to instil all the trade unions in receipt of its financial support with an appropriate reverence for the market economy. As will be argued below, this had a damaging effect on the unions concerned, and did nothing to foster an effective trade union response to the dilemmas of the transition era.

The main errors of the AFL–CIO's approach can be illustrated by reference to Hungary and Russia, where the most acrimonious 'trade union wars' were waged. As mentioned above, the American unions channelled significant financial support to small independent trade unions of Eastern Europe and the CIS through the FTUI, much of which was obtained from the US government for the promotion of democracy. In Hungary, the small confederation known as the Liga, was the main chosen beneficiary of American largesse, while in Russia a number of independent unions benefited, in particular the Independent Miners' Union (NPG). It is doubtful that many trade union organizations within the region have received more foreign financial assistance than the NPG and the Liga, certainly relative to their size, but now both organizations are hollow shells on the verge of collapse. The financial support they received not only failed to foster the growth of these unions, it also made a crucial contribution to their decline. The most important reason for this was that it allowed the recipients of financial aid to survive without their members: recruiting members and collecting dues was far more time-consuming than producing 'politically correct' policy declarations to please American donors. As well as fatally distracting them from the task of organizing workers, the financial assistance also sowed the seeds of scandal and conflict, and quarrels over fax machines and dollars divided and weakened union leaderships.[11]

No less damaging was the political education provided by the AFL–CIO. The main problem was that the obsession with securing the total defeat of communism led to an almost uncritical acceptance of all the neo-liberal reformers had to offer. By encouraging the unions it supported to support the efforts of their reformist governments the Americans effectively prevented the unions from responding to the mood of their members. For example, under strong pressure from the AFL–CIO[12] the NPG gave firm support to the Russian government, dropping its stance of 'constructive opposition' in November 1992 in favour of positive support for the government, at a time when the miners were becoming increasingly dissatisfied with reform. This only served to illustrate the gulf between the union and its members. Had the union been more in touch with the mood in the mines it is difficult to see how they could have continued to support President Yeltsin: in the Russian mining regions of the Kuzbass and Vorkuta, once seen as bastions of the reform movement, support for the communists and nationalists began growing in 1993 and by the 1995 elections the Kuzbass had become renowned as a communist stronghold, while the polar coalfield of

Vorkuta, with its strong anti-communist traditions derived from its gulag past, voted heavily for the extreme right-wing party of Vladimir Zhirinovsky. Meanwhile, in addition to supporting the government, the NPG, encouraged by their American trainers, responded favourably to the World Bank proposals for restructuring the Russian coal industry, seemingly blind to the devastating consequences that awaited their members if the plans were enacted. Thus, the perpetuation of Cold War struggles in relation to trade union assistance in the former Eastern Bloc contributed to the increasing isolation and irrelevance of the independent trade unions, which, while workers' living standards were being slashed, were still fighting the spectre of communism.

The activity of the organizations which worked with the former communist trade unions was less damaging, though scarcely more effective. Within the polarized post-communist context organizations working with former communists were on the defensive. It was therefore politically difficult for Western trade union organizations to address the very severe limitations of the 'reform' conducted by the former communist trade unions, since their justification for aiding such organizations in the first place was that they could not be equated with the 'transmission belts' of the past. In fact, however, all the detailed research on the reform process within the former communist trade unions testifies to how *little* these organizations have changed since the fall of communism, in particular in terms of the way in which they operate at enterprise level.[13] Thus, much of the assistance which was given to these organizations was ineffective because it failed to address the key problem that the former communist unions had reformed little more than their rhetoric, in particular at enterprise level where they were structurally dependent on enterprise managers. All the training programmes on collective bargaining were of little use when the unions at enterprise level had no interest in bargaining anything.

Events in post-communist Eastern Europe are thus the most recent demonstration of the damage that the ideological divides in the international trade union arena have inflicted, and the limitations they imposed on the definition of wider trade union strategies. As the next section will show, however, this experience was also instructive for the ICFTU.

AFTER IDEOLOGY: COMING TO TERMS WITH STRUCTURAL ADJUSTMENT

As economic reform began to bite the political position of the independent trade unions as champions of the reform process became increasingly untenable. Former communist parties were democratically re-elected across the region in 1993 and 1994.[14] This shift in the popular mood meant that the status of the independent trade unions as 'pure' anti-communists became progressively less attractive to potential members. Similarly, their support for economic reform increasingly came into conflict with their trade union function of defending their members' interests, and their alliances with reform parties came under increasing strain.[15] Meanwhile, since, among other things, the support of the

AFL–CIO had rendered them increasingly 'independent' from their (declining) memberships, what distinguished them from the former communist trade unions became less distinct. Meanwhile, both types of union were facing similar problems, namely, in the words of the Bulgarian independent union, Podkrepa, 'recession and unemployment . . . growth in the private sector (particularly small enterprises and illegal recruitment) . . . general impoverishment and massive company and factory closures, [which] have all resulted in . . . a significant drop in the level of trade union membership' (ICFTU–Phare Democracy Programme, 1995). In this situation, the ideological divides between ICFTU affiliates became increasingly irrelevant.

The ICFTU began to recognize this as early as 1992. In the summer of that year it held separate 'evaluation meetings' for donors and East European aliates. The purpose of these meetings was to move away from debates about the ideological predilections of trade union organizations, and to define a far more practical approach to the problems that all types of union across the region faced in dealing with structural adjustment. It was also admitted that all types of organization had problems in communicating with and retaining their members – part of which stemmed from the difficulty of defining an effective trade union strategy in the transition period. These meetings certainly did not solve all the problems, and divisions and distrust between the donors persisted. Nevertheless, the meetings did underscore the recognition, shared by most of the donor organizations except the AFL–CIO, that the obsession with ideology had proved counter-productive.

From this time the situation began to improve, although the AFL–CIO remained an obstacle to the formation of co-ordinated strategy. What completely transformed the situation was the forced 'retirement' of Lane Kirkland as president of the AFL–CIO in 1995 after 16 years in office. Like his predecessor George Meany, Kirkland's trademark was unwavering anti-communism, and this accordingly informed the position of the AFL–CIO international department. Moreover, one of the 'achievements' of the Kirkland administration was the co-creation of the 'National Endowment for Democracy' through which US government funds were provided to the AFL–CIO foreign policy groups, including the FTUI which funded the damaging bonanza for 'free' trade unions in the former Eastern bloc. Kirkland's replacement by John Sweeney led to a dramatic reorientation of the international policy of the AFL–CIO, and the die-hard cold warriors within the organization were squeezed out.[16] The demise of Kirkland finally marked the end of the Cold War within the international labour movement.

The initial response of the international trade union movement to the collapse of communism was thus both parochial and over-ideologized, but once the heat went out of the crusade to ensure that communism was firmly confined to its coffin, it became possible to view developments in the former Soviet bloc in a wider perspective. The post-communist trade union movement was facing problems experienced by unions in the rest of the world, in particular membership loss and the need to define a trade union response to structural adjustment. The ideological divides in the international trade union movement had previously imposed limits on the discussions within its ranks since any new initiative could have unwelcome political implications in terms of the struggle for a 'free' trade unionism.[17] The change in ideological environment in international trade union circles was therefore very important in that it created a far more open political environment in which issues that concerned trade unions, not just in Eastern Europe but elsewhere, could be addressed. It also provided a powerful incentive for the ICFTU to define a new *raison d'être* now that there was no longer a role for an international defender of 'free' trade unionism.

THE CHALLENGE OF THE GLOBAL MARKET: NEW DIRECTIONS IN INTERNATIONAL TRADE UNIONISM

With its major affiliates all suffering from declining membership and revenue, the ICFTU has come under increasing pressure to define a new agenda for the international trade union movement, and in particular to develop a trade union strategy in the face of the global market. National and sectoral trade unions are becoming increasingly aware of the need for more effective representation of labour at the international level, but the ICFTU is not the only organization to which these organizations can turn. In Europe, the ETUC (European Trade Union Confederation) is becoming increasingly significant, especially in the light of the institutionalization of social dialogue with employers at a European level. Meanwhile, the ITSs are the natural international focus for affiliates of the major confederations. Although the ICFTU does have a defined niche as the forum for national trade union confederations, it nevertheless has to prove that it is capable of providing a form of leadership appropriate to the post-Cold War era. The following sections examine the ICFTU response to these pressures by, first, considering the content of recent ICFTU policy and campaigns and, second, by charting the changing institutional context of international trade unionism in the post-Cold War era.

The ICFTU has responded to the dilemmas posed by globalization within the limits of its form as a federation of national trade union organizations.[18] Its proposed strategies draw on a range of different traditions of trade unionism some of which are at least implicitly in conflict with one another.[19] This eclecticism is in some senses realistic: since it is difficult to predict either how campaigns will develop or what their eventual implications will be, a multi-faceted (even if somewhat contradictory) approach at least spreads the potential risks and opportunities for success. Three main themes in recent policy and campaigns are identified and examined: global rule making, social partnership, and organizing and alliance building.

GLOBAL RULE MAKING

A natural and appropriate role for the ICFTU would seem to be that of interlocutor with international financial and government institutions. In the

Cold War era, the international trade union movement was too preoccupied with its divisions to devote much attention to this area. Now, however, attaining greater prominence as a respected 'player' in international policy fora has become a priority. This can be seen clearly in the ICFTU's current Campaign on Labour Standards and Trade, the focus of which is to fight for the enactment of a workers' rights clause within the World Trade Organization (WTO).[20] Such a clause would be implemented jointly by the WTO and the ILO through the establishment of a joint advisory body in which the International labour Organization (ILO) would assume responsibility for setting standards and supervising their application, and the WTO for ensuring that failure to enforce the basic standards should not lead to unfair competition. The campaign uses the argument that 'the global economy needs global rules' (ICFTU, 1997: 56), an idea which recalls the classic pluralist view of industrial relations as a process of rule making (Dunlop, 1958). The ICFTU is thus aiming to take up a position as one of the principal parties in the global rule-making process, in order to challenge the global *diktat* of neo-liberal institutions and engender a more pluralist approach to international economic decision making. Success in this area would not only give the ICFTU a clear global role for the post-Cold War era, it could also provide a focus for international trade union co-operation and campaigning.

What are the prospects of such aspirations being realized? Clearly, it is not within the ICFTU's power to force international financial and government institutions to listen to the trade union point of view. The organization claims, however, that there is a growing awareness among policy makers that 'the free market cannot be simply left to operate unchecked and ungoverned' (ICFTU, 1997: 47). It does indeed seem to be the case that governments and the international financial institutions are in the midst of a mini-crisis of confidence regarding the potential negative effects of liberalization. The World Bank, for example, sounded a cautionary note in its 1995 World Development Report. The report admitted that the dismantling of trade barriers appeared to pose a threat to jobs, wages and support for the elderly, had the potential to increase the gap between rich and poor, had so far done nothing to reduce world unemployment and seemed to imply increased risk and insecurity worldwide (World Bank, 1995: 1–2). Predictably, it went on to assert that such fears were 'mainly without basis' (p 2), but it was clear that officials at the Bank perceived that there was a case to be answered. Running through the report was a tension between the need to define a social dimension without compromising the unfettered global market. Interestingly, trade unions were identified as just the kind of 'social dimension' that could be tolerated. Unions, it was argued, could play a positive role in improving the efficiency of labour markets by providing workers with a collective bargaining power which 'matches that of the employer', by monitoring 'employers' compliance with government regulations', and helping to 'raise workplace productivity and reduce workplace discrimination' (p 79). The right sort of unionism was also identified as a defence against populism – for, it was argued, where workers do not have the freedom to organize, governments try to pacify them and gain support for state-controlled unions through excessive intervention and regulation. Thus, the report conceptualized trade unions as a potential buttress of the free market, arguing that they were the best defence against government intervention in the labour market in the form of such practices as 'regulations on minimum wages and restrictions on hiring and firing' (p 83). In this sense, the chapter devoted to trade unions did not depart from neo-liberal orthodoxy, but it did at least recognize the legitimacy of trade unions, claiming that 'free labor unions are mostly democratic institutions' (p 5). Although the report's acceptance of a role for trade unions was distinctly qualified and uneasy, its importance lay in its recognition that there was a genuine problem with the integration of labour into the world market to which the World Bank did not have a ready-made solution. This was also reflected in the 1997 World Development Report which conceded that the state had to play a greater regulatory role, a position which in turn implied the necessity of channels of political representation, of which trade unions are clearly the main form as regards labour. It is this new touch of humility that has defined a new space for the intervention of the international trade union movement.

This less triumphalist, more questioning mood has also been reflected at a number of international gatherings. For example, the convening of the March 1995 UN World Summit for Social Development in Copenhagen, attended by 115 countries, was in itself an admission that global capitalism could not be left to regulate itself. The countries present at the summit signed a number of commitments, the third of which was to promote the goal of full employment as a basic priority of social and economic policy. The national action promised under this commitment included the safeguarding of workers' rights in line with the relevant ILO conventions, including those on forced and child labour, free-dom of association, the right to organize and bargain collectively and the prin-ciple of non-discrimination. These principles were reiterated at the September 1995 UN Fourth World Women's Conference held in Beijing. Meanwhile, issues of labour standards also arose at the December 1996 WTO ministerial summit in Singapore. Despite the conflicts at this meeting the final Declaration did include a paragraph in which participants 'renewed' their 'commitment to the observance of internationally recognised core labour standards', which should be set and dealt with by the ILO. The ministers also affirmed their support for the work of this institution and its work in promoting labour standards.

So it seems that there is at least the potential for the ICFTU to attain a new prominence in world politics, but this is not simply a question of gaining the ears of the powers-that-be. The other issue is that of content: how far will affiliates be able to agree on a common policy for the ICFTU? Issues such as minimum labour standards have the potential to open up divisions between trade unions from the developed and developing world. The ICFTU has been able to secure consensus over the campaign for the workers' rights clause in the WTO.[21] But the operation of any workers' rights clause would partly depend on the activism of affiliates, many of whom may be either indifferent, hostile or simply too weak to mount an effective campaign around the issue.[22] In short, what can be achieved by an organization representing such a diverse range of interests may be rather limited. Nevertheless, were the ICFTU to gain recognition as a legitimate interlocutor at an international level, it would at least serve to challenge the abstract terms in which the international economic debate is commonly conducted by forcing workers and their all too concrete sufferings on to the agenda.

Indeed, the main merit of the pluralist vision of global rule making is that it implies the possibility of challenging the current form of 'globalization'. The creation of an unregulated global market is not, as is often implied, inevitable, it is a neo-liberal *policy*. The participation of the trade unions in a process of global rule making could therefore make a real difference: the unions could challenge the *lack* of rules in the present global economic environment. Notwithstanding the qualifications outlined above, it should be acknowledged that the attempt to introduce a workers' rights clause in the WTO is at least a first step in this direction.

SOCIAL PARTNERSHIP

The ICFTU-prescribed response to the new liberal environment at a national level is far more traditional. The organization faithfully intones the established ILO mantra of social partnership in which the three social partners (trade unions, employers and the state) co-operate and negotiate with each other to mutual benefit. ICFTU documents are always littered with references to the advantages of social partnership, and their latest publications on globalization are no exception. The main distinctive feature of the recent discussion is that social partnership is predominantly portrayed as a 'pain-sharing' exercise in which the neo-liberal version of the global market is accepted as a *fait accompli*. The rhetoric is tough and similar in tone to that of the World Bank. In its 1995 report, the World Bank made an exception to its preference for plant-level collective bargaining, noting that 'when large-scale structural adjustment and rapid disinflation are needed' national trade union federations could (on rare occasions) rally the workers behind 'social pacts' in order to facilitate stabilization (World Bank, 1995: 84). Similarly, the 1996 ICFTU conference document, *The global market,* emphasized the importance of tripartite systems in managing change, arguing that such consultation was the best way to ensure that labour markets responded smoothly to change and achieved steady growth and competitiveness, and to make 'tough choices about the distribution of scarce resources without destabilising government budgets and within the restraints of global competitive pressures' (ICFTU, 1996a: 63). This implies a form of 'responsible' trade unionism in which unions discipline workers to accept the necessity of 'tough choices'.[23]

This strand of the ICFTU's current approach is the most problematic both in strategic and logical terms. First, it is utterly uninspiring. Given the pessimistic terms in which it is couched, social partnership is unlikely to prove a beacon around which the world's trade unionists will unite. It promises only a mildly attenuated status quo, and imposes a duty of 'responsibility'. Second, it faces the logical problem that it minimizes the tension between democracy and the market. What if trade union members do not accept the necessity of the choices thrust upon them? What if they 'democratically' oppose structural adjustment, rather than selling it to their members as the only alternative?[24] This is a major unresolved problem in such prescriptions. In contrast to this, the idea of global rule making offers far more scope for trade unions to define strategies which respond to their members' concerns.

TOWARDS SOCIAL-MOVEMENT UNIONISM? THE ICFTU BRANCHES OUT

The most novel element in the ICFTU's current strategy is its emphasis on organizing new types of workers, and on co-operating with NGOs in campaigns for workers' rights. The recognition of the need to organize workers in the informal sector, including women and young workers, is not new, but it is being treated increasingly seriously: rather than being part of a ritual incantation of good intentions such issues are now central to ICFTU campaigning.[25] (The current campaign on child labour and the ICFTU's work on Export Processing Zones[26] are examples of this.) The idea of co-operating with other NGOs is a new departure, however, and is something that has been facilitated by the change in the international trade union climate in the post-Cold War era. During the Cold War, the ICFTU was highly suspicious of working with other NGOs and of sponsoring union co-operation with other forms of organization, mainly because the politics of such organizations could not be relied upon: they might harbour communist sympathizers or favour policies avowed by organizations supported by the Soviet Union. Members of the ICFTU secretariat had a tendency to portray other organizations as run by politically naïve idealists who did not understand the complexity and significance of Cold War politics. This lack of love was mutual: it was War on Want which produced the famous denunciation of the ICFTU, *Where were you brother?* (1978), which in particular highlighted the destructive and corrupting influence of the AFL–CIO's anti-communist obsession on the international trade union movement. War on Want also voiced traditional radical criticisms regarding the élitism of trade unions, their neglect of unorganized workers and their lack of involvement in, and occasional hostility to, wider emancipatory campaigns:

> Worker and peasant struggles are characterised by their dynamism and verve. ... There is not a trace of any corresponding spontaneity or inventiveness within our international labour structures. ... The ICFTU, for example, is shackled by a constitution which means that it can only work with and through national trade union centres. ... Many of these centres in the Third World don't represent more than the government and

the few workers' movements allowed to survive to present a democratic image. . . . Many of these ICFTU affiliates are opposed by genuine worker and peasant movements (Thomson and Larson, 1978: 33–6).

The ICFTU still has a number of highly dubious affiliates in its ranks, and this continues to hinder its campaigns. Nevertheless, the organization has become far more amenable to co-operation with other organizations, and has openly declared that

> one modern development that trade unions should not ignore is the rise of NGOs to become powerful lobbyists nationally and internationally. The ICFTU should be ready to build relationships and alliances with those NGOs whose principles and practice do not conflict with trade unionism (ICFTU, 1996a: 70).

This new openness also extends to encouraging affiliates' co-operation with other types of organization.

One example of this greater openness is the ICFTU's willingness to harness the rise of ethical consumerism in its campaigning. The ICFTU sees the formation of alliances between union organizations, consumer organizations and human rights groups to draw attention to abuses of workers' rights as a positive development. For example, it cites as a model initiative the action taken by trade unions, religious, consumer, women's and student's organizations in the USA to highlight the abuses being perpetrated by a sub-contractor of the Gap clothing company in El Salvador, the Korean owned Mandarin clothing company. (These included forbidding workers to talk while they were working, beatings, sexual abuse and the suppression of trade union activity.) This campaign led to an acceptance by Gap of responsibility for working conditions where its products are made, and to it agreeing to independent monitoring of its sub-contractors by a third party (ICFTU, 1996a: 41).[27]

The Cold War environment did not only encourage a closed and somewhat paranoid attitude to organizations and movements outside the 'free trade union family', it also influenced relations within the international trade union movement. Most importantly, the concern with political control and ideological correctness did nothing to foster genuine co-operation between the ICFTU and the ITSs. In the immediate aftermath of the collapse of communism, for example, there was tension between the ICFTU and some of the ITSs regarding policy in Central and Eastern Europe. Initially, the ICFTU approach in the region was informed by an anti-communist agenda, while the ITSs adopted a far more pragmatic policy of co-operation with the unions which existed, without much regard to the independence of these organizations or the veracity of their claims to represent their members. This created a mutual suspicion which made co-operation difficult, even though the need for better co-ordination was a constant theme of the Co-ordinating Committee on Central and Eastern Europe. Such tensions have been dramatically reduced by the ideological relaxation within the ICFTU. This can be seen, for example, in the 1997 ICFTU campaign on the non-payment of wages in Russia which did involve genuine co-ordination between the ICFTU and ITSs. This was facilitated by the ICFTU's decision to work with all the Russian national trade union confederations: previously conflicts over the appropriate trade union partners in Russia had made co-operation far more difficult. Co-ordination took the form of the ICFTU assuming responsibility for the overall running of the campaign in co-operation with the Russian national trade union centres, while the ITSs supported the conduct of sectoral seminars within the framework of the campaign and participated actively in the final conference. Such a division of labour provides a means by which the ICFTU can overcome the 'shackles' of its constitution and co-ordinate campaigns which involve workers at the grass roots as well as lobbying in international fora. Combined with the new willingness to work with NGOs, such an approach removes some of the institutional barriers to effective international labour solidarity.

CONCLUSION

The foregoing discussion is not intended to convey the impression that the ICFTU has been transformed overnight into an organization capable of taming the beast of global capitalism. It is in the process of 'downsizing', which in turn reflects the decline in union membership worldwide. The ICFTU campaign on non-payment of wages in Russia may have been an example of more effective co-ordination between the ICFTU and ITSs, but what it also highlighted is that international campaigns can only make a significant impact when they are backed up by the action of trade unions in the relevant countries. The conservatism and timidity of the Russian national trade union centres proved a major obstacle in the non-payment campaign: a fact dramatically highlighted when, at the conference planned as the climax of the campaign, the head of the former communist trade union confederation, Mikhail Shmakov, (quite incorrectly) asserted that the problem of non-payment was under control! Although the Russian trade union movement is in a particularly bad shape, unionism worldwide is hardly in its heyday. The other side of the weakness of the non-payment campaign was the failure of the ICFTU to persuade Western national trade union centres to take up the issue within their own countries so that the initiative could develop as a global campaign over what is becoming a global issue. Instead the outcome has been a series of discrete campaigns in discrete countries (with Croatia and Ukraine currently taking the campaign forward).

It has to be recognized that the achievements of international trade union organization have not been very considerable, and a wide range of issues which have a fundamental impact on labour have not even been addressed by the trade unions. This chapter has argued that the Cold War divisions within the international trade union movement have been a major barrier to the development of effective international labour organization. It is only very recently that these barriers have finally dissolved so that international solidarity can move up the trade union agenda. But solidarity cannot be created from above international bodies can at best provide a favourable environment for the development of solidarity action. Nevertheless, particularly given the mini-crisis of confidence on the part of the international financial institutions, the structures and opportunities are now in place for national and sectoral trade union organizations to come together and to confront the challenge of the global market.

8

ENVIRONMENTAL NGOS AND GLOBALIZATION

THE GOVERNANCE OF TNCS[1]

Peter Newell

Those standing up against globalism or its effects are not governments (who mostly approve, having given the corporations the authority) but non-governmental groups, which are being pushed into the role of social justice watchdogs, moral arbiters and spokespeople for those without a voice (Vidal, 1996: 260).

Many claims have been made on behalf of the globalization process. One of the most prominent has been the effect of global economic changes on traditional structures of authority, particularly the nation state (Cerny, 1990; Ohmae, 1990; Sassen, 1996; Strange, 1996), leading to assertions for instance about the 'retreat of the state' (Strange, 1996). The starting point for this chapter is the withdrawal of the state from practising certain regulatory functions with regard to multi-national enterprises, particularly in relation to the environment (Clapp, 1997). It can be argued that this 'retreat' creates a crisis of governance, in that while traditional methods of regulation and oversight of companies' activities fall away, new forms of government intervention are not replacing them. In the vacuum left by this gradual retreat of governmental control of the environmental impact of companies' activities, environmental NGOs, through a wide spectrum of co-operative and confrontational strategies, have been targeting companies themselves. This has produced a new and interesting set of relationships; the dynamics and limits of which are explored in this chapter.

Given the perceived unwillingness or inability of national governments to impose adequate environmental safeguards and the failure of internationally orchestrated attempts at the regulation of TNCs,[2] environmental NGOs (ENGOs) have increasingly been adopting non-traditional means to impose accountability upon TNCs by forging alliances with consumers, institutional investors and companies themselves. This chapter aims to explore this emerging trend towards the informal regulation of the environmental impact of the activities of TNCs. It also seeks to *account* for the significance of this phenomenon and to suggest some implications of it. An assessment is made about whether or not the environmental movement, as it currently stands, is in a position to consolidate and extend such regulatory functions without addressing broader questions of accountability and representation which arise when NGOs perform 'state-like' functions. The chapter explores the dimensions of NGO–TNC relations through reference to a broad (and expanding) range of co-operative ventures and sites of confrontation which illustrate the increasing use of a range of policy tools designed to regulate the behaviour of TNCs.

The increase in the use of these instruments is informed by a number of political and economic developments associated with globalization. The point is not that these strategies have not been adopted before in other contexts, but that there has been resurgence in their use, and that they are increasingly important in a contemporary context. Their use at a time of heightened globalization, coinciding with a perception in the environmental movement of the limited nature of existing regulation of multinational companies, offers an interesting example of the way in which social movements adapt their strategies to changing political and economic circumstances. From an international relations perspective this is also interesting because it illustrates an area in which NGOs are seeking to bypass the state and lobby companies directly on the basis that the state is either unwilling or unable to restrain aspects of corporate environmental conduct. This displaces the state as the central unit of analysis and denotes a perceived shift in the locus of power in the global economy.

This is not to suggest that NGOs are superseding states, even if it might be argued that they are increasingly performing functions traditionally associated with the state. They may create inducements and penalties to reward and punish deviant or positive social practice, but they cannot command or compel firms to adopt certain practices. That remains the role of the state. Nevertheless, investigating the role of the environmental movement in the global economy contributes to a less state-centred understanding of the importance of NGOs in global affairs. It also simultaneously tells us something useful about the role of social movements in creating mechanisms of regulation in the global economy and about the way the process of global economic change impacts upon the activities of social movements. By contributing towards the re-regulation of investment patterns, such practices provide a different reading of the globalization process and the role of social movements in shaping its contours.

The chapter proceeds in three parts. First, a number of academic debates within global environmental politics and global political economy are outlined which help to place these 'governance' practices in context. Second, a range of strategies employed by environmental groups targeted at TNCs are explored and discussed and finally the problems associated with the environmental movement performing such governance functions are addressed.

BACKGROUND

The background to the growth in relationships between ENGOs and TNCs is informed by twin developments in global environmental politics and the global political economy. Firstly, there was been an increasing questioning of the effectiveness of traditional mechanisms for achieving environmental protection. The international institutions set up to deliver international action have come under fire as a result of the disappointment felt by many at the outcome of the Rio de Janeiro conference. This disillusionment was heightened by the 'Rio+5' evaluations of 1997, which demonstrated a lack of progress in implementing the goals of the UN conference on Environment and Development (UNCED) five years on (Dodds, 1997). Existing mechanisms for environmental governance are often thought to be little more than an 'institutional bandage applied to a structural haemorrhage'. Often international agreements are vaguely worded, slow to negotiate and difficult to enforce. The greatest indictment of all is that despite the proliferation of inter-state accords relating to the environment the rate of environmental degradation in most areas proceeds unabated (Conca, 1993; Wapner, 1995).

Critical attention has focused on the way in which states and TNCs have carved out a role for themselves as the appropriate agents for articulating a response to the challenges posed by sustainable development (Finger, 1993; Chatterjee and Finger, 1994).[3] Corporations help to obscure their role in causing ecological degradation by providing the expertise, technology and capital for environmental protection. Dependence upon corporations to perform these functions means that, 'states, some more so than others, are finding it nearly impossible either to regulate or to extricate themselves from the global economic relationships associated with environmental harm' (Clapp, 1997: 127). Further, if there exists a structural relationship between the state and capital (Newell and Paterson, 1998), then the limits of NGO strategies pursued through the state are real and need to be acknowledged. Paterson argues in relation to the environmental movement that

> the politics of globalization is not adequately dealt with by looking to the state for reforms, since states themselves are part of the globalizing dynamic. There is little fundamental difference of interest between state élites and those organizing and benefiting from a globalized economy' (1997: 10).

It is unsurprising therefore that the impact of business group lobbying on the state's environmental policies is also considered significant (Chatterjee and Finger, 1994; Newell and Paterson, 1998). Business groups are involved in drawing up environmental agreements, and often sit on government delegations at international negotiations. The involvement of the Business Council for Sustainable Development and ICC (International Chamber of Commerce) with the UNCED (United Nations Conference on Environment and Development) process is credited by some with derailing previous attempts at regulating TNC activity such as the UNCTC's (United Nations Centre for Transnational Corporations) proposals for a code of conduct (Humphreys, 1997). More broadly, some writers have referred to the 'privatisation' of the UN system, a trend towards corporate influence over decisions and activities that are traditionally the prerogative of states at the international level (Lee *et al.*, 1998).

The increased attention of ENGOs to TNCs may simultaneously reflect a frustration with the pace of inter-state reform and the capture by business interests of the institutions set up to address environmental problems. Targeting companies directly also offers the prospect of higher 'returns', given that the investment decisions of major TNCs now dwarf those of many states (Korten, 1995). The appropriate focus of NGO activity is continually contested within the environmental movement. Indeed, the effectiveness of the traditional lobbying approaches of the big environmental NGOs has received more critical scrutiny in recent years. The increasing institutionalization and bureaucratization of the environmental movement (or certain parts of it) has, according to some (Finger, 1993; Chatterjee and Finger, 1994; Sklair, 1994), led to a degree of co-option. Sklair refers for instance to the emergence of a 'transnational environmentalist élite' (1994: 211).[4] There is a perception that NGOs have given more (in terms of legitimacy conferred upon the process) than they have received (in terms of concessions to their demands) by being part of the UNCED process.

In broader terms this 'strategic turn' comes as a result of the singular failure of governments, to date, to regulate the activities of TNCs at the international level. Clapp refers to this as the 'deliberate disengagement of states from attempting to regulate global economic processes' (1997: 126). The issue of TNC regulation was conveniently dropped from the UNCED agenda at the insistence of the USA and others (see Chatterjee and Finger, 1994) and so in a single sleight of hand, the role of the world's most powerful economic agents in perpetuating environmental degradation were removed from global scrutiny. Similarly, while Agenda 21 includes recommendations that affect TNCs, it does not take the form of a code of conduct.

The subject of an international code of conduct to regulate the activities of TNCs has been on the international agenda since the 1970s. The UNCTC was set up in 1973, but after two decades of failed negotiation in 1993, the centre was closed and has been replaced by the Division on Transnational Corporations and Investment located within UNCTAD (United Nations Conference on Trade and Development). In place of binding commitments at the international level, there has been a growth in voluntary agreements, self-monitoring and the proliferation of sustainability audits of corporations by external consultants. The best known voluntary guidelines on the environment are those endorsed by the ICC (International Chamber of Commerce) known as the *Business Charter for Sustainable Development*, a document of 16 principles produced prior to UNCED (Schmidheiny, 1992).

To return to the start of the chapter, this is not a 'sovereignty at bay' argument (Vernon, 1971; 1991) as much as a 'regulation at bay' argument. As Litfin

(1993), Doran (1993) and others make clear, environmental change may well have the effect of extending sovereignty in new directions.[5] The point though is that when it comes to state regulation of TNCs and their impact upon the environment, there has been a notable shift towards voluntary self-regulation, a move away from 'command and control' approaches and a failure of internationally orchestrated attempts at regulation though codes of conduct.

The globalization process clearly makes it harder for states to adopt unilateral environmental actions, for fear of capital flight (a fear which industries have exploited to great effect) and the relocation of industry to areas with lower environmental standards, however exaggerated the 'pollution haven' phenomenon is. Unilateral or even regional environmental standards become less desirable in a context in which the state is competing with rival states and firms for a share of the world market. The extent to which globalization *actually* constrains the ability of states to pursue more far-reaching environmental programmes is difficult to assess. It is clearly also convenient for governments to use the threat of economic losses at the hands of competitors to justify cut-backs in environmental programmes which are desired for other reasons.

Nevertheless, whatever the outcome of the debate over the 'actual' extent and reach of globalization, in broad terms, these patterns imply a growth in the power of TNCs and a reduction in restraints upon the terms of their investment. This can be argued to create a 'crisis' of governance where institutions have not kept pace with the demands and needs for new protection to which economic globalization gives rise. As Vidal argues 'Corporations have never been more powerful, yet less regulated; never more pampered by government, yet never less questioned; never more needed to take social responsibility yet never more secretive. … To whom will these fabulously self-motivated, self-interested supranational bodies be accountable?' (1997: 263). TNCs are said to wield power without responsibility. They are often as powerful as states and yet less accountable. At the same time, because they are simultaneously more anonymous than governments and often more financially powerful, they are increasingly attracting the attention of social activists. For corporations this means 'their own globalism is being actively turned against them by the emerging civil society' (Vidal, 1997: 265). ENGOs perceive power relations to have changed in a way that privileges the position of TNCs to such an extent that they are now equally, if not more important, targets for pressures towards reform. This then provides the space for a new form of governance in which ENGOs adopt a role as regulators by setting standards, creating norms and providing sanctions for 'deviant' behaviour.

The failure to regulate TNCs also coincides with a changed context of NGO–TNC relations informed by organizational and perceptual changes within both the business and NGO communities. The space for more co-operative solutions to develop has been occasioned by a more 'solutions-oriented' approach adopted by many NGOs, and a perceived need among many NGOs to move beyond awareness-raising functions and engage directly with reform by demonstrating its plausibility by pursuing 'DIY' solutions, sometimes by collaborating with TNCs (SustainAbility, 1996; Murphy and Bendell, 1997). The growth in the size of many ENGOs (particularly during the mid-late 1980s) also means that they cannot afford the risk of litigation undertaken by companies against their direct actions. They now have sizeable assets that would be threatened by successful court action against them. Hence, despite the ongoing role of Brent Spar style confrontations, more co-operative approaches become more important for some groups in order to develop credibility among those able to generate reform and to avoid financial loss.

Businesses have also become more proactive in the debate rather than resisting government-led controls or lobbying against legislation post-hoc. Their approach to environmental issues has clearly also shown a transition from the late 1980s onwards (Fischer and Schot, 1993; Hoffman, 1996). As Haufler notes, in order to pre-empt government regulation, firms may decide it is in their interest to construct their own regulatory framework. In so doing they make it more difficult for governments to regulate or they make it easier for governments simply to legitimate the company's own framework and incorporate it into law (1997: 7).[6]

ENVIRONMENTALISM IN AN AGE OF GLOBALIZATION

The challenge for ENGOs is to monitor the global activities of TNCs, made more difficult by the fact that, as Saurin (1996) argues, globalization permits increasing distance between the source and site of consumption. Vidal notes 'the increasingly global economy allows [TNCs] to operate with their own ethics and a social responsibility that may have nothing to do with the people who use their products' (1997: 241). Re-territorializing the obligations of companies is a difficult task for NGOs to perform.[7] This problem is exacerbated by the development of pollution leakage, or 'pollution havens', and the relocation of TNCs to areas with lower environmental standards.

The compression of time and space that is often associated with globalization also means, however, that flash points can spread rapidly around the world and so instead of having to deal with a single and more manageable source of opposition, corporations today have to deal with simultaneous co-ordinated actions of an international nature. The conflicts over the Brent Spar oil rig and Shell's involvement in Nigeria illustrate how 'local incidents can soon develop into international crises' (Vidal, 1997: 240). The boycotts of Shell petrol stations spread quickly across Europe in response to these two incidents. Ken Saro-Wiwa and the MOSOP (Movement for the Survival of the Ogoni People) were able to globalize the plight of the Ogoni by drawing in the support and mobilizing resources of Greenpeace International and the Body Shop (Fabig and Boele, 1999). Communications technologies that globalization has brought in its wake have also enabled NGOs to organize more quickly and effectively and to extend the reach of their surveillance of TNCs, so that ironically TNCs have provided the means for their own monitoring. Public relations disasters can be ignited easily and with global ramifications.

An expansion in consumer markets and international trade in goods also brings choice and heightens the power of the concerned consumer by allowing her/him to exercise the threat of taking business elsewhere; of buying differently (consumer flight). Consumers, unlike voters in a government election, make a series of votes, often on a daily basis about what they think of a TNC's product and which TNC they will 'vote for'. Companies feel the repercussions of these choices, directly and economically.

The 'new' governance

In the context of this 'crisis' of governance, with the opportunities that are presented by altered global circumstances and shifting patterns of business–NGO relations, a number of strategies have been employed by environmental NGOs in recent years targeted towards TNCs. It is not that these are new strategies, indeed there is a long history of the use of consumer boycotts (e.g. Smith, 1990). Other mechanisms of restraint such as exposure of corporate misconduct and non-compliance also have a (relatively) long history. Shareholder activism, and the emergence of stewardship councils, as they are applied in the environmental area, do seem to be a largely new phenomena, however. The point though is that all these strategies, whether new or not, appear to be being applied more frequently than was the case even ten years ago.

Some are more reactive in nature and others more proactive, some confrontational and others collaborative. The strategies should not be considered as stand-alone discrete responses. They are often employed alongside one another and are intended to supplement the strengths and build on the limits of other strategies. One may find consumer boycotts being used alongside shareholder activism, an information war being waged in conjunction with a project collaboration. Nevertheless, while there is overlap and some groups are simultaneously willing and able to use co-operative and confrontational strategies at the same time, others more obviously engage in what will be referred to as either *liberal* or *critical* governance.

Both uses of the term are consistent with a definition which implies some measure of government (of practising governing) without the necessary involvement of governments, where government may be one player among many, *primus inter pares* or absent altogether (Rosenau, 1990; Rosenau and Czempiel, 1992). An emphasis on governance provides a useful starting point because of its twin emphases on governing mechanisms which do not rest on recourse to the authority and sanctions of government and the shifting negotiation of responsibilities between the state and civil society (Stoker, 1998). This permits us to think about NGOs conducting the business of government without resembling the state in fulfilling that role.

Liberal governance

There has been a growth since the late-1980s in a range of collaborations and interactions between NGOs and TNCs that fall under the umbrella of 'liberal governance'. Such strategies of engagement seek to work within the current economic system, to improve the way in which it functions and to offset its worst ecological excesses. They do not require a radical rejection of the current global order; the preference is for responsible management rather than ideological confrontation. They share the aim of rewarding good business practice with financial endorsement (as in the case of ethical consumerism), or awarding companies a symbol of responsible environmental practice (as in the case of the codes of conduct and stewardship regimes). A few brief examples will help to clarify the dimensions of liberal governance.

ECO-CONSUMERISM

'Green' consumerism exploded in the 1980s in the USA. In promoting eco-consumerism groups such as Greenpeace have tried to provide companies with 'carrots' in the form of financial incentives to pursue particular markets by showing that markets exist for environmentally sound products. Greenpeace's promotion of the 'greenfreeze' refrigerator, which runs without the use of ozone-depleting chemicals, is a prominent example. The scheme is a direct threat to TNCs' own products given that the pressure group is competing in the same market and hence serves to force the agenda and draw (in this case chemical) companies into dialogue about how their own products are produced. Attempts to promote social reform through purchasing power (Smith, 1990) have a long history. The ethical consumerism that appeared in the late 1980s was of a different order, however, responding to different impulses and targeted towards different actors and centred around a different set of issues. The magazine *Ethical Consumer* captures its contemporary form:

> We argue that the rise of ethical consumerism is closely connected to global-isation and the pressures this puts on democratic governments to avoid corporate regulation. So unless something occurs to reverse this process, we would certainly predict no early demise for ethical consumerism. Indeed, with few ideas on the horizon which so directly address the social and environmental consequences of globalisation, most evidence points to increasing levels of activity in this field (*Ethical Consumer*, 1997/1998: 25).

The inside cover of the magazine continues:

> It is becoming widely accepted that the global economic system should be able to pursue ethical as well as financial goods. In a world where people feel politically disempowered and where governments are becoming less powerful than corporations, citizens are beginning to realise that their economic vote may have as much influence as their political vote. This is true both for individuals and institutional purchasers (*Ethical Consumer*, 1997/1998: 3).

Under the heading 'Democratising the Market', the same source declared that it aimed 'to enable purchasers to assert their ethical values *through* the market by providing information' (emphasis added).

The important aspect of this strategy in respect of liberal (as opposed to critical governance is the use of the market to express political will and the harnessing of consumer power to the goal of corporate reform. Hence, while the impact of consumption is an issue, the strategy for reform is different consumption and not less consumption.

PROJECT COLLABORATION

One of the most famous examples of NGO–TNC co-operation is the project undertaken between the EDF (Environmental Defence Fund) and McDonald's corporation, often held up as model of NGO–TNC collaboration. The focus of concern was the company's 'clamshell' polystyrene container for hamburgers. The background to the story is that 'Most targets for recycling and solid waste reduction have tended to be fairly loose with little in the way of teeth on the enforcement side. Public pressure has had a far greater influence on company policy' (Murphy and Bendell, 1997: 193). In August 1990, representatives of McDonald's and the DF signed an agreement to establish a joint task force to address the company's solid waste issues. The agreement retains provision for EDF to criticize the company, and if parties disagreed on research findings in the final report on the project, separate statements from EDF and McDonald's could be produced. McDonald's also required EDF task-force members to work in one of its restaurants for at least a day each.

Broader issues relating to rainforest destruction and global warming were strictly off limits. The mandate was deliberately narrowly defined to avoid broader conflicts of interest. The pay-off for the company was obvious. By January 1991, a Gallup poll found that McDonald's was regarded as the most environmentally responsible food chain. McDonald's also gained access to the waste-management expertise of EDF (Long and Arnold, 1995). For EDF, the partnership is seen as a model for other environmental groups to pursue, though involvement with the task force did attract attention away from some of its ongoing projects.

The project was liberal in its emphasis on pooling expertise, avoiding conflict and the belief in the reformability of a company, which necessarily has an enormous ecological impact through the nature of its business.

CODES OF CONDUCT

In 1989 a coalition of environmental, investor and church interests known as the Coalition for Environmentally Responsible Economies (CERES) met in New York to introduce a ten-point environmental code of conduct for corporations. One month later CERES, along with the Green Alliance, launched a similar effort in the UK. The aim was to provide criteria for auditing the environmental performance of large domestic and multinational industries. The code called on companies to minimize the release of pollutants, conserve non-renewable resources, use sustainable energy sources and use environmental commitment as a factor in appointing members to the board of directors. The principles are known as the *Valdez principles* (named after the Exxon Valdez disaster in 1989) and have been used by groups such as Friends of the Earth to enlist corporations to pledge compliance. Companies endorsing the CERES principles are required to report annually on their implementation of the principles. The approach is one of self-regulation as companies have the option of non-endorsement, though public and NGO pressure supply incentives to join.

The principles have been used to foster shareholder pressure on companies to improve their environmental performance, to help investors decide on socially responsible investments, to encourage graduates to be aware of the environmental credentials of companies with whom they may seek employment (Wapner, 1995) and as a benchmark by which to assess reform in company behaviour. Wapner argues, 'The CERES Principles represent a new set of institutional constraints on companies and thus another instance of going outside the states system to institutionalise guidelines for widespread and transnational behaviour' (1997: 82).

The principles open up new channels of reform and avenues of pressure upon company conduct. They enable companies to legitimize their activities by signing up to principles co-drafted with environmentalists and therefore to represent their activities as ecologically responsible. While they also provide a useful lobbying tool that environmental groups can use to pressure companies to remain faithful to their promises, companies have been able to use them as a way of avoiding government regulation.[8]

PRIVATE REGIMES[9]

Stewardship regimes that bring together environmental groups, companies and other interested parties, to formulate accreditation procedures to identify good corporate conduct, have also begun to develop in recent years. These are more formalized and institutionalized than codes of conduct. They provide an ongoing arena in which dialogue and review take place. The Forestry Stewardship Council (FSC) provides an interesting example of this form of governance.

The background to the Council's creation was WWF–UK's decision to pursue an alternative strategy in its campaign for sustainable forestry; a direct response to the 'lack of commitment and progress being observed at the international policy level' (Murphy and Bendell, 1997: 105). It was decided to pursue a campaign aimed at ensuring that all tropical wood and wood products traded in the UK would come from well-managed forests by the end of 1995. Directors of targeted companies concerned about the public relations and commercial implications of the protests, decided that signing up to the target offered a way of retrieving some lost ground in the debate. To join the 1995 club companies had to agree to phase out by the target date the sale and use of all wood and wood products not sourced from well-managed forests.

Manufacturers' misuse of claims about forestry management led to pressure for the establishment of a standard-setting body with a system for verifying product claims. Hence, the FSC was established in 1993. The founding group consisted of environmental NGOs, forest industry representatives, community forest-groups and forest-product certification organizations. The FSC set up an independent forest accreditation programme to alleviate consumer confusion about environmentally friendly wood products. Members of the FSC agree to nine principles of forestry management. An FSC logo denotes that the product was sourced from an independently certified forest according to FSC principles. There has been a proliferation in similar such schemes elsewhere in the world with NGOs initiating buyer groups and FSC working groups. In each case 'a lack of effective government action was a significant factor in making environmental groups turn to the industry itself' (Murphy and Bendell, 1997: 130).

The emphasis once again is clearly upon exchanging the perceived legitimacy of environmental NGOs as the appropriate arbiters of what constitutes sustainable practice for company concessions on forestry reform. The strategy also plays on the power of the consumer to alter corporate practice and upholds the market as the appropriate mechanism by which to pursue change.

Critical governance

In contrast, alongside the proliferation of NGO initiatives aimed at engaging with corporations in order to strengthen their environmental programmes or encourage their more efficient and responsible use of natural resources, there has also developed, simultaneously, another and altogether different range of strategies. What sets them apart from more liberal strategies is the goals they adopt, and the forms they take.

The growth in consumer boycotts, of campaigns specifically targeted *against* TNCs and the proliferation of groups whose principal aim is to document and expose corporate malpractice, such as 'CorporateWatch' and 'OilWatch', provides evidence of a counter-corporate culture. The struggle is more ideological, there is less scope for compromise and dialogue is reduced. Hence whereas groups engaged in liberal strategies such as the EDF seek dialogue with companies such as McDonald's and are willing to trade their expertise, or perceived reserves of legitimacy, in order to get an improved outcome, those engaged in 'critical governance' tend not to compromise and are less inclined to discuss ways in which environmental activists and company executives may be able to help one another. They are also less likely to offer 'rewards' for participation in private regulatory ventures through accreditation with a logo which denotes responsible practice, or help to promote joint projects or markets for companies which have signed up to codes of conduct or are attempting to reform their production process. Their aim is more to punish and expose what they consider to be irresponsible corporate conduct.

The consumer boycotts during the Brent Spar and Nigerian episodes make clear the no-compromise stance often employed in critical governance strategies. The aim was abandonment/withdrawal (respectively) and not dialogue about limiting the impact of operations. Similarly, groups pursuing these strategies are more willing to confront the company about its activities and make damaging public claims about them. The issue is not worked out in closed-door meetings between business and NGOs, but in the public arena (through the media or at garage forecourts) aimed at exposing and punishing environmental (and other) abuses. The 'McLibel' case (below) provides perhaps the most extreme form of critical governance. The aim of the London Greenpeace group which fought the campaign against McDonald's, was not a commitment on behalf of the company to reduce its waste (although they would support such reforms), but to resist the very existence of multinationals. Their campaign constitutes a refutation of the practices and goals of transnational corporate activity grounded in an eco-anarchist critique of contemporary capitalism. In this instance, therefore, the term resistance rather than governance may be more apt. Nevertheless, in as far as the company responds to the criticisms, reforms its behaviour in the light of the confrontation or adopts new working practices, a form of (informal) regulation has taken place, albeit not through open channels of discussion. The examples below help to illustrate the forms that this type of governance takes.

COUNTER-INFORMATION

Advertising of consumer products is clearly a key component of the ability of TNCs to project themselves globally. To build a transnational base of loyal customers who associate a company's product with quality requires good public relations. Acknowledgement of the importance of this aspect of corporate power has led some environmental NGOs to engage in what I have loosely termed counter-information, or perhaps more appropriately propaganda wars. This strategy centres on attacking a company on the basis of the claims it makes about itself and encouraging customers to sever their loyalties with the company through boycotts. Such campaigns are intended to expose perceived corporate misconduct, force the company to defend its reputation in public, and dent its political and economic power.

The most recent and prominent example of such a campaign was the 'McLibel' case between the McDonald's corporation and London Greenpeace. The case against McDonald's, orchestrated initially by London Greenpeace and delivered through the distribution of leaflets within the UK under the title 'What's wrong with McDonald's?', was that the McDonald's corporation was exploiting its workforce, cruelly treating animals and engaging in practices destructive of the environment (including excessive packaging, litter and the clearing of tropical forests for use as ranchland). The leaflet led to the McLibel two, pinpointed for their involvement in the authorship of the leaflet alleged to be libellous by the corporation, being taken to court to face the longest libel trial in British legal history. The different assets that the two parties brought to the conflict is revealing of the new politics. McDonald's had enormous financial muscle, good political contacts and access to the best libel lawyer in the country. The McLibel two on the other hand relied on their portrayal as victims of corporate suppression of their right to express their opinions, successfully manipulating 'David and Goliath' parallels.

Now the trial is over and the corporation feels it has cleared its name. This is in spite of the fact that the judge found in favour of the claims that the company was investing in practices considered to be cruel to animals, targeted children with misleading claims about the nutritional content of its foods through its advertising and was to some degree exploiting its workforce. The campaign continues through the distribution of materials aimed at exposing the alleged malpractices of the company, and the McLibel two are contesting the verdict in order to attract further public scrutiny to the company's activities. The attempt by the company to silence its critics appears to have provoked a strong backlash against what many consider to be suppression of dissent and an act of corporate bullying. The McLibel case suggests the importance to TNCs of their reputation, to the extent that they are prepared to take legal action against their critics. The publication of the leaflet served to engage McDonald's in a critical dialogue in which it was forced to respond to critics and defend its reputation. The McLibel case was, however, as much about *resisting* the culture of globalization which the activists felt McDonald's to be propagating, as it was about controlling the environmental impact of the company. It was an attack on the increasing 'McDonaldization of society' (Ritzer, 1993).[10]

TNC MONITORS

Another trend within the environmental movement has been the growth in organizations solely devoted towards the surveillance of the activities of TNCs. These organizations are at the front line of action against TNCs by exposing their implication in acts of environmental degradation and disseminating this knowledge to the broader community of activists, who then employ the sorts of strategies described above to effect change in the company's behaviour. Examples of groups that fit into this category are 'CorporateWatch' in the UK, 'Multinationals Resource Center' in the USA, 'The Transnational Information Exchange' in the Netherlands and the 'People's Action Network to Monitor Japanese Transnationals' in Japan. There are also sector specific monitors such as 'OilWatch' which has offices in a number of developing countries in which oil companies operate. Based on the premise that what companies say about their own activities is not to be trusted and that government surveillance of their operations is limited, TNC monitors seek to deter companies from violating their legal and perceived social obligations by threatening exposure and the activation of campaigns by other NGOs against them. Such criticism and exposure helps to pave the way for confrontational campaigning including demonstrations and company boycotts.

SHAREHOLDER ACTIVISM

In recent years, particularly in the USA and UK, there has been a growth in what has been referred to as 'shareholder activism' whereby environmental and other groups buy a small number of shares in a company and encourage their supporters to do the same as a way of obtaining access to the annual general meeting and to a fora therefore in which they can influence company decision-making. Oil and road-building companies have been the principal targets of this strategy for environmentalists. The sponsorship of resolutions at company meetings is aimed at overturning management decisions or at the adoption of a social responsibility measure (Vogel, 1978). They play on the 'hassle factor', forcing corporations to devote a disproportionate share of their resources to defend a small part of their global operations where the alleged offence is taking place (Rodman, 1997, 1998).

Shell transport and trading, the UK arm of Shell International had an embarrassing confrontation with institutional shareholders in April–May 1997 over its environmental (and human rights) record in Nigeria. A group of shareholders holding just 1 per cent of the company called upon the company to improve accountability by establishing new procedures for dealing with environmental and human rights issues (Lewis, 1997). The resolution called for a named member of Shell's committee of managing directors to take charge of environmental and corporate responsibility policies and for an external audit of those policies. The resolution, supported by groups such as WWF and Amnesty, called on Shell to publish before the end of the year a report on its controversial activities in Nigeria. In May 1997 the company hired an environmental expert in an attempt to pacify its critics. Before that in March, in an attempt to pre-empt the shareholder motion, Shell revamped its Statement of General Business Principles to include human rights and sustainable development and published its first report on worldwide health safety and environmental activities in an attempt to 'ward off further trouble' (Caulkin, 1997).

It is apparent then that the difference between liberal and critical governance amounts to more than a distinction between 'insider' and 'outsider' strategies. The same strategy can serve different purposes for different groups. There are also areas of overlap between the strategies and they are often used to complement one another. Ethical consumerism is the positive reforming side of the more punitive consumer boycott for instance. The same group can also simultaneously pursue liberal and critical strategies, so that while Greenpeace is encouraging consumers to boycott Shell petrol, it is also working with companies to develop ozone-friendly refrigerators. Critical and liberal strategies can even be used by the same group at the same time with the same company. Greenpeace has mounted a hostile public relations campaign against the food company Monsanto on the basis of its promotion of genetically modified organisms, but has been in dialogue with the company about developing a PVC-free credit card for its supporters (Fabig and Boele, 1999). Clearly then it is particular campaigns or strategies that are liberal or critical and not the groups themselves who often seem to transcend such categories.

LIMITS OF THE NON-STATE GOVERNANCE

There can be little doubt that pressures on TNCs to subscribe to principles or sign up to codes of conduct for instance, do have the effect of creating checks and balances in a system in which the pressure of competition may encourage their removal. They have the effect of encouraging TNCs as private actors to justify their actions to broader public constituencies of shareholders, consumers and civil society at large. Such practices introduce, therefore, new dialogues and forms of authority. The pursuit of profit alone increasingly requires justification. In this sense, the politics that the groups practice contribute towards a new code of ethics and a (limited) framework of norms about how companies should view their impact upon the environment. In as far as governance describes the way in which social activity is rule-bound and socially regulated, then the interactions between NGOs and TNCs of which these 'new' strategies of engagement are a manifestation, can be couched in the language of governance.

However, as the environmental movement evolves and engages with TNCs in these multifaceted ways, it will face a number of challenges which it will have to address and which will, in many ways, determine whether it can legitimately develop these 'public' functions in the absence of state regulation of TNCs. It is important to emphasize, therefore, the limits of this 'strategic turn' as being indicative of a longer term and tenable reconfiguration of the goals and practices of the movement. The extent to which these strategies will play a central part in future campaigning efforts will be a feature of the ability of the movement's ability to address a spectrum of concerns around their own accountability to, and representativeness of, society.

It is arguable that to be legitimate in terms of acting in some notion of the public interest, NGOs will have to act upon directly and respond to the concerns of a broad base within society, and yet there are few mechanisms for channelling supporters concerns into the work of pressure groups. Even 'mass' membership organizations only represent a fragment of the broader population who may not share their concerns with the activities of TNCs and may perceive themselves to be benefiting from their activities, even where they impose environmental costs. There is a danger here not only of paternalism in terms of an assumed understanding of what is in the public interest, but also of an élitism where the agenda of international politics is driven by the concerns of a small, often white middleclass western section of society. Some 'governance' strategies depend upon largescale popular support in order to make an impact. Boycotts in particular, if they are to be successful, have to be undertaken by a significant number of people in different markets if TNCs are to take them seriously. Private collaborations between NGOs and companies are not open to wider participation and scrutiny however, and may fuel concerns about who the NGOs are claiming to represent in these relationships.

It is also doubtful that the targets for NGO campaigns will necessarily be those companies which inflict most damage upon the environment. NGOs' ability to act in defence of 'the' public interest can be offset by their own internal organizational imperatives. There is some suggestion for instance that some of the pressure upon Greenpeace to target Shell over the Brent Spar oil rig disposal derived from membership pressure to re-establish its credentials as a direct-action organization against a background of scepticism about increasing professionalism (Dickson and McCulloch, 1996). Actions in future may need to be more transparent if they are to avoid charges of being guided exclusively by media opportunities and popular panic.

At the moment, these strategies tend also to be *ad hoc* and limited in geographical scope, as well as focused on particular TNCs. Boycotts have to be adopted in these markets of greatest importance to the TNC. Fortunately for the environmental movement, many of these TNCs that have been the target of consumer action have been dependent for their profit margins on success in western markets, where the environmental concern is strongest. The case of the campaigns against Shell in Nigeria and McDonald's in Brazil suggest that operations set up in less developed countries often still ultimately depend on western markets for purchase of the final product. Often, however, there are fewer checks and balances in place to restrain perceived 'deviant behaviour' in non-western societies, and if the pressures for reform originate from outside the host country, from western NGOs, they may be regarded as interference. It can be expected, however, that as TNCs invest further in the 'south', similar mechanisms of restraint will crop up which go beyond existing patterns of resistance. Programmes such as the 'NGO–Business partnership' run by the Asia Foundation, for example, provide incentive grants to NGOs working with the urban industrial business sector to develop initiatives that demonstrate environmentally responsible behaviour.

It is also clear that many TNCs, and often those whose activities have the largest environmental impact, are relatively insulated from NGO campaigns as an effective form of regulation, further suggesting the limits of these strategies. The conflict over Shell's operation in Nigeria demonstrated the failure of activists to exact a price high enough to elicit compliance with their demands (Rodman, 1997: 36). The companies access to technology, expertise and distribution networks cannot easily be replicated by firms from other regions, encouraging the host nation to provide extra inducements to encourage the company to stay. Campaigns likely to be most successful are those targeted against particular projects which are of negligible value to the overall operations of the company, so that fear of loss of profits and damage to reputation in other (more important) markets may be enough to make the targeted operation a liability. Only those TNCs vulnerable to NGO pressure and where consumer preference really matters are being affected by these strategies. In this sense the scope of the surveillance is restricted to 'easy' targets.

At the moment then, rather than constituting a consistent tier of governance, a blanket standard that if TNCs violate or transgress they can expect to be penalized, the pockets of restraint are just that, a patchwork of often unorchestrated activities and campaigns aimed at regulating and resisting the environmental impact of TNCs. It is perhaps unreasonable, or even undesirable, for them to be more than this, but this fact does curtail the impact of these strategies as a result. Moreover, unless NGOs working with and against companies are able to address some of the issues raised above about transparency, accountability and representation, it is difficult to envisage a model of corporate environmental governance which goes beyond this current ad hoc structure.

CONCLUSIONS

States will continue to be targets of NGO lobbying as participants in environmental regimes, as enforcers of environmental agreements, as regulators of industry and as important investors themselves in the process of environmental degradation. In this regard, as Wapner notes, 'The governing capability of global civil society complements but does not replace that of the state system' (1997: 67). However, the analogy drawn between NGO strategies and the tools of statecraft makes sense only in as much as boycotts are a form of economic sanction, in so far as codes of conduct are a form of legal regulation and to the extent that the formation of stewardship councils count as a form of regime which NGOs sign up to and help to police. While connections with state power have been made in this chapter, what is notable is that NGOs exercise a different form of power 'over' corporations. Theirs is a less coercive power aimed at changing consciousness and creating mechanisms of accountability. They employ norms, moral codes and knowledge rather than law and forced compliance, tools which the state has at its disposal. These are forms of control which the state does not exercise a monopoly over – non-formal channels of political engagement (Wapner, 1995).

Often it is the case that pressures directed towards the state are regarded as ineffective or limited. Indeed, it was suggested at the start of the chapter that many of these mechanisms or encounters result from frustration with the formal political process and the incapacity or unwillingness of the state to act in defence of the environment. These activities supplement the inherent weakness of state responses to environmental problems in important ways.

What these strategies suggest therefore is the development of a thickening web of 'moves' in a Polanyian sense which seek to re-embed the market within a framework of social norms and expectations about the responsibilities corporations have in relation to the environment.[11] Their emergence, it has been suggested, derives from a concern about the unregulated nature of corporate activity in a globalized economy. It denotes a shift in the environmental movement away from such an exclusive focus upon exposing the weakness of government regulations and lobbying states to redress the deficit, and towards a proactive attempt to create mechanisms to check and restrain corporate power in various ways. As well as highlighting, as others have done, pockets of resistance to globalization (Gills, 1997), these relationships illustrate the impact of economic change upon the goals and practices of social movements which react to perceived power shifts in the global economy.

9

SHELL, A SURE TARGET FOR GLOBAL ENVIRONMENTAL CAMPAIGNING?

Steve Yearley and John Forrester

The environmental movement celebrates its global character. From the first 'Earth Day' to the 'Gaia hypothesis',[1] to the names which many environmental groups choose for themselves (Earth First! or Friends of the Earth) there is a strong emphasis on equating the earth or the globe with the environmentalist project. Invoking the globe is inclusive; it embraces everyone, as well as all creatures, habitats and even the inorganic world.

In part, this global identity can be attributed to the notion that the environmental problems that the movement aims to combat are themselves global. Though they supposedly have 'global-ness' in common, environmental problems may be global in several different ways. In some cases this appellation appears justified because the problems themselves seem inherently global; global climate change is perhaps the most obvious case, though pollution of the oceans and the hazards of certain kinds of nuclear contamination would seem to qualify also. In other cases an environmental phenomenon is made global by its worldwide repetition; contaminated land might be an example here or pollution from sewage or the majority of toxic pollution from motor vehicles. In each case, the impact is local or regional, but international duplication makes the problem globally inescapable. Finally, some issues are rendered global by conceptual means; the transformation of concern for individual species (the panda or tiger and so on) into the worldwide loss of biodiversity is such a case.

However, this confidence that environmental problems are truly global and the associated assumption that environmental groups operate in the globe's interest can themselves lead to difficulties. First, these factors can readily encourage environmental groups to be utopian in their assertions about global unity. If one can claim to act on behalf of the world as a whole, one might expect there to be no dissenters from the position adopted. As Yearley (1995: 215) explains:

It has clearly been in the interest of environmental philosophers and activists to claim that they are working for a global mission and that they represent the interests of the whole of humanity, perhaps the whole of the biosphere. But some of these claims are open to question. Even apparently global physical problems, such as the depletion of the ozone layer, are more severe in some areas (the poles) than in others. Claims about humankind's universal interest in solving environmental problems cannot necessarily be taken at face value.

Second, the world's most powerful and well-resourced environmental groups, and the ones most successful in mobilizing global imagery, are based in the 'North'. It has been suggested that they may accordingly contribute to the presentation of the North's view of environmental problems as the 'global' or as 'everyone's' position (see Bramble and Porter, 1992: 350–1; Yearley, 1996: 134–40). Indeed, the very assumption that we are 'all in one boat' might be contested by spokespersons for the South, who may deny that they share the same craft or, at least, argue that they are unwilling travellers on a Northern-crewed voyage (see Sachs, 1994).

At the same time as these doubts about the genuinely global character of the environmentalist project beset the greens' embrace of global imagery and planetary rhetoric, there is an additional worrying possibility. In specific cases it appears that the very processes of cultural globalization can be identified as the source of major environmental threats and harms. In particular, the WTO has been identified as a problem by environmentalists because of its propensity for ruling in favour of free trade and against the protection of markets or products on environmental grounds. The WTO favours liberalization and has been inclined to view defences of trading policies in terms of environmental or humanitarian objectives as an excuse for protectionism. This worry is compounded by even more recent steps to harmonize internationally the rules for dealing with companies making transnational investments; TNCs are increasingly pressing to be able to take legal action against governments which appear to block their commercial 'rights', even on environmental or ethical grounds. In all, these steps are seen as evidence of global trends inimical to environmental protection.

From the point of view of Northern environmentalists and environmental movement organizations therefore, globalization is double-edged. In devising a campaign and political strategy in a globalized context, they are faced with a number of tactical options. The majority of campaigns and social movement/ NGO actions in the environmental arena are focused on particular problems such as biodiversity loss or the climate negotiations. But an alternative trajectory for global activism demands that one identifies a global enemy. Although in some cases environmental problems arise from the acts of consumers or (as with the WTO) from the actions of policy-setting agencies, more often companies are the authors of environmental harms. It is accordingly tempting for movement organizations and activists to take global companies as the focus for campaigns and movement activities.

In the run-up to the Kyoto climate change negotiations in December 1997 a renewed emphasis was placed on the conduct of the world's leading oil companies. As Rowell (1997: 99) notes:

> Technological advances and the maturity of existing oil fields have spurred oil companies to explore for oil and extract it from previously inaccessible or 'frontier' areas, both offshore and onshore. In many cases, such prospecting and production will have severe environmental impacts and serious social, ethical and cultural consequences. The challenge [for environmentalists, indeed for society] is not just to halt such exploration and extraction, but to halt oil consumption itself.

On this analysis, oil companies cause and encourage pollution locally and internationally; they favour the short-term use of irreplaceable natural resources; they demand transport infrastructures which frequently lead to major spills and ensuing despoliation of the marine environment, and their global pursuit of new reserves leads them into conflict with the interests of indigenous peoples and the guardians of relatively untouched habitats. They are both global and major 'enemies' of the earth. Accordingly, in this chapter our objectives are to record the development of environmental protest against one particular oil company (Shell) as an indicative example of this process, and to reflect on the sociological implications for the movement of strategies which focus around particular, global (oil) companies.

SHELL AS A TARGET FOR INTERNATIONAL ENVIRONMENTAL CAMPAIGNING

Probably only Rio Tinto Zinc (RTZ) and, much more recently Monsanto, compete with Shell as international icons of far-reaching environmental harms and as a focus for environmental protest. RTZ secured its position by the despoliation associated with its workings and by virtue of the repetitive environmental problems with which it was linked. Monsanto is regarded as the leading industrial proponent of agricultural biotechnology, particularly on account of its genetically engineered soya, cotton and rape seed. However, it is also notorious among environmentalists owing to its association with the generation of dioxins (particularly as contaminants in herbicide products) and the manufacture of polychlorinated biphenyls (persistent and toxic fluids chiefly used in insulating electrical components). In late 1998 the campaigning British journal *The Ecologist* devoted almost an entire issue to critical articles on the company (1998). However, Shell appears to have overtaken RTZ both for the variety and thus 'depth' of the problems with which it is linked and because of the topicality of the problems with which its name is associated in the public consciousness. Moreover, it is more widely known and accessible than Monsanto and has, to date, been involved in a broader range of controversial policy arenas.

Though the catalogue of contentious issues is well known, it is worth recapping on them all briefly as a preliminary to subsequent discussion:

- Shell is associated with prospecting for oil in the seas off East Timor. TAPOL, an Indonesian human rights campaign, held a protest meeting outside the official Shell Birthday Party on the company's centenary on 18 October 1997 (*The Ecologist Campaigns & News*, 27 (6) 1997, C1).[2] Oil company interests in southeast Asia persist.
- In 1997 it was announced that Shell planned to start drilling for gas in an area of rainforest set aside by the Peruvian government as a homeland for nomadic Indian peoples. The project is forecast to last for some 40 years. Of the ten trial drills reported to date, two have been in areas reserved for peoples with virtually no exposure to outside populations; early contacts with incomers are reported to have caused epidemics of whooping cough and serious influenza (Rowell 1997, 105). Though Shell maintains that it will use helicopters and waterways for transport, thus avoiding the construction of roads which themselves can provide the means for further deforestation, Rowell asserts that: 'if Shell finds gas, however, a pipeline will have to be built which will entail building a road and which will in turn open up the forest for loggers and other colonisers' (1997: 105).
- Shell was, until 1998, a General Member of the Global Climate Coalition (GCC). Though 'general membership' is a second-class form of membership which limited the company's role in policy formation (*Corporate Watch*, 4 June 1997: 13), the GCC's *raison d'être* is to lobby for the limitation of measures taken to lessen CO_2 emissions and to combat climate change. The GCC was said to be influential in encouraging Clinton to take a reluctant attitude towards far-reaching greenhouse gas emission targets at the Kyoto meeting. During 1997 Friends of the Earth organized a letter-writing campaign to the head of Shell UK and had a 12-foot shell 'demon' (with a demonic face and horns on the Shell 'shell') stalk petrol station forecourts.
- Shell also belongs to the World Business Council on Sustainable Development (WBCSD), an extension of the Business Council on Sustainable Development, which was inaugurated in the run-up to the 1992 Rio Summit (Finger and Kilcoyne, 1997: 141). The original BCSD had some 50 members and promoted a form of ecological modernization. Its first major publication, *Changing course* (Schmidheiny, 1992), offered a 'global business perspective on development and the environment', and included a list of case studies of good practice and business contributions to sustainable development. The Shell case study dealt with training and personnel development in its (now-notorious) Nigerian operation (see below). WBCSD now responds to the UNCED agenda through the promotion of its 'overall conceptual framework, namely that the market offers the best solution for global environment and development problems, and that regulations are inefficient because they distort free trade' (Finger and Kilcoyne, 1997: 141).

- Shell has become part of environmental campaigning folklore through the Brent Spar incident. The company had a 14,500 tonne oil-storage platform in the North Sea which had reached the end of its useful life and accordingly needed to be disposed of. Despite their initial undertakings to bring the installation back on to land for dismantling, Shell came to the opinion that the Best Practicable Environmental Option (BPEO), a formal estimation of the best realistic course of action, was to strip the Spar as far as possible of contaminants and then to sink it in the Atlantic off the coast of Scotland. In 1995 Greenpeace spearheaded a well-focused campaign against this decision, involving an occupation of the platform itself, the provision of video footage of the mid-ocean struggles over the Spar, and a European boycott of Shell goods. Since consumers show little brand loyalty to particular varieties of petrol, the consumer boycott was very successful, particularly in northern Europe where sales (notably in Germany) reportedly fell by some 50 per cent. Greenpeace Germany provided the largest amount towards the costs of the campaign and German consumers were the most vociferous objectors: two service stations were firebombed while a further station was 'raked with bullets' (Thomas and Cook, 1998: 7). Under pressure from Shell executives in northern continental Europe, the British wing of the company revoked its policy. Greenpeace celebrated its victory while the platform was towed to Norway for storage in a fjord. Only in 1998 were the revised plans for the Spar announced after a very widespread public consultation exercise: the platform is to be cut into sections and these sections used for a quay extension near Stavanger in Norway.
- Possibly the most notorious case concerns Shell's involvement in Nigeria, specifically in Rivers State on the Niger delta. Shell is accused of running its operations in an unusually ruthless manner, sharing few benefits of its economic success with local people, allowing repeated pollution incidents to contaminate river and coastal waters, treating the needs of local people with disdain in matters of siting its pipelines and other plant, and of flaring off gas in a way which is wasteful but also dangerous and polluting. In an area which is home to many local peoples, Shell has faced a series of protests during its decades of involvement with the Niger delta. The most vociferous, associated with the Ogoni, led Shell to withdraw from much of its Ogoniland site in 1993. The antagonism was further heightened by the stance the company took over the imprisonment and eventual execution (in 1995) of a leader of MOSOP (the Movement for the Survival of the Ogoni People), Ken Saro-Wiwa. Many commentators believe that Shell could have exerted sufficient pressure on the government of Nigeria to have Saro-Wiwa's life spared. But during his final days, Shell took the line that it could – not as a mere foreign business – interfere in the country's internal legal and political processes. It is further pointed out by the company's critics that the viability of Shell's operations came to depend on protection from the state paramilitary forces and that Shell appears to have armed certain of these forces, thus providing a means for implicating the company in the killing of civilians.

Shell is believed to be planning to resume operations in Ogoniland though it is also part of a partnership (with a 40 per cent holding) with plans to develop oilfields in southern Chad. In order to export the oil a pipeline will be needed, and this will run through Cameroon to the coast (Rowell, 1997: 105). According to the Rainforest Action Network's 'Action Alert 135' of February 1998:

> The World Bank plans to fund an oil pipeline through Central African rainforests that will bring huge profits to Shell, Exxon, and Elf while causing environmental havoc and threatening local populations – all with US taxpayers backing the deal. The oil companies are about to build a 600-mile pipeline from the Doba oil fields in Chad to coastal Cameroon, slashing through fragile rainforest that is home to the Baaka and Bakola peoples, communities of traditional hunters and gatherers. 'Once construction begins, we'll see an uncontrollable influx of people in search of work the result will be deforestation, wildlife poaching, and the loss of community land,' says Environmental Defence Fund economist Korinna Horta.

The Rainforest Action Network goes on to claim that:

> Observers fear that the project will create another Ogoniland, the Nigerian region devastated by decades of oil extraction and brutal military rule. Shell has worked with Nigeria's dictatorship to crush non-violent environmental organising among the Ogoni, who have watched more than 2,000 of their people killed during the last five years. Even as the plight of the Ogoni has come to public attention, the World Bank seems to have learned little from the oil conflict as it pursues funding the Chad–Cameroon pipeline in the neighboring countries. In Chad, the pipeline will likely escalate current conflicts as it traverses Doba, an area where the government is locked in a long-standing ethnic and regional struggle. In Cameroon, laying the underground pipeline will require moving into rainforest areas that are home to farmer and hunter-gatherer peoples, creating a climate for environmental [resistance].

Overall, therefore, Shell through its status as a global petroleum company would appear to qualify as a target for comprehensive environmental campaigning and as a rallying point for globalized pressure. In certain circles the company has become a watchword for a model of unscrupulous and environmentally harmful business. Thus, John Vidal gleefully reported in *The Guardian* (14 March 1998: 15) that the Centre for Philosophical Studies at King's College London was having trouble attracting the most prestigious academics to its conferences because of its links with Shell (Shell funds the centre to the tune of £60,000 annually). In the remainder of this chapter our task is to examine the practicalities of social movement activities which have adopted Shell as a transnational target for globalized environmental campaigning.

MAKING A TARGET OUT OF SHELL

This case study of anti-Shell protests has been based on campaign and associated literature from leading movement organizations, secondary sources and a limited number of group interviews with locally based campaigners in Britain and Ireland. Our analyses suggest to us that the globalization of campaigning through the selection of a global target is faced with two principal sorts of difficulty.

Issues of orchestration

Shell is such a focus for campaign activity precisely because it appears to be a transgressor on virtually all counts: it causes pollution in developing countries, fails to stand up for (or even offends against) human rights, injures the cause of indigenous peoples, opposes international environmental reform agreements and attempts to capture the international environmental agenda. But the very things which make Shell such a powerful stimulus to protest also offer practical impediments to successful campaign activity. Campaigning organizations have grown up with a sophisticated division of labour and with specialized expertise; in the UK those environmental organizations with the most sophisticated campaigning teams have advanced skills in particular fields but have, correspondingly, to limit their campaigning in fields where they are less qualified (Yearley, 1993). To be adequately documented, Shell's 'offences' require the expertise of various environmental groups as well as Amnesty International, the World Council of Churches, Survival, the Rainforest Action Network and campaigners on trade. Except on extraordinary occasions, this would require a disproportionate investment of campaigners' time. At present the sense of an integrated campaign in the UK is maintained through the activities of *The Ecologist*'s 'Campaigns Section' which operates by referring readers to the web site (or other information resource) of the appropriate NGO and through other similar *ad hoc* arrangements. In other words, precisely because of its diffuse organizational structure and the complexity of its political linkages Shell has no NGO 'mirror image'. There has yet to develop a concerted, global anti-Shell or anti-oil company campaign organization.

Furthermore, not even the techniques for opposing Shell can necessarily be carried over from one arena to the next; the largely successful tactics adopted by Greenpeace to address the company's attitude to the Brent Spar were specific to that protest. As was mentioned above, the oil platform was out of the public eye; that isolation and the resulting fact that the Greenpeace boarding party could monopolize accounts of the conditions on the Spar was a peculiarity of the case. The international dimension of plans for marine disposal, particularly when media discussions of the Brent Spar often implied that the proposed dumping site was within the North Sea (as opposed to the Atlantic, west of Scotland), also gave environmentalists and publics outside the UK a vested interest in the outcome. Accordingly, campaign lessons may not be portable. Social movement organizations (SMOs) compete and have to focus on specific targets. Most of these targets cannot be maintained indefinitely; in the end they have to move on. This point relates to our second observation, that the most conspicuous campaign achievements directed at Shell have come from specific, restricted campaigns. In that sense, it appears significant that the Brent Spar campaign was clearly very successful but was also conducted in a limited way. It was dedicated to overturning one particular decision of Shell's and thus could be treated (not least by Shell itself) as separate from the overall shape of company policy. Our supposition is that the kind of integration which an assault on a globalized company appears to offer does not sit easily with the proven campaigning strengths of SMOs.

These issues of orchestration also arise in relation to local activism. According to one informant in our study,[3] local movement activism was characterized to a large extent by individual participation:

> I would say EarthFirst! [was my first point of information] ... I think an interesting part of it was, how it was very much a lot of people, not groups, that came together.

This view was supported by another interviewee:

> I felt it was very much individuals, I mean you could identify people from different groups there, and presumably different groups networked. I mean the telephone network that I got part of at that particular time, I just literally rang everybody I knew who cared about justice.

Moreover, the groups cited as important to mobilizing participants were sometimes atypical or unexpected ones:

> *Interviewer* So it would be, for want of a better word, informal networks, it wouldn't be a recognized group.
> *Respondent* Well, the most recognized group that I can recognize was my choir, a socialist choir ... because that was one I could, you know, hit the button with quite fast, eh, and I knew people cared. That was probably sort of top of my list, after that it was just individuals, friends.

Given the informal nature of the protest, the question of co-ordination arises not only in relation to participation but also with regard to the activities selected:

> *Interviewer* So I suppose the next logical question would be did you feel that there was anyone co-ordinating action against Shell here [locally]? Was there anyone telling people what to do or was it simply an agreement: this is what we ought to do? With the Greenpeace action for example Greenpeace, Brent Spar, there was a very public face but there was also a lot of other things going on. Was there a sort of central co-ordination of action against Shell or was it simple groups of people who had this common interest and? –

Respondent 1 I would have said the latter and I was very happy about that in the sense that that there was no, em, bureaucracy about it.

Respondent 2 Right, I think also it provided scope for individuals to present something in some way, such as the action which involved the mannequins, you know that was – like, you could hand out leaflets but make your protest in your own way, you think, those things that would have an impact.

Respondent 1 I think those protests never had anybody's badge on.

Interviewer How?

Respondent 1 Until very late on when Survival kind of took it on because they had a particular tie-in, I mean that was not a take-over, I don't mean that.

Respondent 2 They could.

Respondent 1 They were plugging into something and they were using Survival's name and that was fine. But during the whole meat of the protest we never found people trying to badge it, that was good.

It appears that individual participation was highly valued. One of the respondents even talked about their communication to the public in individualized terms:

> most of the time it was direct appeal to passing traffic to hoot if they thought Shell should clean up its act in Nigeria. It was a very simple message.

Though this spontaneity is prized, without a co-ordinating body one runs the risk of the protest diminishing in an unplanned way:

> we had a very very big turnout from which we had a presence at the garage every Monday morning at 8:00 the entire winter, and I was there I think just about every Monday morning through the winter. ... numbers dwindled from that huge initial turnout obviously to three or four, but there was always a presence which more or less taken on by Survival, and on particularly significant dates there were various things like the cardboard cut-outs, the nooses, so that there were visual props and stunts at various times.

Additionally, there are limits on the kinds of activities which can be undertaken in a 'spontaneous' way. When asked about local activities, participants responded as follows:

> *Interviewer* We briefly ... mentioned what we did which was essentially a public, visible protest. In front of Shell filling stations, were those the only tactics you used, did you do anything else?
>
> *Respondent 1* And the public meeting!

Interviewer And the public meeting, sorry.
Respondent 2 And there was letter writing.
Interviewer And there was letter writing as well to –
Respondent 2 To the Nigerian government.
Interviewer To the Nigerian government.
Respondent 2 ... and to the English government.

The range of activities they were able to engage in without the support of bureaucratic SMOs was plainly limited.

In this section we have seen that, though Shell serves to coalesce and concentrate a great many environmental problems, the company does not necessarily offer itself as a ready or straightforward target for globalized opposition. Campaigners, at both local and national levels, face significant problems of co-ordination.

Theorization

Our second point is that generalized opposition to Shell (indeed to the oil industry) faces difficulties because opposition does not appear to be based in a consistent ideology or analytical understanding. For some campaigners, for instance, Shell's involvement in Nigeria and the plight of the Ogoni now appear to stand as a self-explanatory paradigm of environmental and socio-economic wrongdoing. The iconic status of this example seems almost to mean that the specifics of the case need no further examination or explanation. The rhetoric of the Ogoniland suffering has become an identifiable and easy shorthand for problems ensuing from TNCs' involvement. As noted above, the Rainforest Action Network identified people's 'fear that the project will create another Ogoniland' in southern Chad. Rowell (1997: 105) uses the same wording to comment on the Chadian case even though the colonial history, the ethnic characteristics of the divisions within local society, and a range of other geographical and technical factors may differ.

Earth First! (in its *Action Update*, No. 41, July/August 1997: 1) observed the need to tackle a more theoretically integrated target, and called for '100 days of action against fossil fuels'. The text goes on to explain that:

A coalition of anti-oil campaigners are calling on activists to strike at oil targets over the next 3 months in a concerted 100 days of action. The message is simple: we need an end to the dependency on fossil fuels. Activists involved with RTS, Delta, Corporate Watch, Platform, 90 per cent Crude, Greenpeace, Oilwatch and Cardigan Bay EF! and others will hold the oil industry accountable for their crimes. The hundred days will begin on August 23rd [1997] and end with the Kyoto Climate Summit, where world leaders may begin limiting CO_2 emissions but will fail to tackle the real cause of climate change our mad quest for oil. Up until now, anti-oil action in the UK has been either in disconnected bursts or focused on the effects of oil: Shell in Nigeria, the Brent Spar, exploration in Cardigan Bay, BP in the Atlantic Frontier, Mobil in Peru, Milford Haven, The Braer and Sea Empress Disasters, pollution, workers' rights, oil spills, petrochemical toxins. Now with the threat of rapid climate change we must end it before it ends us. The oil industry is large but cumbersome and has never before dealt with an all out assault on its right to exist!

Even here, the key charge against contemporary patterns of consumption trades on the identification of 'our mad quest for oil'; yet the meaning of this central phrase is left unexplicated. Without some analytical understanding of the source of our 'fixation' on oil it is very difficult to determine which course of campaigning action to adopt. Anti-Shell campaigners devote little public attention to addressing this problem, at least in part – one assumes – because it is easier to agree that oil companies are in the wrong than to secure agreement about what precisely is wrong with Shell or the industry as a whole. The pervasiveness of the oil companies and their products was discussed by one respondent:

> Well so maybe it boils down to plastic bags? Making people aware of the connection between what happened to Ken Saro-Wiwa and that plastic carrier bag you've just picked up in the supermarket. [At the] basic level, because even people who said OK I'll use my car less, I'll think about, I mean that [aspect] of culture has come into their consciousness, will still pick up six plastic bags at Waitrose, Sainsbury's – that hasn't, that was the message that we actually finished the public meeting, that it's as simple as that plastic bag.

This observation appears to acknowledge that the oil industry is only being challenged in its most obvious manifestations.

Associated with the problem of 'theorizing' the opposition comes the question of how to judge the success of one's ventures. When local activists were asked about this, they answered:

> We felt connected with people in other parts of the world, and it is my observation that we didn't ever try to blockade the [Shell petrol station] forecourt. People were free to drive in and they did. That wasn't, the purpose was not to blockade it was to raise awareness, and one of the great joys for me was that a coach of schoolchildren came by every week while we were demonstrating and they were all shouting away and they were looking for us, cheering, and I thought they've seen us week after week, they'll be asking questions about that's, that is a success in itself.

Responses of this sort are commonly tied to a defence of the value of action in terms of the worth of political action *per se*. In McKay's work on informal environmental protest, such a view is succinctly espoused by 'John' of the radical political theory magazine *Aufheben*:

[B]y adopting direct action as a form of politics, we ... look to ourselves as a source of change. ... Therefore the key to the political significance of the ... campaign lies less in the immediate aims of stopping the road [or whatever is the focus of the protest] and in the immediate costs we have incurred for capital and the state (although these are great achievements and great encouragement to others), and more in our *creation of a climate of autonomy, disobedience and resistance.* ... Thus, this life of permanent struggle is simultaneously a *negative* act (stopping the road etc.) and a *positive pointer* to the kind of social relation that could be (quoted in McKay, 1996: 127, his italics).

This communal and community action helps protesters feel empowered in the face of globality and its success cannot be gauged simply by whether the protesters' preferred outcome is followed or not. Further, the rationale behind 'corporate' protests such as that orchestrated by single issue groups like Greenpeace over Brent Spar is fundamentally different from the protest against the corporate, global lifestyle which is engendered by TNCs.

CONCLUDING NOTE

On the face of it, Shell offers an attractive, global target for campaign activity. It offends broadly and, given its global reach, it offends widely. One might suppose, therefore, that global campaigning might target a global quarry. Through its public commitment to environmental causes (for instance its 'Better Britain Campaign' and its recent WWF award for environmental reform in Canada) Shell is clearly 'asking' to be judged by lofty standards. But it appears to us that there are sociological reasons for scepticism about the ability of a global target to nucleate sustained global protest or campaigning. The target is too diverse, too unwieldy and demanding of too great a variety of experts to be readily amenable to this approach. Ironically, therefore, aside from their rhetorical value, global environmental 'sinners' may not be the unifying opportunity for global environmental action that one might have anticipated. The 'struggles' against global enemies may become iconic, but it is hard to press the advantage home.

10

THE ISLAMIC REVIVAL

ANTINOMIES OF ISLAMIC MOVEMENTS UNDER GLOBALIZATION

Paul M. Lubeck

ANTINOMY –

1. A contradiction in a law, or between two equally binding laws. 1592 DEE in Chetham Misa ...
2. A contradictory law, statutes, or principle; an authoritative contradiction. Obs. 1643 MILTON Divorce II. iii. (1847) 139/2 That his holiest people might as it were by his own antinomy, or counterstatute, live unreproved. 1649 JER. TAYLOR Gt. Exemp. Add. iv. 48 The signes which the Angel gave ... are direct antinomies to the lusts of the flesh. 1656–Deus Justif., An Antidote, and Antinomy of their great objection.
3. A contradiction between conclusions which seem equally logical, reasonable, or necessary; a paradox; intellectual contradictoriness. (After Kant.) 1802 H.C. ROBINSON Diary I. 144 The antinomies of pure reason. 1857 T.
WEBB Intell. Locke ix. 175 The imagination was distracted on every side by counter inconceivabilities, the Mind was divided against itself; Antinomy was its very law. 1877 CAIRD Philos. Kant II. svi. 566 Criticism must discover the nature and extent of the antinomies of reason, and must show that they are dogmatically insoluble; or that, whichever of the alternative solutions we adopt, we are led into absurdity and contradiction.

– The Oxford English Dictionary, 2nd edition

That we are on the cusp of entering the second millennium under a ruthless, unregulated, polarizing regime, one that simultaneously integrates the more advanced and marginalizes the weaker regions of the world, is surely now indisputable. Like it or not, globalization is the determinant material and social force of our time. To be sure, as a long-term historical process global integration originated in the fifteenth century. But globalization is never linear, for its impact is always mediated by specific, historically situated local institutions. Thus, globalization reflexively suggests *localization* of the global. Nor is globalization continuous: rather it is characterized by rapid spurts of growth, followed by tension, resistance and stagnation. In its current phase, dating from the early 1970s, globalization is characterized by the hyper-competitive integration of finance, production, trade, communications and culture across the boundaries of once hegemonic national states – themselves creations of earlier moments of Western European expansion.

Well, then, what's new? Contemporary globalization compresses time–space relationships creating what Castells calls 'the space of flows': that is, intense networked interaction among geographically dispersed groups, occurring in immediate 'real time'. Accordingly, everyday-life human interaction communicated over vast distances now becomes routinized, indeed even 'natural' for the minority of actors communicating within this new globally integrated sector (Castells, 1996). What's new, therefore, is the microelectronic revolution and the global networks – production, cultural and social – which drive the deepening and geographical reach of globalization processes.

Indeed, global economic integration and time–space compression across increasingly porous national boundaries exists only because of the rapid innovation cycle constantly generated by the electronic informational infrastructure. What is the new global electronic infrastructure? The electronic infrastructure is a multilayered web of firms, services and networks: that is, transnational computer networks, microelectronic-driven production linkages, 'on-line' financial systems, fast and cheap air travel, and satellite-based telecommunication systems like the multi-satellite Iridium system. This last system ranks as the apotheosis of 'spacelessness'. Systems like the Iridium link any geographical location on the globe with immediate, direct, satellite access to the global communications and information system. This is radical change by any standard.

Critics often conflate globalization processes driven by the microelectronic revolution with neo-liberal economic and social policies implemented by economic and political élites from dominant states and multilateral organizations (Hirst and Thompson, 1996). While neo-liberalism is the hegemonic policy in this conjuncture, the microelectronic revolution is the technological force that renders the neo-liberal version of globalization a feasible economic and social policy, albeit since the Asian financial crisis was increasingly questioned by less dogmatic and more realistic economists (i.e. Krugman, Rodrik and Sachs). True, neo-liberalism and the microelectronic revolution emerged on our consciousness simultaneously and are obviously interwoven especially in the global financial industry. Nonetheless, the two should not be conflated nor merged as critics often do. If, to stretch one's imagination, we were to abolish neo-liberal economic and social policies, global integration would continue, for the global is now institutionalized within the new electronic infrastructure which an increasing proportion of all actors now must utilize. Indeed, the global communications infrastructure is critical for democratic reform. For it must be mobilized in order to resolve global social, economic and environmental problems whose solutions lie outside the sovereignty of any single national state.

Daunting as the new global regime may be for social movement theorists and activists concerned with social justice, equality and environmental sustainability, critical social theorists must never forget that the material structures of globalization were, in fact, predicted by Marx, Weber and other Enlightenment-inspired social theorists. To be sure, the structural logic and tendency of global capitalist expansion – commodification, deregulation, rationalization, transnational integration and social polarization – is inherently world-historic, expansive and universal in impact. However disconcerting the cruel facts of globalization may be for those social movement theorists committed to the nation state as a foundational concept for social mobilization, global technical and economic integration now appears irreversible, barring some unforeseen catastrophe. Yet, while the structural and material consequences of globalization correspond to the predictions of Enlightenment social theorists, the social and cultural movements resisting globalization fail to fulfil the Enlightenment profile of increasing secularism, rationality and evolutionary progress.

What was not predicted by Enlightenment theory, of course, is the startling degree of weakness and fragmentation now so evident among secular, emancipatory social movements inspired by the Enlightenment, most of whom are valiantly trying to oppose the polarization, insecurity and misery wrought by the hyper-competitive logic of global neo-liberalism. To be sure, 'hard times' now reign for Enlightenment-inspired social movements in Western societies, where large segments of the population tolerate, vote for or even embrace enthusiastically the fruits of globalization. Looking elsewhere in the non-Western periphery – regions formerly providing inspiration (i.e. Third Worldism) for social movement activists elsewhere – does not offer much solace to 'progressive' social movement theorists.

Nowhere are standard Enlightenment expectations dashed more severely than in Muslim majority countries, or what Hodgson (1974) calls 'Islamdom': a diamond-shaped geographical agglomeration extending across Eurasia and Africa, forming what Ernest Gellner called the 'Qur'an belt'. Muslim majority states stretch from southern Russia to Tanzania on the north–south axis and from Morocco to Indonesia on the east–west axis. Viewed in global terms, Islam is the world's fastest growing religion, accounting for approximately a quarter of the world's population, and one concentrated in some of the world's poorest countries (i.e. Sudan, Bangladesh, Pakistan, India, Nigeria, Mali and Tanzania). And, fueled by global immigration, Islam is growing rapidly in European and North American cities.

Even more challenging to Enlightenment theory is the fact that the triumphal expansion of global forces appears to be *correlated* with the intensification of Islamic practice as well as the simultaneous migration of Muslim communities into new states and regions via the new global infrastructure. In turn, this gives rise to Islamic social movements of great diversity, complexity and contradictoriness. Spatially, these movements are concentrated in the exploding cities of Islamdom and their diaspora networks. Yet, neither theories inspired by liberalism nor Marxism, the contested children of the Enlightenment, predicted the correlation between globalization and the strength of the militant Islamic revival. More difficult for progressives anchored in the West to accept is the stark fact that at the global, national and local level, Islamic social movements have increasingly become the most militant expression of anti-imperialist nationalism. By becoming the voice and assuming the leadership of anti-imperialist nationalist movements – what Wallerstein (1983) calls 'anti-systemic' ethno-nationalist movements – Islamic movements have now largely displaced secular nationalist and leftist movements as the primary mobilizing force of resistance against real and imagined Western political, economic and cultural domination.

Accordingly, given this unexpected shift in social movement leadership at the global level, the central problematic of this chapter is to explain the paradoxical correlation between the intensification of globalization processes and the rising power – discursive, organizational and political – of Islamic social movements. This outcome, however, was not predetermined, nor entirely derived from the strategic and ideological orientation of secular movements. For, as Zubaida (1989) and Beinin and Stork (1997) emphasize repeatedly, the discursive and leadership shift in Muslim majority states was possible for two reasons: internally, the repression of democratic leftist forces by authoritarian regimes, and externally the lavish financial and political support given to Islamic movements by the USA and its client states (Saudi, Gulf States, Brunei) as a counterweight to advances made by the secular left. The case in point is Afghanistan, but elsewhere, too, Islamist groups were fostered by Israel, Egypt and Algeria before they became threats to the dominant powers. According to Richard Murphy, Assistant Secretary of State under two Reagan administrations: 'We did spawn a monster in Afghanistan' (Hiro, 1998: 20). Bin Ladan and the Taliban confirm the adage that the enemy of my enemy is *not* always my friend.

THE PARADOXICAL RELATIONSHIP BETWEEN GLOBALIZATION AND ISLAM

Viewed from the perspective of Western Enlightenment theory, the strength and practices of Islamic social and intellectual movements display rampant contradiction, absurdity and paradox, suggesting the term 'antinomy'. Confronting what Burke (1998) insightfully calls a 'discursive shift', i.e. from Enlightenment-inspired secular national to Islamic-inspired social movements, critical social movement theorists must deconstruct the paradoxical correlation between the Islamic revival and the deepening of globalization.

Thorny questions arise ubiquitously. Why, given the claim of post-Cold War-warrior spin-doctors like Fukayama that globalization is the embodiment of rationalism, efficiency, material abundance and liberal democratic values, are Islamic movements thriving under the extension and deepening of globalization? Alternatively, if these movements are merely backward, vestigial, reactionary movements inspired by seventh-century patriarchal values mostly attractive to marginalized and *lumpen* groups, then one responds with the question: why are Islamic movements so prominent in urban–industrial centres and not in the countryside? Furthermore, why have Islamic movements been able to recruit the best educated: the natural science graduates, the engineers, the urban professionals and even the women of many Muslim majority states? If Islamic movements are essentially and invariably authoritarian and anti-democratic, what explains their sustained popular support and why have they won elections in Turkey and Algeria, only to be kicked out of office by the military to the applause of Western democrats? Continuing our query, why is the Islamic presence so visible in the infrastructures of the new global system, that is, in the commercial networks, electronic communication systems and migrant communities within the global cities of Europe and North America? Haven't these Muslims read Fukuyama's *The end of history* (1992)? Don't they understand his *pronuncio* declaring that the only route to modernity is the neo-liberal democratic path under global capitalism? If we turn to Kant, who coined the term 'Enlightenment', the paradoxical correlation between globalization and Islamization that has produced 'global Islam' is nothing less than an *antinomy*: 'A contradiction between conclusions which seem equally logical, reasonable, or necessary; a paradox; intellectual contradictoriness'.

ANTINOMIES ON THE STREETS OF ISLAMDOM

Let us explore the antinomies and paradoxes of 'global Islam' by turning the ethnographic dial to the rapidly growing cities where Islam and globalization confront each other. The general term for these New Social Movements is 'Islamism', or integralism, or 'political Islam' (Beinin and Stork, 1997). On the streets, rebellious, unemployed urban youths are shouting a Hegelian-sounding teleology: 'Islam is the future.' Or 'Islam is the solution.' In Turkey, one of Islamdom's most industrialized states – and its first secular nationalist state – a young female medical student attempting to take a surgery exam was expelled for wearing a head scarf (*New York Times*, 17 March 1998: A4). Elsewhere in Islamdom, especially in comparatively industrialized Malaysia, younger middle- and working-class women are voluntarily covering themselves in opposition to the dictates of authoritarian, secular-minded regimes. Faced with gerontocratic, arbitrary rulers, political activists are calling for *shura* – the Islamic right to be consulted by rulers – and usually insisting on the opportunity to compete in democratic elections. Kramer's study (1993: 80) of Islamist notions of democracy does not support Western conceptions of Islamist political practice:

> The moderate pragmatic Islamists whom I consider to be the mainstream of the 1980s and early 90's have come to accept crucial elements of political

democracy: pluralism (within the framework of Islam), political participation, government accountability, the rule of law, and the protection of human rights.

Islamism represents the emergence of a new intelligentsia and leadership stratum in Muslim majority states. Note that Islamists are not recruited from the traditional, clerical status-honour group, the *ulama*, nor from Sufi brotherhoods (*tariqa*), two social groups who led earlier periods of Islamic renewal. Instead leaders and followers are recruited from graduates of modern national, or even Western, universities. Unlike the *ulama* who are accused of rote learning, imitation and stagnation, Islamist intellectuals embrace science and are constructing new political discourses and disseminating them on audiocassettes, videotapes, e-mail and web pages. (Cyber-Islam is a reality, see: *www.ou.edu/cybermuslim.*) Not only do they employ modern organizational tools and 'cell' structures borrowed from Western anti-systemic movements, but they also assert that they are pursuing an alternative route to modernity, one that self-consciously intends to 'Islamize modernity' (Ghamari-Tabrizi, 1998).

WHO THEN ARE THE 'ISLAMISTS'?

For those navigating these waters for the first time, it may clarify the paradox to describe empirically the social structural base from which the new Islamist social movements recruit their followers. The social base is generally middle class, often from provincial towns, and employed in, or seeking employment in, the service sector, not the manufacturing nor the entrepreneurial sectors. Beginning with Mitchell's study of the Egyptian Muslim Brothers in the 1950s, virtually all research confirms that most Islamists originate from the lower middle to mid-middle class fractions, with remarkable strength from the professional classes in large cities like Cairo (Mitchell, 1969). Indeed, paradoxically, when allowed to compete in open elections, Islamists tend to win the leadership posts in that bastion of modernist activism: urban professional associations (engineers, lawyers, doctors, teachers and university students) (Wickham, 1997).

Again, paradoxically, the Western-origin University is the bastion of Islamic activism. According to Roy (1994), secondary school and university students whose aspirations for security and social mobility are frustrated by economic stagnation, widespread corruption and bureaucratic incompetence, form a 'lumpen intelligentsia' poised for easy recruitment. Richards and Waterbury paint a grim picture of the Middle East and North Africa (MENA) region. MENA is second only to Africa in rates of population growth; the region's population is expected to double in 27 years; and Islam and fertility are positively correlated universally (Richards and Waterbury, 1996: 80–5). 'Most Middle Easterners are less than twenty years old' (p 89). 'Everywhere in the region the labor force is growing faster than the demand for labor' and in most cases exceeds 3 per cent a year (p 91). State educational budgets are biased toward tertiary and secondary education, geared to the state employment of males. In Egypt, for example, increases in secondary school enrolments average 14 per cent annually, tertiary enrolments roughly doubled between 1971–84, and universities consumed 38 per cent of the education budget in 1984–5, while nearly a quarter of the girls were not enrolled in primary school (pp 119). Nor is this phenomenon limited to the Islamic world. Muslims attending universities overseas, especially Malaysians, discover that militant Muslim organizations, like branches of the Muslim Brotherhood, dominate international Islamic student associations at Western universities. Hence, in practice, exposure to Western education often links Muslim students to the communication networks fuelling the global Islamic revival.

Consider Algiers, now a site of a brutal civil war. A survey found that 75 per cent of youth aged 16–29 were seeking work while, at the same time, 'the educational system produced 270,000 unemployed diploma holders. Some 80 per cent of this age group continued to live with their families, often eight persons to a room' (Eickelman and Piscatori, 1990: 116). Richards and Waterbury (1996) confirm the universality of this pattern elsewhere in the Middle East: high population growth, bloated secondary and university enrolments, stagnant state-managed economies and dismal employment opportunities for new entrants into the labour force. In general, the failed developmental policies articulated by repressive regimes in the region will generate an endless supply of new recruits from the middle classes for the Islamist programmes. To be sure, less privileged strata – the unemployed, migrants and fractions of the urban working classes and informal sector – are also recruited into Islamist organizations, especially in Algeria, Turkey and Iran, or gratefully accept valuable health, educational or welfare services. Nonetheless, the heart of the Islamist social base and its leadership arises from the service sector, that is, the middle strata structurally located in government, schools and markets.

To return to our antinomy theme, observe the challenge to Enlightenment assumptions when one tries to explain the paradoxical fact that a high proportion of Islamists were formerly militant members of Marxist organizations. For instance, a survey of *Hamas* activists in Gaza found that 60 per cent acknowledge prior membership in Marxist organizations (Eickelman, 1997: 34). This antinomy suggests great similarity to Latin American liberation theology, where the left and the popular church overlap significantly. According to Burgat (1997), from Cairo to Tunis the 'leftists' and Islamists have been for a few years now sending signals that effectively opened the door to approaches that are quite different from the open warfare that has existed up to recently. Thus, ' . . . part of the secular intelligentsia has already begun to reposition itself in a way that brings it much closer to the cultural preoccupations of the Islamist approach' (Burgat and Dowell, 1993: 83).

Grasping the profound significance of the discursive shift toward Islamic culture, leadership and organizations is crucial for understanding the paradox presented by globalization and the Islamic resurgence. This discursive shift enables Islamists to assume the mantle of what has proved to be the most powerful anti-systemic discourse in post-colonial, Muslim majority states:

populist, anti-imperialist nationalism. Among the politically active population, this discourse remains the most powerful lever for mobilizing oppositional social movements. Formerly, until the rise of the Islamists, the nationalist, anti-imperialist discourse had been the property of secular nationalists: Nasserites, Ba'athists, Marxists and other Western-inspired movements. As global restructuring intensified, especially after the collapse of the Soviet Union (1989) removed it as a model and threat to globalization, secular nationalist ruling groups lost what little shred of legitimacy these gerontocratic regimes once possessed. Indeed, Islamism surged once these regimes accepted global neo-liberalism's dictate to implement structural adjustment programmes (SAPs), thereby smashing living standards, increasing unemployment and privatizing national industries. Of course, SAPs are an ideological windfall for Islamists, like manna from heaven. For they confirmed the illegitimacy of the regimes implementing SAPs, while allowing Islamists to consolidate their control over the mantle of populist, anti-imperialist nationalism within civil society. Let us now turn to explanations for the correlation between the deepening of globalization, experienced most acutely as neo-liberalism, and the consolidation of Islamic social movements as Islamdom's most influential social movement.

CULTURAL EXPLANATIONS: WHY ISLAMISM THRIVES UNDER GLOBALIZATION

Antinomies and contradictions abound both within and among Muslim beliefs and movements as well as between globalization processes and Islamic movements. Space not permitting an elaboration, suffice to say that a wide spectrum of Islamic movements, not only Islamists, now compete for a following. Recalling that the problematic to explain is the rise of the Islamist movements under the structural condition of rapid globalization, let us turn to some theoretical tools to explain this contradictory movement.

Wallerstein's (1983) concept, 'reactive ethno-nationalism', is valuable for situating Muslims in a broader global context. By assuming that anti-imperialist social movements are a dialectical combination of new identities formed in reaction to world systemic forces, reactive ethno-nationalism explains how subject peoples simultaneously invent new identities, in order to contest the costs exacted by the accumulation processes of the capitalist world economy. Islamic identities, while subject to these processes, are more complex. In practice, Muslims are socially constructed, multiply situated subjects.

Historically, in the broadest sense, individuals could claim and benefit from a global identity as members of a universalistic community of observant believers – the *umma* – a trans-ethnic identity that neither privileges ethnicity or nation among Muslims. Over the long historical *duree*, the networks of the global *umma* are renewed annually by the pilgrimage to Mecca and, in the contemporary era, by the infrastructure of global capitalism. At the level of the territorial political unit, the emirate, sultanate or the nation state, Muslims have an identity defined by the polity that administers Islamic law, *Shari'a*. While the ideal is the abstract norms governing the universal *umma*, once symbolized by the Caliphate that ended in 1924, Muslims recognize that state-administered political institutions are necessary to enforce Islamic law. In practice, at the national and regional level vast differences of interpretation and proposed solutions prevail; largely because of sectarian differences and four legal schools among the majority Sunni there is an absence of a unified code of Islamic law. Remember that Islamdom does not possess a centralized authority like the Roman Catholic Curia to rationalize and enforce a consistent and universal code of (canon) law. And finally, Muslims may have a locally or family-derived identity based upon membership in a sect, a brotherhood affiliation, and local saints (*wali*) or particular local traditions.

Membership in a universalistic, global community of observant believers – the *umma* – is the broadest possible boundary of the Muslim national identity. Globalization, quite ironically, stimulates a militant reactive ethno-nationalist opposition to the hegemonic state responsible for the management of global structures (i.e. the USA). In a contradictory way, however, the new global infrastructure actually integrates the disparate members of the global *umma* by encouraging Muslims to communicate, study, trade and travel to fulfil the diverse Muslim obligations.

Turner (1994: 86), a theorist of global civil society and social citizenship, correctly perceives the relationship between globalization and Muslim self-conception of communication within the global *umma*:

> It is the availability in modern times of effective global communications systems which makes possible for the first time a globalization of Islam. . . . While Islam had always claimed universalistic status, it was, prior to the emergence of contemporary communications systems, actually unable to impose this type of uniformity and universalism. The paradox of modern systems of communication is that it makes Islam simultaneously exposed to Western consumerism and provides the mechanism for the distribution of a global Islamic message.

STRUCTURAL EXPLANATIONS OF GLOBAL ISLAM: THE POLITICAL PROCESS MODEL

Thus far we have reviewed the multiple situational identities available to Muslims and the tensions generated by their contradictory relationship to globalization processes. Having outlined the cultural basis of identity and social action, let us now turn to the central problematic of this chapter: explaining why Islamic social movements thrive under a regime of intense globalization. Although paradoxical from the Enlightenment perspective, this correlation must nevertheless be explained theoretically. Accordingly, after reviewing the analytic power of several explanatory models, it is readily apparent that the *political process model* pioneered by Doug McAdam offers a cogent framework to explain the relationship of globalization and Islam. Indeed, McAdam (1982) and Smith (1991), writing on the American civil rights movement and Latin American liberation theology movements respectively, make a convincing case for the explanatory power of the political process model (PPM) for all social movements. Distilling key factors from a complex explanatory theoretical schema is, of course, always difficult to accomplish in a short chapter. But six essential factors drawn from McAdam and Smith's use of the PPM suggest some key factors, analytical concepts and underlying processes that explain why Islamic movements thrive under globalization. Briefly, the PPM provides six sequential factors.

1. *Broad socio-economic changes*: These refer to large-scale structural economic, political and social changes that disrupt social continuity and generate social tension. In turn, these create social instability, disrupt existing power arrangements, create status inconsistencies and thus offer opportunities for new actors desiring to restructure existing power relations, that is, urbanization, industrialization, booms, busts, wars, state centralization and new political transformations. For Islamdom, the seminal changes are national independence and the petroleum boom of the seventies.

2. *Expanding political opportunity*: In turn, given the disruptions associated with socio-economic changes, new political opportunities emerge for an aggrieved group; this change is measured by, first, the increased awareness of and, second, assertion of claims by insurgent groups for real political power. Sooner or later insurgents mobilize themselves in order to seize rewards and advantages arising from the increase in social space for them to exercise leverage with lower risk of punishment.

3. *Strength of indigenous organizations*: To develop a successful, anti-institutional social movement, however, aggrieved groups must mobilize indigenous organizational resources by creative incentives of 'either a solidarity or material nature' (McAdam, 1982: 46). In the Islamic context, this refers to mobilizing the vast networks of mosques, schools, teachers and 'pious foundations' (*waqf*) to heighten communal solidarity, to provide welfare services and to support the Islamist political programme.

4. *Linkage of organizational resources to insurgency*: Long standing, strong indigenous organizations offer insurgent movements unparalleled resources: a membership base, a veneer of legitimate cover, communication networks, established leaders, incentives for solidarity and 'enterprise tools' such as telephones, staff, meeting places (mosques or schools) and the material means for publicizing their message. Islamic organizations and institutions possess vast, multilayered resources that are invaluable for insurgent movements.

5. *Cognitive liberation*: Mobilization must simultaneously construct an oppositional, insurgent consciousness, one that can be reinvented as a meaningful oppositional culture liberated from the constraints imposed by the ongoing institutionalized discourse. Once a new discourse is constructed, aggrieved groups are able to dismiss the authority of existing rulers and institutions, inculcate memberships with a new discourse, and reduce fatalistic reasoning in favour of asserting legitimate rights. Ideally, insurgents convince members

to believe that, if they act collectively, they can create, to some degree, highly desired outcomes. 'Insurgent consciousness is a collective state of understanding which recognises that social change is both imperative and viable' (Smith, 1991: 62).

6. *Social control response*: Once mobilized as a threat to the existing institutionalized order, the social movement's viability and ultimate success will be shaped by the capacity of the now threatened institutionalized groups (i.e. secular élites, the post-colonial state, the Western powers) to respond effectively either by concession or repression to the demands of the insurgents.

In the remainder of this essay, we shall apply these concepts to explain the rise of Islamic social movements in the late twentieth century, the era of rapid globalization. Historically, this period consists of three distinct phases. As we apply PPM theory to each phase, one must focus on how global structural change, state capacity and Islamist insurgency interact and shape one another. Above all, the following analysis focuses on the reasons why insurgent Islamists were able to mobilize their organizational and cultural resources, networks and alternative vision in spite of the triumph of neo-liberalism and global integration under US military and economic hegemony. The first phase begins with the collapse of the Ottoman Empire and the abolition of the Caliphate at Istanbul.

PHASE I: SECULAR NATIONALISM AND STATE-CENTRED DEVELOPMENT

The end of the First World War, the establishment of Atatürk's model of a secular state and his abolition of the Ottoman controlled Caliphate (1924) mark the commencement of a wave of secular nationalist movements in Muslim majority states. Although aspiring to achieve the 'modern' ideal of a secular national state, support for this project was largely limited to urban centres, the western-educated intelligentsia and other politically active groups. Above all else, the nationalist political project called for the construction of a modern, quasi-secular nationalist state. The euphoria of this phase promised an end to the humiliation of European colonialism, the implementation of a modern, secular-national, state-centred economic development programme, and assertion of an authentic modern nationalist identity. Furthermore, the nationalist discourse promised a bevy of distributional benefits associated with Enlightenment-sponsored modernity such as freedom, democracy, health, education and rising incomes. The Gulf States, Pakistan and, to some degree, Malaysia, are exceptions to the secular nationalist model.

In terms of economic change and the disruption of the existing social order, largely because under Fordism the international oil firms administered petroleum prices, state intervention into society and culture was the most disruptive feature of Phase I. Islamic education was displaced by modern secular education while the state institutionalized a security apparatus that intruded into family and household relations to a degree unprecedented in Islamic history. Oppositional Islamic groups were repressed with impunity as long as the secular modernist discourse was unchallenged by disruptive political events or major social dislocations. The defeat of 1967 and the loss of the Muslim shrines at Jerusalem, together with the crisis of state-centred import substitution industrialization (ISI), generated widespread disillusionment, thus setting the stage for the transition to the second phase. The OPEC-initiated petroleum boom served as the disruptive structural force for Islamic social movements.

PHASE II: THE DEFEAT OF 1967, CRISIS OF ISI AND THE PETROLEUM BOOM

The second phase emerged under the shadow of the Muslim defeat in the 1967 war – marked by the loss of Jerusalem and the Islamic shrines – and the generalized crisis of ISI. With the onset of the petroleum boom of 1973–4, Phase II was in full swing. One cannot overestimate the disruptive effect wrought by the petroleum boom: it distorted the economies of both oil producers and regional suppliers of labour and materials to oil-exporting states. Unlike Fordism, Phase II is marked by international economic instability, a crisis of global hegemonic leadership, rampant inflation and a surge in petro-dollar financed state industrial development projects, especially in oil exporting states. Initially, the price revolution was a windfall for the political élites in the Organization of Petroleum-Exporting Countries (OPEC). Recall that nine of the original fourteen OPEC states had Muslim majorities with the Saudis possessing a veto. Indeed, petroleum rents now funded Saudi and other Gulf states' support for their vision of the Islamic revival at the expense of the more populated and poorer secular states. Indeed, the nationalization of the oil industry and the price revolution shifted unprecedented economic power to the élites managing the state sector. Unfortunately, the petroleum boom not only increased the autonomy of state élites, it reinforced their propensity to favour large-scale, state-controlled, non-competitive, Fordist industrial projects and unrealistic macro-economic policies (i.e. exchange rates).

Rents granted state élites not merely control over the national economy, but also personal wealth through kickbacks, bribes and vast resources used to sustain a profligate rentier coalition around the petro-state. Hence, at a time when the east Asian newly industrializing countries were restructuring their economies and societies toward state-guided, but market-augmenting, export-oriented industrialization, thereby adjusting to increased internationalization and global competition, the euphoric élites of oil-exporting states were institutionalizing an inflexible, centralized statist model of industrial development – peripheral Fordism. Sadly, once the petroleum boom crashed in the mid-1980s the social dislocation was even greater for Muslim majority states dependent directly or indirectly on petroleum rents. These states had so far to fall because the rents were an unearned windfall like manna from heaven, rather than arising from a disciplined social structure of accumulation like east Asian export-oriented industrialization. In contrast to east Asia, states dependent on petroleum rents pursued classic peripheral Fordism: highly protected, centrally managed, state-owned enterprises such as refineries, steel mills, and deep import substitution industries like autos. Of course, none of these industries achieved competitiveness, typically requiring subsidies from the public purse after falling prices and global neo-liberalism reduced the relative autonomy of the rentier petro-state.

Given the swollen city as incubator of Islamism, the truly destructive urban bias of the petroleum boom deserves emphasis. Focusing on dislocation in the highly populous agrarian sector, Alan Richards (1987) reminds us that oil booms (i.e. the Dutch disease) raise urban incomes, stimulate construction booms, spike inflation rates and encourage rent-seeking behaviour. In turn, these changes encourage a decline in the terms of trade for rural producers, increase rural-to-urban migration, tighten rural labour markets and raise rural wages in order to compete with the booming urban wage rates. Food production must decline. Cities, meanwhile, absorb enormous numbers of unskilled, rural migrants attracted by higher wages; these workers then often labour on vast construction projects overseen by the rentier élites (who then profit from the kickbacks associated with construction contracts). Subsequently, food imports rise as a result of the change in tastes in favour of imported food (i.e. sugar, white rice and white bread). In response, a regime awash with petrodollars typically initiates capital-intensive, state-managed irrigation schemes and encourages its allies (the urban merchant–bureaucrats–military officer stratum) to invest in luxury food production such as poultry and meat. Aided by their connections to the state, they are allocated state-subsidized capital-intensive machinery, imported fertilizer at subsidized prices (the Green Revolution) and, in Nigeria, even privileged access to state-financed agricultural development projects managed by the World Bank.

Over time, the petro-boom produced a highly combustible social cocktail in Muslim majority states. Key factors included: widespread official corruption, organizational indiscipline, rent seeking, the expansion of higher education regardless of demand for graduates, and the intensification of state intervention into society. All of this eroded the legitimacy of secular states even before the crisis of the 1980s. Elsewhere, labour shortages in the Gulf States brought the migration of Arabic speakers and other Muslims into contact with the radical discourses of a highly politicized Islam while, at the same time, internationalizing the labour forces and economies of the non-oil producing countries. All of which generated instability and change, severely disrupted existing power arrangements and laid the foundation for the social forces exploding as the Iranian Revolution.

PHASE III: URBAN REVOLUTION, THE PETRO-BUST AND GLOBAL NEO-LIBERALISM

After the collapse of oil prices, that is from a high of $41/barrel in 1981 to less than $8/barrel in 1986, societies already disrupted by the petroleum boom entered the wrenching phase of the petro-bust. Multilateral institutions soon administered structural adjustment programmes (SAPs) a neo-liberal prescription that continues more or less until today. Before elaborating the changes associated with neo-liberal structural adjustment, the political effect of the Iranian Revolution must be put into perspective. The volcanic political event, of course, was the urban insurrection known as the Iranian Revolution (1978–82). Not only did the revolution exert a powerful 'demonstration effect' on other Islamic insurgents, it thoroughly transformed a Muslim's imagination regarding what was politically possible to construct from an innovative Islamic discourse as articulated by Khomeini. It was, in short, a hegemonic rupture for Islamism of global proportion. Here was an authentic Islamic revolutionary transformation, yet one of the few that ever survived the active belligerence of the global hegemon, the USA, who, together with Saudi and other patrimonially governed Gulf States, financed and supported Iraq's attack on the Islamic Republican government of Iran. Ironically, despite the ravages of the First Gulf War, Iran has survived and is liberalizing its institutions, while authoritarian, secular Iraq is isolated and in ruins.

Zubaida (1989: 40) captures superbly the electrifying effect of the Iranian Revolution on Muslim popular consciousness:

> Here was an Islamic Revolution which was populist and anti-imperialist, which had sported some of the vocabularies and slogans of the left. For some it seemed that, unlike the 'imported' ideologies of Marxism or nationalism, Islam in its political and progressive form is more accessible to the people, springing as it does from their historical cultural roots. Political Islam acquired many recruits, a political respectability and viability, it became firmly established in the mainstream.

Concurrent with the institutionalization of the Iranian Revolution, yet much more important for stoking the flames of Sunni Islamic movements, are the petro-dollar surpluses distributed by conservative, royalist Gulf States (Saudi Arabia, Kuwait, UAE). Patronage distributions from the Saudis throughout Islamdom shifted discursive power away from the urban modernist thinkers living in secular states and toward very conservative interpretations of Islam favoured by the Saudis, that is, the royalist, Wahabbi-Hanabali interpretations. Al-Azmeh (1993), for example, asserts that 'Petro-Islam ... has broken the secularist and nationalist cultural, mediatic and, to a lesser extent, the educational monopoly of the modern Arab state.' Again, once petroleum rents crashed and thereby reduced the secular states' leverage on Islamic actors, Saudi patronage became even more influential among Islamic groups for funding mosques, schools, universities, medical clinics and welfare services.

Turning to the implementation of neo-liberal structural adjustment in Muslim majority states, the decision of Federal Reserve Chief, Paul Volker, to restrain credit in order to rediscipline the world economy soon led to the Mexican default in 1982 and the onset of the Third World debt crisis. The

International Monetary Fund (IMF) and the World Bank aggressively advocated a transition from a regime of state-led ISI to privatized export-led development and integration into the world capitalist market. The economic conditions of the early 1980s allowed the IMF and the World Bank to promote this programme – the neo-liberal Washington consensus – even more forcefully by attaching conditions to the loans it offered to ease the debt crisis. The typical IMF/World Bank debt relief and SAP raised the cost of food and other basic consumer goods, cut government spending on social, health and educational services, diminished the role of the public sector, and promoted integration with the world capitalist market through export-oriented development.

By emasculating state capacities, structural adjustment provided a windfall of new political opportunities for Islamist movements as well as an infusion of insurgent consciousness, enabling Islamists to don the mantle of nationalist resistance to foreign domination without rival, thanks to the suppression of the secular left. The social disruption caused by structural adjustment cannot be overstated. As a result of structural adjustment, state capacity to co-opt oppositional movements declined and services were increasingly restricted to urban middle-class and élite areas. Income distributions polarized. Structural adjustment meant that states were unable to provide previously established levels of services or to insure adequate supplies of commodities to all sectors of their territory and population, undermining the terms of the social compact established during the Fordist phase of secular nationalist and populist authoritarian state-led development. The political and moral vacuum opened up great political opportunities that were seized by the Islamists, who established a social base by offering social services that the various states had failed to provide (Wickham, 1997). Insurgent Islamists reshaped the populist nationalist content of their insurrectionist discourse. Most importantly, they linked the corruption, authoritarianism, human rights abuses and moral degeneracy (associated with the importation of Western cultural commodities such as television serials) of the existing state élites to their inability to provide adequate social services and economic opportunities for new entrants into the labour force. Triumphant neo-liberal economic and social policies, to the chagrin of informed observers, became the midwife to Islamist ascent in civil society.

Popular resistance to SAPs has been common in a number of Muslim states with widely varying political ideologies, i.e. Morocco, Algeria, Egypt, Tunisia, Nigeria, Malaysia, Indonesia, Senegal, Pakistan and Jordan (Walton and Seddon, 1994). Neo-liberal restructuring of Muslim economies has enraged populist sentiment and rallied moderates to support the radical Islamic opposition to the deflationary policies forced upon secular élites by their global paymasters. From the Muslim perspective, by reducing state subsidies and curtailing state investment for employment, SAPs impoverish the most vulnerable in the Muslim community, i.e. the poor, aged and weak. The latter is perceived as an outrageous intrusion and challenge to Islamic principles of charity. Furthermore, not only do SAPs violate Muslim prohibitions against paying interest on debt, as well as the state's obligation to provide alms to the poor (*zakkat*), typically

understood as state subsidies for basic needs, the transparently foreign management of the SAPs rapidly evaporates any residual fig leaf of legitimacy retained
by secular political élites.

Imagine empathetically, for a moment, the anxiety of a treasury official from a
Muslim majority state who has just signed off on an IMF debt-restructuring
agreement at IMF headquarters in Washington. Upon returning he must justify
administering a programme that militant Muslims perceive as usury-driven,
foreign controlled and mired in a dependency that merely reproduces a corrupt,
illegitimate, secular state. Equally important, SAPs not only limit the state's
ability to co-opt adversaries, but they also encourage the economically weak in
urban centres to rely on redistribution of basic needs (food, medicine, etc.)
dispensed by Islamic charities rather than state social-service agencies. In some
situations the Islamic organizations have become a parallel state-welfare service.
The Islamist mobilization of civil society under SAPs can only confirm to the
popular classes the abysmal failure of the post-colonial secular state to meet their
aspirations. Most of all, the Islamist discourse is global as well as local, authentic
and accessible, for there is no need for militants to teach the foundational
concepts of Hegel, Marx or Locke. All know the vocabulary of the Islamic alternative, which they already understand as a local culture. An avowed antagonist
of Islam, the conservative Samuel Huntington, recognizes the power advantage
of indigenous organizational resources for Islamivts as compared to liberals:

> The latter [Islamists] can operate within and behind a network of mosques,
> welfare organizations, foundations, and other Muslim institutions, which
> the government feels it cannot suppress. Liberal democrats have no such
> cover and hence are more easily controlled or eliminated by the govern-
> ment. (Huntington, 1996: 112.)

GLOBAL GOVERNANCE, NEO-LIBERAL DOGMA AND THE QUESTION OF DEMOCRACY

Despite truncation due to space limitations, our analysis confirms how global
economic and social changes articulate with the Islamic revival during three
distinct phases. Islamists took advantage of the political opportunities offered by
the multiple crises of the post-colonial secular state and the petroleum boom
and bust cycle. It is readily apparent that Islamist groups are adept at mobilizing
indigenous organizational resources, from schools to mosques, and providing
both material and moral incentives to their followers. Of course, Islamist power
has received an enormous boost from global financial managers and multilateral
policy makers who have failed to heed Polanyi's warnings regarding the way
unregulated market forces generate insecurity and extreme social movements
(Polanyi, 1944). The latter's unrealistic insistence on implementing deflationary
structural adjustment programmes worldwide, regardless of their failure to
deliver policy goals (i.e. Indonesia), suggests a dogmatic theology rather than
a falsifiable social science. For, as we have demonstrated, SAPs function as a

veritable recruitment campaign for the Islamist movement. Locally, efforts by secular state officials to license mosques and to exert social control over insurgent Islamist groups have proved extremely ineffective and very costly in terms of human lives.

Despite lacking the hierarchical organization associated with Western churches, Islamic movements are organizationally adept and pragmatic. They rely on networks often created by scholarly and student affiliations. And they construct the dense webs of Muslim associations connecting mosques, schools, welfare associations, pilgrimage associations, clinics, missionary activity, community development associations, student associations, and Islamic versions of most kinds of organizations found in the West (Sullivan, 1994). When Islamic social movements mobilize these associations and networks, they fulfil the criteria advanced by McAdam's and Smith's use to explain social movement success. On the political front, it is readily apparent that, when repressed by authoritarian regimes, Islam's civil society organizations form a parallel organizational alternative to the state, and when allowed to compete, they are very successful in pluralist democratic elections. When Western powers support authoritarian regimes (i.e. Algeria, Egypt and Turkey) the obvious hypocrisy fuels ultra-nationalism and undermines democratic tendencies within the Islamist movement.

When these parallel organizations of civil society are allowed to compete in elections, as in Jordan, Algeria, Turkey and Malaysia, Islamists have succeeded beyond most expectations. Since Islamists combine modern organizational discipline, a protean communal identity and pragmatic tactics, their effort to convert their strength in civil society into electoral power has been remarkably successful. In Algeria and Turkey, achieving power by liberal democratic means was blocked by the secular military alliances with tragic results in the former. When blocked from participating in electoral politics, as in Egypt, Islamists shifted to organizations within civil society and won control of many professional associations, only to be put under judicial control by the state.

In Tunisia, despite affirming democratic pluralism and agreeing to abide by the rules of Western democracy, the Islamist Party (MTI) was banned and its leader, Ghanouchi, arrested for treason, sentenced to life imprisonment and later forced to leave the country. And the recent Iranian municipal elections confirm the generational thrust for democratic change. Note that in the Tunisian, Egyptian and Algerian cases, the French government supported the authoritarian regime, even awarding Mubarak of Egypt an honour: a prize for democracy and human rights (Burgat, 1997: 37). Citing human rights reports, Burgat observes that torture is customarily used against political prisoners in Algeria and Egypt, numbering at least 34,000 in Algeria and probably more in Egypt. Finally, Burgat asserts acerbically that if the Algerian state's tactics were employed against a Western political party, 'I will transform it into the Armed Islamic group within weeks. . . . ' For Burgat, despite the role of Islam, the crux of the conflict is a very ordinary one between a generation that has been in power for the last 30 years and a new political generation that is not permitted to gain access to political power.

CONCLUSION: THE IMPLICATIONS OF GLOBAL ISLAM

Islamic affiliations and networks have global implications beyond insurgent social movements. Compared to rivals, Islamic cultural practices, ritual obligations, and institutions encourage and support an unusually high degree of geographical mobility, arising largely from trading and religious networks simultaneously engaged in commerce, pilgrimage service and missionary activity. Historically, migration undertaken to acquire religious knowledge was an honourable, prestigious and common practice. In general, religious practices stimulated mobility and dispersed Muslim communities across trading and pilgrimage networks (Eickelman and Piscatori, 1990). Most importantly, the obligation to undertake the pilgrimage to the Hijaz (*hajj*), required of all Muslims who are capable, constructed a dense network of Muslim trading and pilgrimage communities throughout Asia, Europe and Africa prior to the modern age. For readers in the West, the global message is 'Islam is coming to your neighbourhood soon', if it's not there already. Historically, such networks institutionalized a distinct tradition of Muslim global 'cosmopolitanism' and encouragement of geographical mobility prior to the era of globalization. Thus the way in which globalization processes articulate with this tradition of Muslim cosmopolitanism in a given social context contributes to the formation of wider, more inclusive identities among Muslims. All such cosmopolitan dimensions of Islam, now interwoven within the infrastructure of globalization, have established a parallel network of international Muslim associations; one result was the mobilization to support Muslim victims in Bosnia. While it may be counter-intuitive to most observers, globalization has actually increased communication and associative opportunities for the once isolated and differentiated Muslim communities of the global *umma*.

The best measure of cognitive liberation and insurgent consciousness is found in the vast, innovative literature now produced by Muslims on modernity, justice, governance and, increasingly, human rights. It is clear that Muslims are shaping the political agenda in many states. In response to efforts by states to exert social control, Islamists are very active. Their actions include: organizing demonstrations, mobilizing civil society against structural adjustment, building and staffing schools, medical clinics and employment centres, protesting American military adventures in the Muslim world, demanding charity (*zakkat*) for the poor, denouncing repression and torture, and, most importantly, constructing parallel institutions to dispense material, social and emotional support to those marginalized by the relentless march of global neo-liberalism.

By strategically seizing the mantle of anti-imperialist nationalism, a discourse formerly controlled exclusively by secular nationalist and leftist movements, Islamism has become the world's most extensive and militant anti-systemic social movement. Yet, Islam has the advantage of being simultaneously an ethno-nationalist identity as well as a resistance movement to subordination to the dictates of the capitalist world economy. Seizing the space left by the shrinking state, Islamists have become the best organized political force in an

urban milieu marked by declining state capacity to deliver services and/or any
other alternative developmental model (i.e. state socialism).

In the cultural domain, on the other hand, Islamism reinterprets and
elaborates on already existing discursive practices integral to the everyday life of
Muslims. It captures and mobilizes for essentially modern ends a deeply felt
desire to belong to a transcendental community the global *umma*. Here is a
subjectivity that can be articulated and identified with at many different levels:
local, national or even global. Hence, in contrast to the secular left, Islamist
organizers do not have to teach Hegelian logic to recruits, for the recruits already
know the basic tenets of the discourse as lived experience. Finally, we conclude
with an insightful comment from one of Burgat's interviewees, an explanation
from a former North African leftist who made the discursive shift to Islam.
Burgat's informant tells him that he has to understand 'that there is no way for
the state to communicate efficiently with society, without the medium of
religious culture' (Burgat, 1997: 44). Just how the medium of Islamic culture will
articulate with essentially modernist projects and problems becomes a pivotal
issue for students of GSMs.

11

RELIGIOUS MOVEMENTS AND GLOBALIZATION

James A. Beckford

It is no exaggeration to claim that religions have been closely associated with the emergence of most of the world's empires, the modern world-system of nation states and today's increasingly globalized social order. Yet, relatively few social scientists have analysed this association closely. Nevertheless, as I shall argue in this chapter, the development of religious movements in the late twentieth century demonstrates the importance of religion, admittedly as only one factor among others, in shaping the various processes contributing to globalization. The chapter falls into three main sections. After some preliminary discussion of relevant concepts, the first deals with the contribution of religions towards perceptions of 'the global circumstance'. The second analyses the linkage between religious movements and global social movements (GSMs). And the third inquires into the implications of globalization for religious movements.

At the risk of sounding trivial I need to begin with a reminder that the concepts of 'social movement' and 'religion' are both historical and contested. The same is also true, of course, of the hybrid term 'religious movement'. The varied ways in which these terms have been used at different times and in different contexts should alert us to the need for some conceptual 'hygiene' at the outset. I therefore need to clarify the different meanings that these terms have carried, and continue to hold, in social scientific discourse. Before doing so, however, I also need to sketch briefly the evolution of sociological thinking about the contribution of religion in general and religious movements in particular to social change.

SOCIOLOGY OF RELIGION

Orthodox views in the sociology of religion between roughly the 1930s and the 1980s tended to be polarized between two extreme readings of religion's contribution towards social change. On the one hand, it was held that religious institutions were normally forces for order, continuity and stability in cultures and social formations. On the other hand, it was recognized that religion could also flourish, albeit without much social influence, on the unstable margins of society in the form of enthusiastic cults and separatist sects. Images of modernity and of the modernization processes usually found space for both of these readings of religion, especially when they were combined under the rubric of secularization. Many theorists of secularization, taking their cue directly or indirectly from Max Weber and Ernst Troeltsch, argued that the significance for social life of heavily institutionalized forms of religion was bound to go on declining while upsurges of cultic or sectarian enthusiasm on the fringes of mainstream social institutions could still be expected (see, e.g. Wilson, 1970, 1976; Dobbelaere, 1981).

Although most of the sociological analyses of religion produced by Western or Western-oriented scholars between the 1930s and 1980s were concerned with developments in the most technologically advanced societies, there was certainly interest in religious change in other parts of the world as well (Worsley, 1957; Lanternari, 1963; Kaufmann, 1964; Wilson, 1973; Bastide, 1978; Pereira de Queiroz, 1989). In fact, social scientists from widely differing theoretical and ideological backgrounds found it convenient to explain religious change in so-called developing societies in terms which appeared to confirm the correctness of their interpretation of 'Western' religion. In other words, the template of modernization, secularization and the contradictions of capitalism was applied to religion in non-Western countries. The results seemed to confirm high-level theoretical expectations that the influence of modern, industrial and capitalist social formations would eventually erode the primacy that religion still enjoyed in some cultures and regions but that, in the meantime, religion could still function as a force either for cultural resistance or for hastening the advent of, for example, democracy, rule of law and a liberal version of civil society. Debates about these issues were particularly lively in relation to India (Mandelbaum, 1972) and the countries of Africa and Latin America (Smith, 1963, 1971, 1974; D'Antonio and Pike, 1964; Willems, 1967; Vallier, 1970), but related variants of this line of reasoning also emerged strongly in relation to Spain, Poland and Israel (Liebman and Don-Yehiya, 1984; Casanova, 1994).

We can see, with the benefit of hindsight, that there was a strong tendency until the 1980s for social scientists to examine the contribution of religion and religious movements towards social change in discrete nation states, societies or regions of the world. This is no doubt because much of the basic theorizing about industrial or capitalist societies took it for granted that each state, society or region had to respond separately to forces emanating from other equally discrete states, societies or regions.

Two significant changes began to occur in the 1980s. The first is that it became increasingly apparent to some social scientists that religion amounted to more than a contingent or secondary feature of modernization. The second is that technological, political and cultural factors combined to generate the reality and the consciousness of a new and increasingly global order of culture and social relations (Albrow, 1996; Castells, 1997). The effect of these two changes is plain to see in the claims that are made below about religion and religious movements, although it is also clear that some of the older interpretations have persisted alongside these changes.

DEFINITION OF RELIGION

There is literally no end to the definitions of religion. Nor do arguments over the question of whether religion is found in all known human societies show any signs of being resolved. It would be inappropriate, therefore, to evade or to foreclose on definitional issues here, but it is still necessary for me to demarcate the kind of phenomena that qualify as 'religion' for my purposes. The need is for a formulation that will avoid the extremes of narrowness *and* of excessive inclusiveness. I think this can be met by conceptualizing religion as beliefs, senti-ments, actions and social institutions informed by perceptions of ultimate significance. This conceptualization draws upon Durkheim's (1967: 274) notion of 'la vie sérieuse' and Tillich's (1958) notion of 'the felt whole'. It errs more on the side of inclusiveness than of narrowness, but this is acceptable to me since nothing essential to the arguments that follow turns on this bias.

Although nothing in this chapter turns significantly on the way that I have defined 'religion', it is worthwhile noting Robertson's (1993: 3) argument that ' "Religion" is largely a category and a problem of modernity'. Only in modern times and predominantly Western societies has religion been categorically separated from the rest of culture. The influence of secularist ideas associated with eighteenth century revolutions in France and America reinforced intellec-tual efforts to conceptualize religion as a separate sphere of societies and of individual lives. In time, however, these efforts ironically strengthened the idea that all national societies needed to have a religion. Thus, says Robertson (1993: 15), religion 'has become a globally diffused mode of discourse which plays an important part in the institutional ordering of national societies and international society'. In short, the very practice of constructing 'religion' as a sociological category is part of a long-term process leading to globalization.

RELIGIOUS MOVEMENTS

It may seem at first glance to be easier to conceptualize 'religious movements' than 'religion', but the task is actually complicated. The main reason for this has to do with the variety of meanings attributable to the term 'movement'. Indeed, the academic study of social movements is still preoccupied with questions about conceptualization, definition and the methodological implications of particular concepts and definitions. For example, even the first, apparently innocent component of Zirakzadeh's (1997) three-fold definition of 'social movement' would be considered problematic by those scholars who insist that the term denotes something much broader, subtler and more inclusive than 'a group of people seeking to build a radical new order' (see, e.g. della Porta and Diani, 1999). I believe that these considerations are particularly appropriate to the case of religious movements.

To confine the discussion to purely sociological considerations for the moment, it would be fair to say that the study of social movements has transcended the focus on 'a group of people' in several important ways. Firstly, it is widely acknowledged that social movements are complex in the sense of mobilizing people who stand in a variety of different relations to movements' central grievances or aims (McCarthy and Zald, 1977). Some are directly affected by the grievances and are therefore likely to benefit directly if the grievances are resolved to their satisfaction ('direct beneficiaries'). Others, however, do not stand to benefit directly but are nevertheless mobilized by their conscience ('conscience constituents'). Still others are 'potential beneficiaries' or even 'bystanders' who lurk on the fringes of social movements. Then there are 'patrons' who may lend their prestige, know-how, social connections and, in some cases, material support. The constellation of actors in social movements is therefore much more complex than is captured by the phrase 'a group of people'. But, allowing for this degree of complexity in personnel, we now have a lot of empirical evidence about the diversity of even the activists at the core of many social movements. They display, for example, heterogeneous motives, intentions, perception of grievance, degrees of commitment, ideological understanding of what is at stake, strategic and tactical ideas, and definitions of a 'satisfactory' resolution of the grievances. In view of this diversity of actors associated with social movements and the heterogeneity of their outlooks, it is increasingly common for scholars to opt for concepts such as 'collective action' (Melucci, 1996) or simply 'mobilizations' in place of the more monolithic and clearly bounded 'social movement'. The search is for concepts which adequately reflect the diffuseness, fluidity and indeterminacy which supposedly characterize today's social movements.

Secondly, there is growing recognition of the importance of material and organizational resources to social movements (McCarthy and Zald, 1977). The underlying claim is that the number of grievances in any society is far higher than the number of social movements. This is explained in terms of the failure of many would-be mobilizations to secure adequate resources to pursue their grievances. In fact, the success of influential movements is attributed to their superior resources and management. Again, the restricted perception of social movements as 'groups of people' runs the risk of overlooking the importance not just of material resources and their management but also of the social networks from which movements draw human and material support. Their 'social infrastructure' is believed to play a major role in influencing movements' chances of success.

Thirdly, social movements amount to far more than individual participants, formal movement organizations and material resources. In reaction against conceptualizing social movements in ways which privilege these concrete and formal aspects, many scholars now favour approaches which give priority to the cultural content and ethos of movements (see, e.g. Johnston and Klandermans,

1995). This type of approach emphazises the meanings, images, values and preferences represented in movements – but not necessarily or exclusively in formal or official guises. Thus, waves of public joy or sadness and currents of indignation or enthusiasm can occur from time to time and can be traced through changes in public opinion or through public demonstrations. Alongside these public instances of changing preferences there are also personal manifestations of the effect of mobilizations. When roughly similar changes take place in, for example, the ways in which individuals construct their personal identity, perceive others, use language or express emotion, it seems justifiable to infer the influence of a social movement (but understood as a diffuse mobilization of sentiment and consciousness).

In sum, social scientific understanding of social movements or religious movements needs to break away from rigid, out-dated conceptualizations. What is required, instead, is an approach which is sensitive to the diversity of participants, the reticulate character of movements' social organization, and the diffuseness of ideas and sentiments at play in many mobilizations. This is not to deny, of course, that formal movement organizations with clear boundaries and relatively fixed ideas have never existed. Movements of this type, such as Jehovah's Witnesses (Beckford, 1975), Seventh-day Adventists (Bull and Lockhart, 1989) and Mormons (Arrington and Bitton, 1979), have had powerful effects in many parts of the world in the twentieth century. But my point is that it would be a serious mistake to overlook the influence of less formal, more diffuse, less exclusive, more inclusive, less homogeneous and more diverse mobilizations of ideas, sentiments, commitments and material resources in the name of religion. In my terms, then, a religious movement is a formal or informal mobilization of people, material resources, ideas and feelings in pursuit of objectives dictated by concerns deemed ultimately significant but largely outside the framework of conventional religious activities.

Perhaps the best way to conclude this discussion of the concept of 'religious movement' is to emphasize that such movements constitute complex 'fields' of social relations, ideas, sentiments and resources. The salience of particular components in each field varies from movement to movement, and from time to time. Thus, formal 'movement organizations' may predominate in some circumstances but may be eclipsed in others by more diffuse currents of opinion and feeling. A good example of what I mean by a religious movement is Pentecostalism (see, e.g. Hollenweger, 1972; Burgess and McGee, 1988). In the course of the twentieth century it has developed into a worldwide Christian movement affecting tens of millions of sympathizers and participants (as well as critics and opponents). Pentecostalism is embedded in formal organizations such as churches, missions, broadcasting and publishing companies, health-care institutions and so on. At the same time, Pentecostal ideas and experiences have permeated churches and denominations which are not based on this particular tradition but which have, in some places, given it a sympathetic reception. Finally, there are individual Christians who have been subtly influenced by Pentecostalism without ever considering that they were part of the movement.

This 'fluid' perspective on social movements, to use Gusfield's (1981) formulation, helps to trace their subtle influences on social relations and culture. It also helps to counter the tendency to identify the success of social movements too narrowly in terms of the strength displayed by their formal organizations.

GLOBALIZATION AND RELIGION

This is not an appropriate place to explore all the different meanings attributed to 'globalization'. Nor is it necessary to rehearse all the arguments for and against the usefulness of this concept. Instead, I shall merely list some of the characteristics commonly associated with the concept so that I can then concentrate on aspects which are especially relevant to a discussion of religious movements.

Globalization, as a contested process, can be characterized by:

- the growing frequency, volume and interconnectedness of movements of ideas, materials, goods, information, pollution, money and people across national boundaries and between regions of the world;
- the growing capacity of information technologies to shorten or even abolish the distance in time and space between events and places in the world;
- the diffusion of increasingly standardized practices and protocols for processing global flows of information, goods, money and people;
- the emergence of organizations, institutions and social movements for promoting, monitoring or counteracting global forces, with or without the support of individual nation states;
- the emergence in particular countries or regions of distinctive or 'local' ways of refracting the influence of global forces.

I need to emphasize that globalization is a process which is far from being clear in its outlines, constant in its progression or uniform in its effects. Indeed, the concept is contestable and heavily contested. But that only makes it all the more interesting to explore how well globalization makes sense of social, cultural and, above all, religious change. Fortunately for me, other authors have already been pioneers in the search for conceptual clarity and theoretical coherence in our thinking about religion and globalization (Robertson, 1985, 1989, 1992; Robertson and Chirico, 1985; Beyer, 1990, 1992, 1994; Simpson, 1991; Castells, 1997; Inoue, 1997; Voyé, 1997). My task, more modestly, is to consider how well the available knowledge helps to explain relations between globalization and religious movements.

My starting point is that it is currently fashionable to claim that globalization is a phenomenon unique to the late twentieth century and that the most interesting aspect of global culture is the predominance of images, technologies and industries controlled by multinational mass communications companies. It is not necessary for me to challenge these claims head-on, but I want to argue that both of them miss the point as far as religious movements are concerned. In other words, if globalization is examined in terms of the contributions and problems presented by religious movements, a different picture emerges. The result does not refute any of the central arguments about globalization but it does show that the phenomenon is actually more challenging and complex than it is often depicted. I freely admit that religion is not the most important aspect of globalization, but equally religious movements undoubtedly bring to light some relatively neglected and challenging aspects.

Two examples of religious movements with origins earlier than the 'global era' will help to pave the way for a more detailed analysis of the multi-faceted contributions of religious movements towards the crystallization of a global circumstance in the late twentieth century. Let me begin with the role played by North European Protestant sectarian movements from the mid-sixteenth century to the mid-eighteenth century in forging ideas and social institutions from which eventually flowed notions of individual conscience, personal freedom, freedom of conscience and, of course, toleration (see Jordan, 1932; Wilson, 1995). Radical Baptists, Congregationalists, Independents and Quakers were among the best known of these so-called dissenting movements. Indeed, the very idea of a civil society composed of freely contracting parties protected from the arbitrary power of monarchs, the military, state churches and the relics of the Holy Roman Empire grew indirectly out of the kinds of religious separatism and experiments with virtuous 'communities of saints', especially in North American territories (Walzer, 1996). These Protestant spiritualities, diverse as they were, nevertheless tended to put in place some of the ideological and institutional foundations for the kind of bourgeois, liberal and capitalist enterprises which, in turn, helped to foster worldwide systems of economic, political and cultural relations. Moreover, the descendants of some of these early Protestant movements were instrumental in establishing missions and communities in those far-flung parts of the world which came to form the infrastructure of colonialist and imperialist capitalism on a world scale (Hammond, 1963; Taylor, 1965; Wilson, 1967). And, although Roman Catholic missions were also part of this infrastructure in America, the Caribbean region, southeast Asia and west Africa, Protestant missionaries were in a stronger position through marriage and child-rearing to inform the development of communities of expatriate traders and settlers.

My second example of a religious movement that has indirectly contributed towards 'making the world a smaller place' is the Watchtower movement of Jehovah's Witnesses. Within 30 years of its emergence in Pennsylvania in the 1870s it was already exploring the potential for growth in many parts of the world (including Western Europe, South Africa, Colombia, the Caribbean region, east Africa and the Middle East). The movement has gone on spreading and growing at a steady rate ever since (Beckford, 1975, 1977). It currently claims 5.5 million regular members, and the astonishing number of 14.3 million people attended its annual memorial service in 1997. But for my purposes the most significant aspect of the Watchtower movement's development is that it has retained rigidly standardized teachings, practices and forms of organization in all the 232 countries and territories where it currently operates. Dissident groups have appeared from time to time in, for example, east Africa and Japan, and there is a dense penumbra of apostate organizations (Rogerson, 1969; Bergman, 1984), but the mainstream of Jehovah's Witnesses remains strikingly uniform and united. The Watchtower movement is truly a 'religious multinational' (Beckford, 1986) with a dense network of communications on a global scale.

But equally important for my analysis is the fact that the Witnesses have also contributed towards globalization by pressing relentlessly in all parts of the world for the freedom to practise their faith without major obstacles or penalties. This is ironic, since the self-image of Jehovah's Witnesses is that of a movement 'in, but not of, the world'. Witnesses constantly assert their lack of involvement in politics, trade unions, social movements and so on, but by their unremitting campaigning for their religious freedom they have actually made a disproportionately large contribution towards legislative change in some places. For example, they have consistently challenged laws requiring them to belong to political parties, join trade unions, salute national flags, undergo military training, refrain from proselytising in public, accept blood transfusions for themselves or their children, or permit their children to participate in collective worship and religious education in schools (Hodges, 1976; Penton, 1985). The Watchtower Society's legal department in the USA and in some other national branch offices has acquired extensive experience and expertise in these political and legal issues. One indirect effect of this legal work is, on the principle that difficult cases make good law, to push for greater acceptance of the individual's right to choose how to practise religion. The other side of the coin is the right to be exempt from practices that might compromise an individual's religious obligations. In short, the Witnesses are a thorn in the flesh of political and military authorities and a tenacious advocate of the basically liberal constitutional principle of the separation of religion and state. Since this principle is closely associated with the idea that freedom of religion is a fundamental human right (Bradney, 1993; Cumper, 1996), it could be argued that the Watchtower movement is indirectly and perhaps unwittingly helping to promote the human rights movement with all its implications for universalism.

Although I have used the examples of dissenting Protestants in the early modern period and of Jehovah's Witnesses in the twentieth century in order to illustrate the subtle contribution of religious movements towards the formative stages of a global order and awareness of globality, it is no less important to see the other side of this equation. For Protestant missions and sectarian religious movements have also elicited critical and hostile responses in many parts of the world especially where these religions accompanied colonialism and imperialism. I shall have much more to say below about local and particularist reactions against the would-be universalising forces of some religious movements.

RELIGIOUS MOVEMENTS AND THE GLOBAL CIRCUMSTANCE

In this first main section of my chapter I want to analyse some of the factors which account for the capacity of religious movements to make the kind of contributions towards globalization that have just been illustrated. My intention is definitely not to claim that religious movements are necessary or sufficient conditions for the emergence of globalization. My much more modest argument is that there has been an elective affinity between some religious movements and global themes and that an indirect spin-off from the activities of some religious movements has been the strengthening of global forces. In comparison, economic and political factors have been more directly and heavily responsible for globalization, in my opinion.

The first part of my argument is strongly informed by the thinking of Robertson (1985, 1992) who was among the first scholars to recognize not only the distinctiveness of globalization as a process but also, and more importantly for me, the salience of religion and of religious movements in globalization. Robertson is particularly insistent on the point that *consciousness* of living in an increasingly interdependent world owes much to the fact that some religious bodies have elaborated the idea of 'the global circumstance' (Robertson and Chirico, 1985) in their ideological work. Two new religious movements (NRMs) with origins in east Asia, the Unification Church[1] (renamed the Family Federation for World Peace and Unification in 1997) and the Soka Gakkai,[2] are credited with giving special prominence to a view of the world as a site of irremediably mutual connections among beliefs, peoples, and the institutions of politics and profit-seeking business. Both of these movements energetically seek to transcend ideological, religious, ethnic and national boundaries in promoting their visions of a harmonious and peaceable world unified by faith in a transcendent religious power. But the Unification Church and the Soka Gakkai cannot avoid constructing their images of globality on the basis of their own partial or particular ideas. In other words, a two-way relationship exists between perceptions of globality and attempts to capture it and elaborate it in particularistic terms.

The tension between universalizing and particularizing forces is characteristic of circumstances in which awareness of globality has outstripped agreement about its significance. Competition and exposure to new ideas have the effect of threatening to relativize all ideological positions, thereby raising the stakes for those movements that strive to impose their particular interpretation of the allegedly new universal condition. One of the marks of globalization is that it puts all ideologies and belief systems under pressure to clarify their place in relation to the new circumstance. They can no longer afford to refuse to consider their position. An interesting case in point concerns the difficulties that suddenly faced the Orthodox Church in Russia when competition from other religious and spiritual ideas was permitted after 1990 (Kürti, 1997). It was no longer enough for the Church to assert its age-old views with renewed vigour: it had to reclaim and defend its position in the face of competition from various minorities with different religious traditions and from 'imported' religions. In Kürti's (1997: 41) words, 'For each nation-state emerging out of the Soviet Empire, the "neighbouring other" assumes the characteristics of the externalised evil'. This was just as true of religious communities as of nation states in the former USSR. This is why some nationalists and leaders of the Russian Orthodox Church pressed so hard for new legislation in 1996 to control religious competition and the relativization of their own previously hegemonic, albeit severely controlled, position. With the protection offered by the new law on 'Freedom of Conscience and Religious Organizations', which discriminates in favour of 'traditional' religious groups and against 'non-traditional' groups, conservative and nationalist elements in Russia are trying to forge an understanding of the country's distinctive identity in an increasingly globalized world (Shterin and Richardson, 1998). Meanwhile, its religious competitors are struggling to defend their right to deploy their different interpretations of global conditions in terms of the allegedly universal and therefore overriding principle of the human right to religious freedom – something that was at least offered by the Constitution of the Russian Federation.[3]

Another characteristic of religious movements that aspire to capture the meaning of globalization is the care that they take to situate themselves in relation to other powerful religious organizations. It is not enough merely to lay claim to represent globality: it is also necessary to show that competing religious ideas and practices are no longer effective or relevant in an age of globalization. Again, the Watchtower movement provides a cogent example because it has always asserted (a) the failure or inability of other religious groups to fulfil their duties and (b) its own qualifications for superseding other groups' partial truths with a would-be universal and exclusive truth. The more global the outreach of the Watchtower movement has become in the course of the twentieth century, the louder has become its claim to have replaced all other religious bodies which owe their origins to particular times and places rather than to the 'end time' and to the transcendence of all national, cultural or 'racial' differences.

In much less strident and exclusivist terms many other religious movements of the late twentieth century have deliberately sought to dissolve the differences between peoples in the pursuit of the universal. There are two main strategies for achieving this result. The first is to claim that a new movement has come, usually in fulfilment of ancient prophecy, to complete the task the other religious organizations were supposed to perform. Central to the Unification Church, for example, is the belief that Jesus Christ failed to marry, to produce perfect children and to restore the 'fallen' world to a state of divine perfection. The Lord of the Second Advent's mission is therefore believed to be to complete Christ's task and, at the prophetically critically point in history, to give humankind at least the opportunity to make the sacrifices on which restoration of a perfected world order would be conditional. The movement's mission is correspondingly universal in scope. The Church of Jesus Christ and the Latter-Day Saints, or the Mormons, is also founded on a belief that Joseph Smith unlocked prophecies in the 1820s explaining the fate of the lost ten tribes of Israel, the division of the world into 'racial' types and the completion of the Christian religion by Mormons.

The second main strategy of religious movements aiming to transform the world is to claim that a highly significant turning point has been reached in the development of human knowledge and that the capacity to make a break-through into a new era of worldwide peace and contentment is therefore at hand. The Baha'i movement offers a nineteenth century example of this predominantly positive outlook which has continued to prosper modestly to the point where its members now number about three million (Smith, 1987). They revere the teachings of an Iranian nobleman whose religious title was 'Bahá'u'lláh'. Break-ing with Shi'i Muslim expectations of a messianic kingdom under the *Mahdi*, he promulgated a message of hope for peace on a world scale and for peaceful relations among all religious communities. Bahá'u'lláh described his message of hope as follows to an English contemporary:

> That all nations should become one in faith and all men as brothers; ... that diversity of religion should cease, and differences of race be annulled ... Let not a man glory in this, that he loves his country; let him rather glory in this, that he loves his kind. (Browne, 1891: x1).

He justified his teachings as a new expression of a timeless and universal God whose divine wisdom had been corrupted in earlier religious traditions. Bahá'u'lláh saw himself as the latest in a line of prophets. The distinctiveness of his particular message was that it allegedly related for the first time in history to the entire world and it offered a new universal standard of justice, equality, rights and responsibilities. In some senses the Baha'i faith foreshadowed globalization, with its emphasis on the interdependence of all peoples and the need for international institutions of peace, justice and good governance to combat 'the anarchy inherent in state sovereignty' (Shoghi Effendi, 1955: 202, quoted in Smith, 1985: 23).

There are echoes of this optimistic 'turning-point' philosophy in numerous parts of the Human Potential Movement and the New Age today. Scientology has probably gone further than most NRMs towards trying to establish a world-wide network of individuals and organizations committed to applying the wisdom of L. Ron Hubbard, the movement's founder and chief ideologue, to the task of transforming the world (Wallis, 1976). But the most explicit claims for the transformative power of a NRM have come from Transcendental Meditation (Bainbridge, 1997: 187–91). The Maharishi Mahesh Yogi's followers believe that the fortunes of any country could be significantly improved if at least 10 per cent of the population performed the approved spiritual exercises. And it was under the auspices of the movement originally called *est* (Erhard Seminars Training) that a project was launched in the 1970s to rid the world of hunger, again by applying the founder's wisdom without regard for national differences.

Whereas the vehicles of pre-modern and modern religious movements with global aspirations were often imperialism, colonialism and capitalism, the late twentieth century has seen the flourishing of numerous movements which contained their own ideological vision of globality and their own organizational motivation to foster a worldwide mission without being adjuncts of attempts to conquer large tracts of the world for political or economic reasons. But it has to be said that, while some of these religious movements have profoundly affected the lives of tens of millions of people, their *independent* impact on political and economic life has been slight in most cases. These movements may have refracted or mitigated the effects of political and economic systems on their followers as individuals, but there is very little evidence that they have independently helped to shape public policy in matters other than the law relating to religious freedom. The world images of some religious movements are distinctly global, but for the most part the movements continue to be marginal to the exercise of societal power. The next section of the chapter will qualify these generalizations in one important respect.

RELIGIOUS MOVEMENTS AND OTHER SOCIAL MOBILIZATIONS

Although religious movements have exercised relatively little *independent* influence over the central concerns of money and political power in the modern world, it would be a serious mistake to overlook their capacity to act in *harmony*, if not necessarily in *concert*, with more powerful forms of mobilization. By this, I mean that the ideological work of some religious movements has either resonated unintentionally with the themes being pursued by various social movements, campaigns, pressure groups, lobbies and political parties or has deliberately tried to inform such themes.[4] Examples of religious movements which have deliberately sought to influence other mobilizations are sketched in Figure 11.1. The names enclosed in inverted commas are generic labels for varieties of specific movements.

The case of the USA is particularly interesting in the sense that its framework of law and politics permits or encourages 'single issue' politics on a scale unmatched in most other countries. As a result, religious movements are an integral part of the political and legislative process. They help to raise consciousness of grievances, to collect resources, to lobby legislators and decision makers, to monitor the actions of their opponents, and to keep their causes in the public eye. While religious movements in support of peace (Pagnucco, 1996), human rights (Morris, 1996), progressive welfare policies (Tabb, 1986) and illegal immigrants (Golden and McConnell, 1986) are active in the USA, conservative movements are more evident in the public sphere. Thus,

> The number of culturally defensive religious interest groups (that is, groups promoting religious fundamentalism and traditional morality) had been growing steadily since the late 1950s and reached a peak only in the late 1970s. These movements, all of which were organized on a national scale, included efforts within denominations to restore fundamentalist theology and traditional morality to prominence, as well as extradenominational organizations aimed at reforming the entire society. [S]tudies conducted largely between 1980 and 1984, continue to document the political mobilization that has come to characterize evangelicals. (Wuthnow, 1987: 28)

Mobilizations	Religious movements
Peace	Soka Gakkai ISKCON* Rissho Kosei-kai Pax Christi USA
Environmentalism	'Green Christianity' FWBO† 'New Age'
Human rights	SCLC‡ Baha'is Base ecclesial communities Scientology
'Moral and religious purity'	NVLA§ Jamaat-i-Islami 'Khomeinism' Communione e Liberazione
'Ethnic, national and religious purity'	'Christian Patriots' RSS‖ Christian Coalition

* International Society for Krishna Consciousness
† Friends of the Western Buddhist Order
‡ Southern Christian Leadership Conference
§ National Viewers and Listeners Association
‖ Rashtriya Swayamsevak Sangh

Figure 11.1   Religious movements seeking to influence various mobilizations

The Moral Majority, the Christian Coalition and Christian Patriots (Aho, 1991, 1996) are only the most publicized of the broad swathe of conservative religious movements seeking deliberately to influence American public life. Yet, for all the attention given to these movements and to other claims of a conservative religious resurgence in the USA, the movements remain internally divided and relatively insignificant in comparison with non-religious mobilizations (Wuthnow, 1987; Manza and Brooks, 1997).

Nevertheless, as I have argued elsewhere (Beckford, 1989), although religion continues to lose significance as a force in the public life of many societies, the strongly differentiated character of many advanced industrial societies oriented towards economic growth and national competitiveness in an increasingly globalized social order actually creates new problems of meaning, identity and integrity, in response to which religion and spirituality retain some credibility. For example, the elusiveness of peace, the popularity of ethno-religious nationalism, the persistence of famine, poverty, torture and oppression, the dilemmas presented by new scientific ideas and medical or technological inventions, and the fear of manipulation by the mass media and unscrupulous governments all reverberate in countless religious movements. So, even in countries where rates of membership of religious organizations or regular participation in organized religious activities are low, there is still plenty of opportunity for the expression of religious and spiritual themes. The situation is more complex than a zero-sum game between religion and modernity. This is why I disagree with the more conventional view that 'Just when humanity most needs an ethical system that enables diverse peoples to coexist peacefully and justly, the traditional source of such guidelines are [sic] being daily undermined by the challenge of modern science and the increased cross-cultural contact' (Kurtz, 1995: 3). In fact, my hypothesis is that as the power of formal religious organizations has declined, religious issues have not necessarily withered away or simply been privatized but have drifted away from their former points of anchorage and become 'cultural resources' (Beckford, 1989). As such, religious language, symbols and imagery are more freely available for deployment in attempts to mobilize public opinion and support against all manner of grievances. But religious personnel are less likely these days to inspire or to lead such mobilizations and more likely to be co-opted for instrumental or symbolic reasons (Beyer, 1994) – sometimes to good effect, as in the case of the Dalai Lama, Archbishop Tutu in South Africa, Bishop Belo in East Timor or Father Popieluszko in Poland. Nobody who witnessed the massive deployment of religious and spiritual imagery at the time of Princess Diana's death and funeral in 1997 could lightly dismiss the idea that religion remains a powerful cultural resource in advanced industrial societies like the UK without being anchored in popular religious organizations.

In countries where sharp contrasts exist between, on the one hand, burgeoning spheres of industrial production and information technology and, on the other, massive spheres of rural and urban destitution, underemployment and unemployment the persisting power of religious symbols and imagery tends to be even clearer. In India, for example, the secular constitution is no obstacle to the formation of powerful movements, which seamlessly combine politics, ethnicity, caste identity and religion. So-called Hindu nationalist movements currently have the highest profile and the best chance of influencing India's political development – at least for the foreseeable future. Reflecting themes adumbrated in nineteenth-century Hindu reform movements, the Rashtriya Swayamsevak Sangh (RSS) or 'National Volunteer Corps', founded in 1925, has fostered a notion of Hindu 'national' identity by means of 'a peculiar Westernized military and boy-scout discipline' (Bhatt, 1997: 198).[5] It favours martial arts training, political education and anti-Muslim sentiment in its drive to claim that the Hindu 'nation' was the indigenous population of India and that 'foreign minorities' (i.e. Muslims and Christians) which refuse to merge with the Hindu majority should not be tolerated. 'The fetishism of order, discipline and organization is at the core of RSS ideals', according to Bhatt (1997: 209), despite the fact that there is very little warrant for them in ancient

Hindu spirituality. In opposition to Mrs Gandhi's imposition of a state of emergency the RSS developed closer links with political organizations and extended its activities by creating the Vishwa Hindu Parishad (VHP) or 'World Hindu Council' and a political party which later became the Bharatiya Janata Party (BJP) or 'Indian People's Party'. With more than two million members and with the support of numerous other ultra-conservative Hindu movements, the BJP has already participated in coalition government and in 1998 was poised to form the India's first Hindu nationalist government in alliance with many smaller parties.

While it would be wrong to describe the RSS as a 'religious movement' it is clearly a mobilization which draws heavily, but selectively, on religious and spiritual themes in the complex patchwork of ideas and practices conventionally labelled 'Hinduism' (Jackson, 1995). For present purposes, the most important aspect of this religio-ethnic–nationalist movement is the consistent attempt to forge not only a Hindu identity but also a '*world* Hindu' identity so that India's position in the global order can be specified and strengthened. This involves, among other things, claiming that Hinduism embraces all the major world faith traditions except Judaism, Christianity and Islam. It is almost as if Hinduism is expanding to fit the space created for it by globalization, in confirmation of Beyer's (1994: 28) argument that,

> Globalisation thus involves a double and somewhat paradoxical process. Because there is no common and dominant model to which societies can conform, each society creates its own particular image of global order by promoting, even inventing, its own national image of the good society in short, its own national identity. The global universal, more precisely, the global concern about the universal only results from the interaction among these images.

This is why movements such as the RSS make heavy investments of effort in relaying myths, archaeological claims and historical revisions as well as religion and morality. What has changed in the last 50 years is the perceived source of threat. It is no longer British colonialism but is now secularism, Muslim neighbours and the global economy. As a result,

> Postcolonial Hindu fundamentalism can thus appear as a new colonialism of the victors. In representing an emergence of Indic group consciousness in new forms shaped by the colonial experience, it can easily lead to a tyranny of the majority. For it keeps the Western idea of religious community as an ideally homogeneous group, but abandons the ideas of equality among communities and protections for minorities introduced with the secular British administration: a flourishing, united Hindu Nation should need no legal protection for any special group. (Gold, 1991: 580).

On the other hand, there is no shortage of examples from Central and South America of religious movements, the emergence of which is related to globalization but the aims of which are far from being ultra-conservative. Varieties of liberation theology (Candelaria, 1990; Smith, 1991), for example, have inspired many local protests, campaigns and movements against perceived exploitation and oppression (Nash, 1996; Nepstad, 1996). Base Ecclesial Communities (Barbé, 1987; Adriance, 1991) and religious movements for communal democracy (Levine, 1986; van Vugt, 1991) have also attracted popular support and opposition. Similarly, the role of churches and religious movements in the search for liberation from multiple oppression in the Philippines and from apartheid in South Africa is well documented (de Gruchy, 1979; Villa-Vicencio, 1990; Borer, 1996).

Globalization has exerted pressure on nations, nation states, ethnic groupings and religions to defend their boundaries and assert their integrity. It has also helped to provide the *organizational and technological means* with which to tackle these tasks effectively. In the jargon used by analysts of social movements it is a matter partly of 'resource mobilization' and partly of 'opportunity structure'. The former is about the need for movements to generate and manage a reliable flow of resources, not just from people who stand to benefit directly if their grievances are met but also from 'conscience constituents' who consider themselves morally obliged to make contributions. The latter concept refers to the way in which the opportunities for mobilization are structured by frameworks of law, politics and mass communications. The effect of applying these concepts to the study of religious movements is to play down the importance of perceived grievances and to play up the importance of organizational strategy and management. The advent of globalization has ambiguous implications for these aspects of religious movements.

IMPLICATIONS OF GLOBALIZATION FOR RELIGIOUS MOVEMENTS

My argument so far has been that globalization has not contributed in any straightforward way towards the eclipse of religion but that it has undoubtedly produced various effects on religion. I consider the overall effect to be *ambiguous* at present. Globalization has opened up some novel opportunities for religion but it has also imposed some constraints. Now is the time to assess the balance of these opportunities and constraints by asking how they have affected religious movements – probably the least stable sector of the field of religion and the one most responsive to changes in its social environment.

Given that religion, by my definition at least, is concerned with questions of ultimate meaning or significance it is bound to make claims about universal values or truths. These claims are usually rooted in beliefs about the origins, history and purposes of the world and its inhabitants. The normative codes or precepts governing human action to which religions give rise also tend to claim universal validity – if not in terms of applicability to all people, then certainly in terms of applicability to all 'time and eternity' in the Mormons' phrase. These features of religion might seem to give it advantages in an age when, for the first time, it is becoming feasible for ideas to achieve truly universal distribution. Indeed, as Robertson (1992) has argued, the very possibility of universal communications elicits religious responses.

On the other hand, however, religions are rooted in particular places, institutions and self-identified communities. That is, they 'come from' somewhere and consequently they filter perceptions of globality through their particularistic meaning systems. For example, Pan-Islamism or 'world Hinduism' may aspire to global outreach but they remain extensions of particular world faith traditions. There is no Archimedean point from which any existing religion can, with any realistic expectation of success, mount a claim to make universally valid statements. They can only offer sentiments, symbols, images, ideas and values that arise from their historical experience. In other words, the emerging global circumstance may call for a universalistic form of religious expression, but the available resources are irremediably particularistic. Nevertheless, religious movements as diverse as the Soka Gakkai, the Unification Church, the Jehovah's Witnesses, the Mormons and the Baha'is continue to press their case for global status.

While a 'global religion' seems improbable, there is plenty of evidence to show that perceptions of globality have generated, or assisted in the development of, particularistic reactions *against* globality (Castells, 1997). The case of the RSS in India was discussed above, but an equally interesting case from the same country concerns the Sikh religion. The diaspora of Sikh communities around the world is extensive (Tatla, 1999), but communication with their homeland in the Punjab remains important to many Sikh individuals and groups. Indeed, political and military struggles for the creation of a sovereign Sikh state of Khalistan have strengthened many bonds of solidarity between Sikhs. Again, whereas some currents of Sikh spirituality have fostered an eirenic outlook and an ethic supposedly valid for all people, other factions have responded to the experience of living in a global diaspora by trying to reinforce the distinctiveness and exclusiveness of Sikh culture and communities and thereby to protect them from global influences. Global forces, in the shape of British colonialism, helped to create not only 'the notion of the Sikhs as a martial "race" and indeed as a distinct and separate nation' (Madan, 1991: 603) but also the Sikh diaspora. Sikh separatists are now using globalized communications media to resist the further effects of globalization on their religion and culture. This is another example of the ambiguity inherent in globalization's effects on religion and a striking instance of 'hybridity' in Bhabha's (1994) terms.

Religious movements have been in the vanguard of *new technology* ever since radical Protestants exploited new printing techniques in order to make the Bible available in vernacular translations to an increasingly literate public in early-modern Europe. The predecessors of Jehovah's Witnesses perfected an early version of multi-media technology before World War I with their mobile Photo-Drama of Creation show. The Witnesses were also among the first religious organizations to make use of portable phonographs in door-to-door evangelism, 'sound cars' equipped with public address systems, and a radio station on Staten Island, New York. Meanwhile, Seventh-day Adventists and Mormons in various parts of the world continue to invest heavily in advanced medical technologies in order to boost their missionary programmes. More recently, the architects of the Moral Majority in the USA pioneered the technology of computerized mailing-lists as a way of communicating relatively easily with millions of supporters and sympathizers scattered across North America. At the same time, aircraft, radio, TV and video media, satellite broadcasting and compact disks have joined the armoury of religious movements. The Internet and the World Wide Web are only the latest developments – albeit potentially the most rewarding *and* problematic.

The speed with which both rumour and reliable information circulate around most of the world in an age of global electronic communications has been clearly illustrated in the case of various epiphanies or manifestations of the sacred. They range from reported sightings of the Virgin Mary, 'weeping' statues and miraculous cures to such apparently unique events as the days in September 1995 when statues of the elephant-headed god, Ganesh, were believed to 'drink' milk in different countries (Bhatt, 1997: 251–2). The effectiveness of Muslim communications networks was also demonstrated beyond doubt as the 'Rushdie affair' began to unfold in 1988 and when the Babri masjid at Ayodha was sacked in 1992. Religious movements have not been slow to exploit the potential of global communications. This is particularly apparent among American evangelical, fundamentalist and sectarian movements operating in South America and Africa. Brouwer *et al.* (1996) captured the essence of this phenomenon with the phrase 'the new spirit of Protestantism and the global consumer'. These authors acknowledge the skill with which conservative Protestantism is currently being exported, mainly from the USA, to the rest of the world but they also recognize that the exports are accompanied by 'other historical Protestant influences that have encouraged authoritarianism, an aggressive tendency to identify US interests with God's interests, and an intolerance of people from other cultures' (Brouwer *et al.*, 1996: 270). Of course, these accusations have often been levelled at Christian missionaries in the past, but my point is that the new technologies seem to have changed the situation. They may be fulfilling some of Tocqueville's worst fears about mass media in the USA, namely, the potential for an élite ruthlessly to manipulate a mass. Thus,

> Under the twin covenants of Americanism and their churches, the new fundamentalists are having a profound effect in promoting both an acceptance of American (US) cultural norms and the kind of civic and psychic orderliness that does not question the rule of the powerful (Brouwer *et al.*, 1996: 271).

Another problematic aspect of the uses to which religious movements put new electronic communications media is that, in addition to conveying values representing powerful cultures rather than genuinely 'global' values, they can exercise forms of control which are less and less accountable to local groups of followers. Indeed, followers become more like consumers or audiences than members. Consequently, dissent and disagreement which have no convenient outlet in movements held together by electronic communications tend to spill over into angry 'flame outs' on the Internet or, more seriously, into organized apostate Web sites. The advent of the Internet has sparked off a massive outpouring of controversy and recrimination on top of the 'normal' level of what I call 'cult controversies' (Beckford, 1985). In short, one of the implications of globalization is that the sector of religious movements has become more uncivil, unruly and controversial. Accelerated and intensified communication at a global level in the field of religion is just as likely to aggravate friction and conflict as to produce reconciliation and harmony. If a global order is emerging in religion it is neither peaceful nor stable.

CONCLUSIONS

My central arguments can be summarized as follows:

- some religions have indirectly facilitated globalization;
- awareness of globalization has elicited some religious responses;
- some religious responses to globalization welcome the opportunity to foster new ideals of universal love and peace;
- other religious responses perceive globalization as a threat to their integrity and influence;
- the advent of a 'global circumstance' and of global media of communication creates as much friction as trust between religious communities;
- religious movements, representing dissatisfaction with conventional religion and commitment to change, tend to be in the forefront of positive and negative responses to globalization.

My speculations about the foreseeable future suggest that, as actors on the fringes of institutional politics, social movements will play an increasingly important role in influencing national and regional 'refraction' of global forces because many of the most perplexing issues will concern identity, solidarity and meaning. Religious movements are also likely to remain important for the intellectual, ideological and emotional resources with which they seek to frame and resolve these issues. The fact that religion functions simultaneously on universalistic and particularistic 'registers' will ensure its continued relevance to life in a globalized future.

12

THE PEACE MOVEMENT

RETROSPECTS AND PROSPECTS

John Mattausch

How and why the peace movement has waxed and waned during this century, and what its future character and significance will be, are questions that may only be addressed by reference to a theory of macro social development. The current pre-eminent discourse emphasizes a 'global logic' which is predicted to override mere regional dynamics. For those of us who remain sceptical over the 'globalization thesis' it is interesting to note that this European conceptual initiative has itself so far failed to make much impact upon North American sociology. Moreover, and as recently noted by Martin and Beittel (1998: 139):

> Much of the focus of the globalization literature has been on the cultural characteristics of the late twentieth century. Indeed, despite the firm material roots provided by accelerating flows of transnational capital and technology, work on globalization has been especially prominent in the area of cultural studies.

Debate rages over the actual evidence and periodization for the globalization thesis, for example, Amin's response (1997) to Hirst and Thompson (1996), but with its non-material emphasis upon cultural topics (religion, identity and consciousness) champions of the thesis would appear to be following the hermeneutic, contra-Enlightenment mode of analysis also favoured by advocates of 'postmodernism'. Yet, this divorce from classic explanatory social theory is, as divorces often are, incomplete and messy for, in common with postmodernists, globalization theorists seem to hold a markedly conventional view of societal change: like their Enlightenment forerunners, these current schools of herme-neutics presume that the global social patterns they identify are destined to supersede older regional sociopolitical formations; in particular, that the nation state with its attendant notions of citizenship will be swept away by a tide of intense, worldwide influences.

This assumption that old sociological patterns are supplanted by new models, an assumption reflected in the titles of books such as Martin Albrow's *The global age* (1996) and in the prefix of postmodernism, betrays, as I shall argue, a legacy of misconceived modernist theory; a misconception arising from the erroneous belief that social life evolves in a successive procession whereby outmoded features, such as militarism and warfare, are superseded by more 'advanced' evolutionary forms, such as legalism and pacifity. Unfortunately, no such simple successive evolutionary process has, in this century, been evident for, despite the optimistic forecasts given by the founders of social science, old societal practices, notably militarism and warfare, have not atrophied but have instead remained stubbornly enduring. Focusing upon the British Campaign for Nuclear Disarmament (CND), a prime component of the wider twentieth-century peace movement and a quintessential new social movement (hereafter, NSM), I consider reasons given for the historical emergence and nature of the Campaign and offer an assessment of its future prospects. This discussion and assessment is made in line with a critique of societal evolutionism still evident in the globalization school. I also take the opportunity to acknowledge mistakes that I made in my earlier research on CND. The lessons to be learnt from these mistakes and from a rejection of the notion that societies evolve informs the conclusions I now draw over the breadth of support, and possible significance, of tomorrow's peace movement.

RETROSPECTS

That international capitalistic enterprise affects our local circumstances and shapes our thinking is, for many, a commonplace. Before the First World War the future renowned playwright J. B. Priestley took his first proper job as a Junior Clerk in a firm of wool exporters. Success in this traditional Bradford trade depended upon accurate knowledge of the international market:

> A man responsible for business of this kind really had to know a good deal, not only about raw wool, tops, noils, yarn, but also about financial conditions in many different countries, which he would visit regularly, calling on his customers.

Priestley, however, never rose to a position of such responsibility and as a lowly Junior Clerk his daily work was 'dull', but nevertheless the firm's international business afforded him perks such as jaunts to Copenhagen and Amsterdam and it could enliven the daily grind of office work with tangible, if peculiar, examples of the firm's global business reach:

> Now and again, it is true, the samples sent to us were not without romantic interest. The muck that came out of the samples of camel hair brought eastern deserts into our office; on the sampling counter was dust from the road to Samarkand. Once I opened a parcel of Chinese pigtails, for

millions of them had been cut off, following a state decree, and somebody in Shanghai was trying to tempt us into a new exotic branch of the trade. (Priestley, 1962: 14)

These exotic examples of international trade were, however, a rare intrusion into the daily office routine, into the tedious, everyday experience of Priestley and most other people whom then, as now, laboured in the world of work fashioned by imperial capitalism.

If the personal experience of international trade was, for Priestley and the majority, dull routine, then the same cannot be said of this century's other forces for global change: war and warfare. Priestley, like too many of his generation, felt the personal and wider impact of war with an intensity that puts the purported effects of the globalization thesis into proper perspective. In later life he reflected upon this impact:

I think the First War cut deeper and played more tricks with time because it was first, because it was bloodier, because it came out of a blue that nobody saw after 1914. The map that came to pieces in 1939 was never the apparently solid arrangement that blew up in 1914 (p 6).

By the time the global map once again 'came to pieces', Priestley had become a successful author: his hopes for the peace found brilliant expression in his best play, *An inspector calls*, written in the final week of 1944. In his final speech the eponymous inspector issues a warning:

We don't live alone. We are members of one body. We are responsible for each other. And I tell you that the time will come when, if men will not learn that lesson, then they will be taught it in fire and blood and anguish.

Tragically, this lesson was not learnt: instead, the aftermath spawned a new condition, the Cold War, a frosty political arrangement of nuclear and non-nuclear capable nation states, made possible by the Bomb. As the thinness of the ice upon which the species now rested became apparent, as knowledge of British nuclear testing was reluctantly revealed to a surprised public, Priestley once again made a moral appeal for a chain-reaction to counter the nuclear one 'leading to destruction'. This appeal, written in 1957, acted as the catalyst to the formation of CND, the Campaign for which Priestley was to become Vice-President.[1]

It might be presumed that given the gravity of the nuclear issue, and the size of the Campaign, the first wave of CND would have attracted substantial research from social scientists. This, however, was not the case. Social science studies upon the first wave of CND (roughly, 1957–64) were small in number and poor in quality. Very few surveys of the Campaign's membership were carried out and these few did not yield reliable data. Analytically, the only notable contemporaneous study was Frank Parkin's well-known work *Middle class radicalism* (1968), a study in political sociology whose title entered the sociologists' lexicon. In common with so many other sociological studies, Parkin had ulterior analytical motives for he was interested more in investigating the activities of middle-class people whom, in obverse parallel to working-class conservatives, held political views seemingly at odds with their class position. This analytical concern encouraged Parkin's neglect of the intrinsic meaning of his respondents' answers to a structured questionnaire in favour of his interpretation that they were evidence of 'alienation' from 'certain dominant social values'. Parkin claimed that middle-class activists had their 'radical' views formed before entering employment and thus sought out work enclaves wherein they would have to make the minimum of compromise, employment in what Parkin termed 'welfare and creative' occupations.

Unfortunately, Parkin only considered male activists, and at the time he carried out his research the Campaign was in steep decline, facing serious internal problems. The net effect of Parkin's theoretical approach led him, as Day and Robbins (1987: 219) later observed, 'to treat support for CND as more or less entirely symbolic of other things'. Nevertheless, Parkin's work had the merit of recognizing the Campaign's socially restricted profile, the lack of any proportional showing from ordinary working people – a crucial stumbling-block for a movement attempting to attract truly mass support, a feature common to all NSMs, and a continuing characteristic of CND when it revived in the late 1970s.

The revival of the Campaign in the late 1970s took social scientists by complete surprise. Indeed, Taylor and Pritchard felt confident to claim (1980: 137) that 'its days as a mass movement had ended by 1964/5', an unfortunate prognosis that was refuted by the rapid resurgence of support evident at the time their book came to be published (necessitating a hasty reconsideration of the Campaign's mass movement potential by the authors in an appendix to their study). Taylor and Pritchard's book, entitled *The protest makers*, was essentially a retrospective study of what they had presumed to be an expired social movement. Their intention was not to produce a history of the Movement, but, rather, an exploration of its 'political and ideological dimensions', the lessons it offered those interested in achieving radical change in Britain, and an analysis of 'the current attitudes and activities of Movement supporters some twenty years later' (1980: vii). Despite these disclaimers their study was, however, informed by a strong historical perspective, unsurprising given Taylor's deep knowledge of the Campaign's political history (the subject of his definitive PhD thesis, 1983). Based upon 400 questionnaires completed by 'core activists' and numerous in-depth interviews, Taylor and Pritchard presented an analysis of what they presumed to be a failed movement, a failure they accounted for in terms of political weaknesses and an evaluation of the Campaign not shared by all of their study sample. For like Parkin, Taylor and Pritchard also took an analytical stance that, by concentrating upon the effects of the activists' campaigning, distanced them from the experiences and stated motives of the early Campaigners: in particular, their chosen analytical approach led them to translate moral positions into political stances (see Mattausch

1989a: 10–14). The broad conclusion they advanced was that CND proved unsuccessful because the Campaign did not pursue 'New Left' political strategies, the only strategies they believed capable of achieving substantive radical change.

Similarly, the Campaign's socially unrepresentative basis of support was explored in the light of political campaigning considerations. Their explanation for the rise of the original CND reflected this orientation: a number of events in the mid-1950s reawakened the radical stratum of British society, a stratum swelled by the 'growth of a new and unique youth culture', feeling 'an increased scepticism and mistrust of the old ideologies and the old institutions' coupled with 'a heightened political atmosphere' (p 6). Several difficulties are contained in this explanation for the rise of the original CND: first, these factors are retrospectively identified and could also be seen as compatible with the growth of any number of dissimilar movements (for instance, they could equally well be used to explain the emergence of an extreme-right organization); second, it cannot account for the limited appeal of CND, limited to only a small percentage of, for example, young people; third, it does not address adequately the avowedly moral character of the first Campaign, a crucial, defining aspect of CND in both of its manifestations (p 3).

The revived Movement came to attract far more attention from social scientists and surveys were larger, more frequent and reliable. This time round the surveys encompassed women as well as men, lay supporters as well as activists. From my own secondary analysis of this survey data (1989a: Appendix C) it is clear that, once again, the Campaign attracted socially unrepresentative support and that this was true of those attending big demonstrations (Nias, 1983), of the national membership (Nias, 1983; Byrne, 1988) and of local CND groups (Day and Robbins, 1987; Mattausch, 1989a). These surveys confirmed the obvious: as noted by Parkin, Taylor and Pritchard and every commentator upon the first CND, the revived Campaign overwhelmingly comprised well-educated supporters likely to be in non-manual employment plus large numbers of younger student supporters. This well educated, middle-class profile was true for both men and women. It seemed to me, when I began my own research in the early 1980s, that I should build upon the findings and insights of earlier studies. Specifically, this seemed to call for an explicit recognition of the Campaign's unrepresentative support and for an analytical strategy that avoided denigrating the supporters' own views over their campaigning (a key failing of Parkin's classic work wherein he argues that CNDers derived psychological satisfaction from their 'expressive politics'). This wish to preserve the integrity of the CNDers' own views stemmed partly from my own sympathy with the Campaign's aims and partly from my adherence to the anti-essentialist argument contained in the later philosophy of Wittgenstein (my covert incentive for studying the Campaign).

On the basis of my interview material I concluded that Parkin had been wrong to assume that middle-class radicals had their views formed prior to entering the world of work; rather the reverse, their education, especially postgraduate professional education, and their experiences at work came to radicalize them. To make this argument I had redefined the occupational sector employing most CNDers, replacing Parkin's 'welfare and creative' tag with my own 'welfare state' label. Thus, education and training for, and experiences of working in, the welfare-state sector as for illustration, social workers, doctors, nurses and teachers, promoted an identification with the ethic of the welfare state, an ethic which spilt out into other areas of their lives such as membership of CND. Working as welfare-state professionals meant imbuing the morality of one's work and thus this group of the population were likely to feel specially affronted by the moral obscenity of nuclear weaponry.

This redefining of the Campaigners' employment, by emphasizing that they were overwhelmingly employed in welfare-state professions allowed me to extend my analysis to embrace the origins, as I then saw it, of the nuclear threat. Drawing upon the then contemporary work by Michael Mann (1987, 1993) and others which drew attention to the 'dual' nature of the state, both domestic and intranational, I concluded that nuclear weapons are always under the control of national states and what had occurred in post-war Britain could be seen as one half of the Jekyll and Hyde state, the highly undemocratic, secret side of the state concerned with international politics and 'defence', generating a danger met with by people involved in the comparatively open, democratic domestic, welfare state. It would seem, on the basis of these conclusions, that an estimation over the future of the peace movement and its possible global dimensions would best be achieved by examining the post-war dual legacy of the reconstructed state that had, in Britain, given us both Beveridge and the Bomb. But such a focus would not be justified for the reasoning, which suggests it is, I have come to realize, mistaken.

That the basis of support for CND, the wider peace movement and indeed all NSMs remains socially specific is in itself unremarkable – is there any organization which does have a socially representative membership? – and may obscure the banal but nonetheless salient fact that, no matter how we may wish to define the supporters, only a small, select *minority* of well-educated, welfare-state professionals or students will sign the membership form. This utterly banal point confounds social deterministic explanation: the correlation between occupational locations, educational status and class position is in fact evidence for a very *weak* causal relationship and one which, in any case, will not address those supporters who do not share these social characteristics.

Similarly with the link between nuclear weaponry and the state: while Weber's observation that modern states monopolize the legitimate use of force finds chilling nuclear expression, an examination of the actual history of the Bomb reveals this link to be delusory. All the major decisions regarding British nuclear weapons have been taken by tiny committees, by handfuls of men, whose purpose and existence has been hidden from governmental scrutiny. Their decisions are only made public when the scale of expenditure demands and then as *fait accomplis*: in the past 50 years this highly secretive non-democratic pattern has been true regardless of which political party held power.

Of course there is influence from the 'military–industrial complex', and as research by Donald MacKenzie (1990) and others clearly shows, there are pressures shaping technological development, but even so crucial decisions remain the prerogative of the (very) few. With respect to nuclear weaponry, crucial decisions are made *despite*, and not because of, the state and its Weberian monopoly upon legitimate force. It is in the light of these earlier errors that I now turn to the second part of this chapter, to the global prospects for the future peace movement.

PROSPECTS

Contrary to Zirakzadeh's three-fold definition of social movements (1997: 4–5), the peace movement did not comprise a group of people seeking to build 'a radically new social order', it did not involve 'people from a wide range of social backgrounds' (a frequent misperception: Mattausch, 1989b), and while some actions may have been 'politically confrontational and socially disruptive', most were well-ordered affairs. Rather, the peace movement comprised people from very limited social backgrounds with widely differing views upon the social order they would prefer (and many who had no such aims). As to unorthodoxy, the form that their political activism took has long, deep roots:

> war resistance in many of its phases was closely linked to notions of egalitarian communal democratisation. Since the seventeenth century, those groups most involved in anti-war activity were those most closely linked to experiments in small-scale democracy of a participatory kind (Young, 1987: 24).

Quite simply, no attempt at definition of the type proposed by Zirakzadeh and other scholars will succeed for they are essentialist in formulation. These definitional strategies will always fail, they will always do injustice to the similarities and differences that, following Wittgenstein, characterize categories. As Bagguley (1995) has shown, in his empirical research upon the British anti-poll tax campaign, even the distinction between 'old' and 'new' social movements is blurred and artificial with campaigners frequently straddling this theoretical divide. Moreover, essentialist positions are incompatible with the dynamic perspective necessary for an understanding of the future of the peace movement in a global context.

Clearly, the appellations 'mass', 'large' or whatever have no real analytical worth when considering the peace movement (when, precisely, does a social movement deserve such adjectives?). What we do know, however, is that even at their height, European and North American peace movements have not been overly popular: membership figures, estimates of informal support or numbers at demonstrations show conclusively that most European and North American citizens are notable by their absence (see Klandermans (1991), for profiles of The Netherlands, West Germany, Belgium, Italian and US campaigns and

Kodama (1989) for Sweden); more people will be at football matches than at meetings or demonstrations. Excepting the small, usually pacifist organizations which persist, the 'peace movement' rises and falls: it is these surges of support which need to be accounted for, periodic surges that are reactive to perceived threats. In order to address the Movement's future prospects, an evolutionary framework which spins both sides of the peace and war coin would be helpful. But, and as is well recognized, theories of societal evolution have kept embarrassingly quiet about war and militarism, *regarding* them as *surpassable* phenomena belonging to earlier phases of societal development an unwarranted belief expressed with characteristic dogmatism by Auguste Comte who, in 1842, felt able to proclaim that 'At last the time has come when serious and lasting war must disappear completely among the human élite' (cited in Aron, 1968: 360). Such sanguine views over the future of 'serious and lasting' wars arose not simply from the general optimism of emerging European expansionism but also, and more profoundly, from an historical misfortune.

Biology only emerged as a separate discipline in the early nineteenth century (helped, ironically by the enthusiasm of Comte who is credited, by his biographer, with championing the new discipline and helping to secure its independent disciplinary status). And, not until more than a decade after the publication of *The cours de positive philosophie* (1893) did Darwin (1985/1865) publish his hypothesis for natural evolution. Consequently, founding theories of societal evolution had been flavoured with erroneous theoretical ingredients including: the notion of acquired inheritance; the belief that the apparent natural order was evidence for planned design; the belief that evolution was a progressive affair; and a progression following a common pattern. Moreover, most clearly expressed in French Positivism, these erroneous evolutionary tenets were married with law-like explanatory methodologies that purported to predict, amongst other things, a pacific future.

The blame for the now apparent failures of these theories of societal evolution and their disproved predictions should not, however, be heaped solely upon social scientists. It was the late development of biology or, and to be more precise, the unfortunate earlier development of sociology which rendered the unity of method claim premature. Indeed, not until Crick and Watson's momentous discoveries, and arguably not until the early 1960s when 'messenger DNA' became identified, did biology deserve methodological emulation from evolutionary social theorists. Which brings us, unavoidably, to the current attempt at a unity of method between natural and social science, to that intellectual parvenu known as 'sociobiology', a parvenu to which I am personally opposed.

Curiously, the High Priest of sociobiology, Edward Wilson, has expressed views on the future of aggression and military conflict acceptable to any nineteenth century optimist:

Although the evidence suggests that the biological nature of humankind launched the evolution of organised aggression and roughly directed its early history across many societies, the eventual outcome of that evolution will be determined by cultural processes brought increasingly under the control of rational thought (1995: 116).

This passage could so easily have been written by Comte: Wilson's optimistic faith in reason extends even unto the nuclear threat:

> Civilisations have been propelled by the reciprocating thrusts of cultural evolution and organised violence, and in our time they have come to within one step of nuclear annihilation. Yet when countries have reached the brink [...] men use reason as a last resort (p 117).

Not only does Wilson echo Comte he, in common with others of a sociobiological persuasion, also makes the same fundamental error of misassuming that 'cultural processes' are comparable to species' transmutations. This attempted methodological emulation is wrong: whereas physical characteristics of a species evolve through a pattern of exclusive supersession, culture (the world of things and customs invented by humans), in contradistinction, incrementally accumulates. Whereas the expression of a genetic complex is always temporally exclusive (at any one time the individual, or the group of individuals, either exhibit a characteristic or they do not), the cultural world always preserves, to some degree, earlier formulations which coexist and may at any time be redeployed (I could have written this using chalk on a blackboard; I need some basic literary skills before I can use either chalk or computer keyboards). Thus, any cultural phenomena bequeathed to offspring will always include, to varying extents, potential earlier models which the individual will also acquire and may redeploy. These earlier models may lie dormant or may be used for limited, specific purposes (we still sign wedding certificates with pen and ink). Older and later models often coexist as, for example, in the case of varying marital arrangements. The individual inherits a cultural repertoire that does not exclude previous forms and so no preservation-or-loss selective process comparable to natural evolution is to be found in cultural developments.

It follows from this picture of cultural development as accumulation that we should not expect, contra Comte *et al.*, social achievements such as wars to be lost in the unfolding of history. So, for instance, when Yugoslavians set out to murder their erstwhile neighbours in the name of ethnic divisions they have not fallen prey to some atavistic drive, rather, they are re-exercising hateful cultural potentials that were never lost but instead preserved as part of the inherited cultural baggage. Cultural development carries forward the nasty as well as the nice achievements of the past.

Past cultural patterns may remain dormant only to be reawoken by the accidental and novel combining of countless small circumstances: some wars and conflict may be planned, to a degree; but equally some, probably the majority, will be just accidental in origin and execution. This common sense view of wars and their origins may be analytically uncomfortable but historically it holds good and thwarts accurate prediction. The events, then, that provoke surges of support for the peace movement cannot with any certainty be predicted. Can, we, nonetheless, specify who will be provoked to protest against war and/or campaign for peace?

Using the example of past upsurges in support for CND, it is clear that simple perception of a threat will not in itself lead to a growth of the peace movement. A further element is needed, a moral call to arms: campaigns for peace assume moral expression which will find only limited appeal from the public. Why is this appeal limited? Why are only a minority moved by these moral messages?

Like the continuation and unpredictability of war and conflict, moral behaviour has proved difficult for social theorists and for much the same historical reasons. Given the Enlightenment legacy of optimism and the erroneous post-Humean view of societal evolution in which it was embedded, knowledge ruled by reason, divorced from morality, became the focus of theory and the stepping-stone for evolutionary progress. To be effective, reason had to be a human universal and a universal which, as Edward Wilson apparently still believes, will come to override other reasons for action including, presumably, ethical ones.

To ask why moral appeals to campaign for peace influence minorities is to ask why some people are more or less susceptible than their companions: this is a matter of *degree* and not some essentialist distinction between those who are influenced from those who are not, nor less a distinction between the 'good' and the 'bad'. Here, natural evolutionary theory does yield useful analogies, for following Darwin, the importance of small differences is often stressed; small differences may yield big outcomes: similarly, very small differences in moral susceptibility may make the difference between joining a campaign or not. Moral susceptibility is like tastes in music; most, but not everyone, will enjoy music, not everybody will dance to the same tune, some will be unusually responsive, some wholly indifferent, a very few will detest each note. Nonetheless, who exactly will be moved to action by moral messages for peace, and how exactly they will act, is conditioned by a host of further factors such as the individual's other commitments, their particular circumstances, the available resources or the attitude of friends. Just as it has not proved possible to predict in advance the threats which provoked the peace movement, so too it has not proved possible to predict the volume of support for the peace reaction nor the precise identity of the supporters (Who knew how many people would oppose the American attack on Khartoum? Were you amongst their number?).

In the past, the peace movement has grown spontaneously in response to a perceived threat. The usual campaigning strategy has been to win over as many people as possible, to build a 'mass' movement for peace. This strategy has never been successful. International links have been formed, specifically pan-European campaigns launched (e.g. European Nuclear Diasarmament – END) and there have been numerically impressive Europe-wide demonstrations (the largest, to my knowledge, having taken place in 1983 when some 5 million people took

to the streets of European capital cities). Nevertheless, such big protest demonstrations are the exception and the growth of support for a pan-European peace
movement appears to have been drawn from a small minority sharing the same
limited social constituency (this was particularly true for END, members of
which were overwhelmingly employed in higher education). Should we expect
the peace movement to achieve greater 'global reach' in the future, and if so,
how? The answers to these questions depends, of course, upon how the present
international situation, and the current position of Europe in particular given
that the peace movement has, so far, largely been a European phenomenon – are
envisaged. NSM theorists appear to be following the current hermeneutic trend
towards cultural analysis, as acknowledged by Johnston and Klandermans in
their Editorial Introduction to a selection of conference papers on NSMs: *Social
movements and culture* (1995: 3). In so doing these NSM theorists, in concert
with social scientists working in diverse other areas, are following the general acceptance of the postmodernist tenet that European societies are entering
(or have already entered) a distinctively new phase of societal development,
a phase calling for distinctively new analytical tools and approaches. Such a view
is, however, still grounded in the erroneous conception of societal evolution
I disputed earlier. It is not the case that 'modernity' has been, or indeed ever
could be, wholly superseded: cultural developments of the past do not just go
away; past patterns of imperialism, nationalism and ethnic identifications do not
have an expiry date (as should be all too clear from the spectacle of change in
Eastern Europe and the former Soviet Union). Instead, what we are witnessing is
the grafting on to the past of adopted cultural features; notably, at present, the
grafting of capitalism on to increasingly disparate national cultures. This accum-
ulative grafting process does not mean, contrary to expectation, that bourgeois
individualism, or whatever, will come to extinguish the earlier ways in which
individuals think of themselves and their companions. Nor should we expect
nation states, imperialism, nationalism, patriotism or religious sentiment to be
supplanted by a new global era.

That we cannot predict the future, and that the condition of the species is the
outcome of countless accidents, are the true, unpalatable lessons of neo-Darwin-
ism when applied in its proper domain of natural evolution. With regard to
societal change, a partly comparable pattern of development is evident although
here, in the cultural sphere, the wayward nature of change is to be explained not
by the selection and preservation of fortuitous random characteristics but, rather,
by the accumulation of alternative cultural technologies influenced by chance
occurrences. It is within this ever changing, ever expanding cultural sphere that
the peace movement must find expression.

CONCLUSION

In this century the peace movement has been largely reactive in character, surges
of protest and dissent that rise and fall. These surges of support have proved
impossible to predict with any accuracy partly because the perceived threats have

themselves been unanticipated. The significance of the Movement has lain less in its specific achievements and more in its bequest to future campaigners. This bequest has included campaigning skills, experience, knowledge and inspiration. In this sense, the peace movement, like other cultural phenomena, never expires; indeed, each reactive surge of protest and dissent adds more to the legacy, to the growing repertoire of tactics and strategies from which future campaigners may select (thus, for illustration, a Hindu caste custom of bargaining through the threat of self-harm was adapted by Gandhi to oust the British, copied by the Black Civil Rights' movement, practised by early British anti-nuclear testing groups, then by the Committee of 100, later by mainstream CNDers and is at present a common weapon in the fight against destructive road development and in countless other protests). The progress of the peace movement is, therefore, conditioned by the heritage of previous campaigns and not simply by the character of the campaigners nor the particular threat which they face.

Contrary to some current expectations, the sociopolitical patterning of Europe will not be governed by global capitalism and nor will a globalized consciousness replace earlier notions of individualism and group identities. Instead, globalism will simply add another strand from which such patterns and identities may be woven. When, in 1980, E. P. Thompson launched the appeal for a nuclear-free Europe (1980: 223–6), the continent was still split by the post-war agreements and in the winter of the Cold War. The continental changes that have occurred in the intervening two decades were inconceivable not simply because the collapse of the Soviet Empire and the Warsaw Pact had been unexpected but also because the re-emergence of national and ethnic groups had not been predicted. We may reasonably expect the future development of Europe and of other continents to follow this unpredictable pattern wherein resurrected and innovative group alliances combine. Excepting in those circumstances that demand their involvement, most people will remain indirerent or apathetic even when confronted by clear portents of war. A few, a minority, will act for peace. Luckily, however, the resources upon which this minority can draw include a heritage from previous campaigns: and, sometimes, calls for peace like other moral messages may find only a small audience at first but with the passage of time become popular when Priestley's *An inspector calls* was first performed at the Old Vic it met with 'a cool, almost hostile, reception' (1962: 195), but subsequently 'it went all over the world' and has become probably his most popular work, the world over. Chance, the true motor of societal development, does not favour war anymore than it does peace.

NOTES

CHAPTER ONE

1   This suggestion was made first, so far as we are aware, by Sylvie Ollitraut, from the University of Rennes, in lectures at the Maison Française, Oxford, in 1998. We regret that we have been unable to consult her published work on the environmental movement.

CHAPTER THREE

1   For example, practices of chattel slavery, apartheid, trafficking in human beings, sex-based discrimination and violence, lynch-justice, the emergent semi-feudal formations of labour exploitation at the very heart of contemporary economic globalization.

2   This caveat is important. International human rights enunciations, being productions of politics of, and not always for, human rights, do not always speak to human suffering and immiseration. See Baxi (2000)

3   When abandoning my work as the Vice Chancellor of South Gujarat University, Surat, I visited Bhopal in the first week of the catastrophe I found swarms of international television people and contingency fee lawyers from the United States in search of clients who would authorize them to file suits. Bhopal was a big story for the international media and an ample source of revenue.

4   These are: Bhopal Gas Peedit Mahila Udyog Sangathan (BGPMUS) and Zahreeli Gas Kand Sngarash Morcha (ZGKSM). The names are revealing. BGPMUS proclaims itself as an 'organization'; ZGKSM as a 'movement' or 'struggle.' BGPMUS emphasizes suffering of oppressed peoples (*pidit*, not being a translatable word in English); ZGKSM directs its struggle towards the epoch or the era of the toxic gas. BGPMUS proclaims itself to be an organization of women victims and develops an overwhelming base among them; ZGKSM is a movement of victims as a class. Associated are at least five other relatively autonomous movements: Bhopal Gas Peedeet Sahyog Samiti (Committee for Co-operation of Bhopal Gas Affected Victims); Jana Swastha Kendra (People's Health Centre); Bhopal Group for Information and Action; Gas Peedit Sangarash Morcha (The Association – lit. platform – of the Gas Affected Peoples in struggle); Gas Rahat Evam Punarwas Trust (Trust for Relief and Rehabilitation of Gas Affected Peoples). In addition, various environmental and human rights groups related themselves to the struggle: Ekklavya (Bhopal); Delhi Science Forum; Peoples' Union of Civil Liberties (PUCL); Peoples' Union for Democratic Rights (PUDR); coalition of medical professionals based primarily at the All India Medical Institute. Retired Supreme Court Justices, notably Justices Krishna Iyer and P. N. Bhagwati, eminent lawyers and public officials (notably P. N. Haksar) and media personalities (notably Nikhil Chakraborty) endowed by their association the Bhopal groups with a national visibility. See, for a contemporary account of diversity of Bhopal movement, contributions to 6 Lokayan Bulletin (1988).

5   These latter comprised The Bhopal Action Research Center (BARC), New York, and the International Coalition of Justice for Bhopal (ICJIB), both owing a great deal to the initiatives of Dr Ward Morehouse, President, The Council of International and Public Affairs, New York. The Permanent Peoples' Tribunal had several sessions (New Haven, Bangkok, Bhopal and London) on Hazardous Industries and Human Rights focusing primarily on Bhopal where victim groups testified to their plight and the spirit of their struggle. In addition, an International Medical Commission reported in 1994 on the long-term and mutagenic impact of MIC exposure. Many groups across the world have maintained web sites on Bhopal, which has sustained sharing of information and planned action, at least on each anniversary of Bhopal.

6   There is a lethal continuity between the project of Green Revolution and Bhopal. Extensive chemicalization of agriculture was the order of the day in the late 1960s when the Government of India decided not to import MIC-based processes or products under the auspices of USAID and

commenced indigenous production of MIC-based insecticides and pesticides. It invited Union Carbide to design and set up a plant in India and allowed the production and storage of huge quantities of MIC on site, contrary to the best industry practices. It allowed (despite conscientious protest by the Chief Secretary, Government of Madhya Pradesh, Mr M. N. Buch) the location of the plant in the vicinity of a growing area where the urban impoverished lived. And the state government took no action whatsoever on an accidental leakage at the plant which killed two employees. The warnings concerning the outdated security system were ignored.

7   On the bureaucratization of suffering see Baxi (ed.) (1986: 30–4).

8   In essence, claiming that hazardous enterprises owe duties of compensation and reparation not mitigated by defences including exculpation on the ground of *force majeure* or acts of God, events beyond rational contemplation. For the precise legal formulation see Baxi and Paul (1985) and Cassels (1993).

9   India states, on a sworn affidavit, that her legal system is undeveloped to justice in situations of mass disasters (Baxi and Paul, 1985: 165–99). The averment that the 'Bar in India does not presently possess the pool of skills, the fund of experience, or the organizational capacity' to pursue efficiently and effectively 'massive and complex litigation' turned out to be more of a toxic insult to the Indian legal profession than the MIC ingested into several hundred thousand victims! As a result, socialist lawyers unsuccessfully challenged the validity of the Bhopal Act before the Supreme Court (Baxi and Dhanda, 1990: 550–635).

10   In the review proceedings of the settlement order where we argued that these be set aside as the court had not heard the violated of Bhopal, who were full petitioners. An exasperated Supreme Court of India had to acknowledge that it gave no due process hearing to victims in passing the orders. But the court, citing the Bard of Avon, observed that at times a little wrong has to be done to accomplish a great right! The violated of Bhopal were not well versed either in Shakespeare or Dicey were wonder-struck at a process where doing of manifest injustice requires reasons! They asked me not to be overly perturbed (until this day I have not written a critique of this judgement) but instead focus on that which was achieved, the conscience-stricken striking down of criminal immunities conferred on Carbide. One of them said to me: 'Bhai (brother) you have worked so hard in this case (review proceedings). Please look at the bright side. After all, did not we bring back *ijjat* (honour) to the Supreme Court?' Her words still resonate. Though the judicial process re-victimized them again and again, to the violated of the Bhopal restoring of the *ijjat* of India's summit court constituted an important part of the overall movement against Carbide.

11   This symbolic power of representation affects, at the end of the day, the judicial review of the settlement orders, which while tortuously upholding these orders, makes the Supreme Court of India cancel the immunities from criminal prosecution granted initially to Union Carbide. Carbide shuns the criminal jurisdiction of the Bhopal Sessions Court and is now declared by it as an 'absconder,' a fugitive felon, the first multinational in the Twentieth Christian Century to 'enjoy' this status. The violated of Bhopal are now seeking to constrain the Indian state to seek the extradition of the corporate management to stand criminal trial. Stockholders of the Union Carbide Annual General Meeting on April 28, 1999, at Danbury, Connecticut, which I addressed (along with Ward Morehouse and Clarence Dias) were heard to say (as we were addressing a television interview after the meeting) 'Let us get away from the fumes of Bhopal!'

12   We lack a history of the Bhopal movement, outside the legal or juridical narrative. But when it is written the significance of my observations will be fully borne out. Women gave voice to human suffering in Bhopal; they provided the movement with a tenacity of purpose, the single-minded pursuit of Union Carbide; they attended public events in large numbers, often outnumbering men; they presented the case of the violated before national and international fora with a poignant dignity; and they, overall, provided integrity to the movement on occasions when the male leaders were tempted by party political processes. I was privileged to witness, and even take part in, the trends I describe. The fact that most women were Muslim also bears a mention. The devout among them brought an element of piety to the entire movement. Their leadership and participation ruptures a whole genre that depicts them as subservient to a tradition that endows men with the exclusive and belligerent occupation of the public sphere.

CHAPTER FIVE

1   There are three levels of status within ECOSOC arrangements: I, or general status, is available to groups which are concerned with most of the activities of the UN and represent major segments of the population; II, or special status, is available to groups with an expertise in only a few areas; and

the Roster is available for those groups which can make an occasional and useful contribution to the work of ECOSOC (ECOSOC resolution 1296, XLIV).

2   The 1995 NGO Forum that ran in conjunction with the Fourth World Conference on Women in Beijing was organized by the established NGOs with consultative status.

3   Many of these were published by 2ed Press in their Women and World Development Series.

4   The information in the following paragraphs was gleaned from interviews with members of the established groups and officials of the UN Secretariat, personal observation at international conferences and a review of several newsletters from established groups including the IAW and Women's International Democratic Federation.

5   At least two new international groups related to women's health emerged in the 1990s – the Global Alliance for Women's Health and the International Women's Health Coalition. Both were very active in the 1994 Cairo Conference on Population and Development and the 1990 and 1995 Cairo meetings.

6   ISIS-WICCE moved to Kampala, Uganda, in 1993. It continues its exchange programme and publishes collected feminist material from around the world for women in Africa. The ISIS International office in Santiago also boosts the Latin American and Caribbean Women's Health Network.

7   Several significant new global women's networks have been created in the 1990s to support women who are interested and involved in using information and communications technologies including the Association for Progressive Communications' Women's Net and Virtual Sisterhood. See Stienstra (1999a).

8   Women from the South have continued to be at the forefront pushing for the recognition of the importance of these issues. DAWN has advocated throughout the 1990s for governments to address the impacts that macro-economic policies have on women.

9   Significant coalitions of women's groups have formed over the 1990s. Alianza or the Women's Global Alliance for Economic Justice began as a boss network in 1990 and continues to work to address feminist gender analysis to globalization. It draws together DAWN, WEDO, WIDE, the Centre for Women's Global Leadership and other national and international groups. WEDO also hosts women taking on the WTO.

10 The Global Alliance Against Trafficking in Women (GAATW), formed in 1994, is a network of over 100 organizations working to end trafficking in women.

11 FINRRAGE was initially known as FINNRET (Feminist International Network on New Reproductive Technologies) but its name was changed during the 1985 emergency conference on new reproductive technologies. (Feminist Forum, 1984, 1985a, b.)

12 My thanks to Joan Grant-Cummings and Marilyn Porter for their first-hand accounts of Alianza.

Bibliographic note

To reduce the number of references I have avoided detailed citations to the following magazines, journals and newsletters, which nonetheless are very important sources of information for scholars interested in the field:

AFSC Women's Newsletter, various dates;
Connexions, various dates;
Forum 80, various dates;
ISIS International Bulletin, various dates;
WIN News, various dates;
Woman's World, various dates;
Women in Action, various dates;
Women's International Network News, various dates;
Women's News, various dates;
Women's Studies International Forum, various dates;
WorldWIDE News: World Women in Defense of the Environment, Newsletter, various dates.

CHAPTER SEVEN

1   Between October 1991 and October 1993 I was employed as the Research Officer for the ICFTU Co-ordinating Committee on Central and Eastern Europe. Some of the information used in this chapter was derived from my experiences working for the ICFTU.

2   This chapter does not consider the issue of international trade union co-operation within multi-national corporations (MNCs). For an account of developments in this area see Ramsay, 1997.
3   For a more detailed description of international trade union structures see Windmuller and Pursey (1998). This section draws heavily on their account.
4   This organization is not considered within this chapter. Competition with the WFTU was what defined the politics of the ICFTU; the far smaller WCL was generally viewed as little more than an irritant.
5   For the classic critique of the ICFTU's activity in the developing world see Thomson and Larson (1978).
6   The only exception to this was the case of Poland, where the flight of millions of members from the official Central Council of Trade Unions (CRZZ) after the establishment of Solidarnosc in 1980 led to the dissolution of this organization and the formation of the nominally more 'independent' OPZZ in 1984 with the express intention of breaking Solidarnosc. In the case of the Soviet Union, the VTsSPS asserted its independence from the Party in 1987 and in 1990 the official branch organizations began to establish republican organizations.
7   For a general overview of the development of independent trade unions in the region see Ashwin (1994).
8   For more details see Ashwin (1994: 141–2).
9   While working for the ICFTU Central and East European desk I frequently felt very uncomfortable when trying to explain to worker activists from independent unions why the ICFTU and many of its European affiliates were co-operating with the former communist trade unions. These unionists certainly saw it as a betrayal, and from the perspective of their invariably cramped and makeshift offices, it was difficult not to be sympathetic.
10 This even-handed approach sometimes proved problematic, however. For example, the former Miners' International Federation (MIF, now part of the International Federation of Chemical, Energy, Mine and General Workers' Union (ICEM)) had big problems in negotiating its relations with the mining unions in Russia which were deeply divided between the anti-communist NPG and the former communist mine workers' trade union. Meanwhile, the Public Service Workers' International, had problems in expanding its activities in Russia because its first affiliate was a very small independent trade union.
11 In Russia, at a national level the principal struggle in which independent trade unions were engaged in 1994 was over individual and collective access to US funds (Clarke et al., 1995: 404).
12 For details see Clarke et al. (1995: 1590).
13 On Hungary see Tóth (1993); on Russia see Ashwin (1995, 1997) and Ilyin (1996).
14 This occurred in Lithuania in early 1993, Poland in autumn 1993 and Hungary in spring 1994, while in countries such as Romania and Slovakia it can be argued that the communists were never really ousted in the first place.
15 For details see Ashwin (1995).
16 An editorial of the theoretical journal of the Communist Party of the USA declared Sweeney's election to be 'nothing less than historic ... the most dramatic expression of the fact that a turning point in the class struggle is now taking place'.
17 This is not to say that the struggle for workers' rights per se was entirely neglected, but it was often relegated to second place after 'political' concerns. Usually, when members of the ICFTU secretariat used the phrase, 'It's political', it had Cold War rather than trade union connotations.
18 Moody (1997) and Waterman (1998), both advocates of social-movement unionism, are critical of the organizational form of the ICFTU, which Moody defines as a 'labor bureaucracy three times removed ... far removed from the reality of today's workplace' (p 229). But although it is possible to imagine international solidarity taking the form of a multiplicity of alliances between different trade unions over particular issues, it is difficult to see how an international confederation of the world's trade unions could be anything other than what Moody disparagingly refers to as a 'federation of federations' (p 229). Any move towards a more horizontal or organic form of organization, while superficially attractive, would raise major questions regarding representation and democracy.
19 Moody (1997) claims that the end of the Cold War has led to 'a shift to the right in the politics of the ICFTU leadership' (p 230). This is an over-simplification. As discussed below, it is difficult firmly to categorize the current political strategy of the ICFTU, but at least part of it – 'a commitment to union growth and recruitment' – overlaps with Moody's own vision of social-movement unionism (p 290). Writing from a similar perspective, Waterman (1998: 111–32) provides a more balanced assessment of the post-Cold War changes in the ICFTU. His main emphasis is on the support policies of the ICFTU in the developing world. He argues that the ICFTU has begun to

shift away from its Cold War criteria, although he notes that in a number of countries it remains bound by some of its more dubious alliances with right-wing anti-communist trade unions.

20 The text that the ICFTU is proposing for the WTO (and similar international agreements) is:

> The contracting parties agree to take steps to ensure the observance of the minimum labour standards specified by an advisory committee to be established by the WTO and the ILO, and including those on freedom of association and the right to collective bargaining, the minimum age for employment, discrimination, equal remuneration and forced labour (ICFTU, 1997: 18).

21 For example, the May 1997 congress of the ICFTU African regional organization (ICFTU–AFRO) adopted a strong statement calling for a workers' rights clause in the WTO. How far this will translate into action supported by trade union members is another question.

22 A report on the campaign at the March 1998 meeting of the ICFTU Co-ordinating Committee on Central and Eastern Europe did not generate a great deal of interest among the Central and East European affiliates present (author's own observation).

23 This parallels the strategy of many branch and national trade unions in the hostile environment created by intensified global competition. British unions have been attempting to counter employer hostility to unions by arguing that they can 'add value' to business through improving employee relations and hence increasing productivity, as well as through 'managing change', by selling restructuring to workers in return for a voice. The problem with this justification for trade unionism is that research into the economic effects of unions tends to show that these benefits to the employer only accrue when product markets are competitive and where industrial relations are not conflictual (Freeman, 1992): that is, where unions are either weak or co-operative, but not when they are assertive and 'demanding'.

24 This is also a key contradiction in the World Bank's discussion of trade unions. On the one hand, its 1995 report recognized that unions might have an important role to play in the political integration of labour in dynamic economies. Moreover, the fact that 'organised labour is often in the vanguard of the movement towards greater political openness and democracy' (p 5) was noted in relation to the role of Solidarnosc and the South African trade unions. But democracy is clearly a dangerous thing for the World Bank if one of its effects is that trade unions decide they do not want to be confined to the minimal role prescribed for them by neo-liberals. The report's implicit answer to this is that democracy has to be balanced by the impersonal discipline of the market. When such discipline is absent and demands go beyond the constraints imposed by the market, organized labour is portrayed as a disruptive force pressing its claims at the expense of unorganized workers. But this is only a formal resolution to a complex political problem. As Elson has pointed out the section of the report which considers public sector workers ignores the possibility that strikes by public sector unions may be in support of the struggles of the general public, while, not surprisingly, the transformatory potential of unions in reshaping socio-economic conditions in ways that benefit non-unionized sectors is not considered (Elson, 1995: 5).

25 In its 1996 conference publication the ICFTU identified the organization of women, young people and workers in the informal sector as among the major factors which would influence the ability of trade unions to defend workers in the twenty-first century (ICFTU, 1996a: 64).

26 See ICFTU (1996b).

27 An example of an ICFTU campaign that drew on increased consumer sensitivity was the initiative supported by number of international union federations to get FIFA, soccer's world governing body, to eradicate child labour in the production of soccer balls. The revelation that the souvenir balls produced for the June 1996 European Championship had been produced by child labour in Pakistan proved highly embarrassing, and, in September 1996, after negotiations with the ICFTU, FIFA was persuaded to adopt a code of labour practice.

CHAPTER EIGHT

1 I would like to acknowledge the useful comments made on earlier drafts of this chapter by Matthew Paterson, John MacMillan, Shirin Rai and Robin Cohen.

2 I use the term transnational corporations here to denote the fact that most of the TNCs being discussed here such as McDonald's and Shell are primarily western owned and therefore control and decision-making is concentrated within the western branches of these organizations. Given that power, resources and authority are not diffused throughout the organizations, the term 'multi' may therefore exaggerate the global scope of the company (Gill and Law, 1988).

3   This process has been aided by the use of metaphors such as 'Spaceship Earth' and phrases like 'Our Common Future' to obscure blame and extend responsibility (Yearley, 1996).

4   It should be noted, however, that for Sklair this elite is not made up of environmental groups alone but green bureaucrats, politicians, professionals and green media (1994: 212).

5   Clearly, in many ways the state has extended its authority in new directions in dealing with environmental problems, defining a new role for itself in the face of a legitimization crisis. This has involved the creation or extension of bureaucracy, increased monitoring of pollution and of course establishing ongoing rounds of international negotiations in which governments themselves are the key players. In broad terms in can be argued that freeing up regulations also strengthens the state because governments become more competitive and are able to accumulate more wealth. See Saskia Sassen (1996).

6   The case of Nestlé is illustrative in this respect where the company was said to have drafted codes of conduct in relation to the marketing of baby milk that went on to be implemented almost verbatim in a number of transition country parliaments.

7   As Sachs argues:

> the emergence of a globe as an economic arena where capital, goods and services can move with little consideration for local and national communities has delivered the most serious blow to the idea of a polity which is built on reciprocal rights and duties among citizens. ... Through transnationalisation, capital escapes any links of loyalty to a particular society' (1997: 10).

8   Humphreys (1997) highlights the case of the Sun company (a petroleum-refining company) who have used their endorsement of the Valdez principles to gain credibility when lobbying against environmental legislation in Congress.

9. It should be noted here that the use of the term by Haufler (1995) to describe regimes in which exclusively private sector agents participate, is different from my use of the term to imply a non-governmental arena for the 'regulation' of the activities of private-sector actors (by NGOs).

10. Ritzer uses the term 'McDonaldization' to describe a 'wide-ranging process ... by which the principles of the fast-food restaurant are coming to dominate more and more sectors of American society as well as the rest of the world' (1993: 1).

11. Mittelman suggests the use of the term 'move' rather than movement to describe similar 'micro-counter-globalizing tendencies' to recognize the proto forms of such activities before the transformative potential of a 'true' Polanyian counterforce can be ascribed to them (Mittelman, 1998: 867). For other applications of Polanyi's work in relation to environmental resistance to globalization, see Mittelman (1998) and Glover (1999).

CHAPTER NINE

1   The Gaia hypothesis, advanced by independently minded scientist J. Lovelock, proposes that living systems are connected in a vast web of symbiosis; in other words, planetary life is somehow 'co-ordinated' in a way which keeps the plant suited to the continuance of life. In a sense, the entire biosphere can be seen as a 'superorganism' which plays a vital role in the regulation of environmental conditions on earth (see Yearley, 1992: 144–7).

2   *The Ecologist* magazine contains a 'Campaigns and News' feature in each issue; no details of authorship are given. Information from this source has been referenced in the text not in the bibliography.

3   The interview data derive from a continuing study of environmentalisms [sic!] in York. These data arose from focus-group sessions designed by both authors but conducted by Forrester. The sessions were transcribed in full and then independently analysed by the two authors before agreed interpretations were advanced.

CHAPTER ELEVEN

1   See Beckford (1973), Bromley and Shupe (1979), Barker (1984) and Chryssides (1991).

2   See White (1970), Hashimoto and McPherson (1976) and Wilson and Dobbelaere (1994).

3   According to Article 28 of this Constitution, ratified in December 1993,

> every person is guaranteed freedom of conscience, freedom of confession, including the right to confess any religion, individually or together with others, or to confess none, to freely choose, hold and propagate religious or other convictions and to act in accordance with them.

4   Some idea of the vast range of interactions between social movements and religious movements could be had at the World's Parliament of Religions held in Chicago in 1993.

5   I owe much of this section to Gold (1991) and to Bhatt (1997).

CHAPTER TWELVE

1   I consider the historical emergence, development and eventual demise of the first wave of CND in Mattausch (1991).

ACKNOWLEDGEMENTS

Warm thanks are due to Professor Richard Higgott, Director of the Centre for the Study of Globalization and Regionalization, University of Warwick, for sponsoring the conference that preceded the development of this book. We are delighted that *Global Social Movements* is published with the support and imprimatur of the Centre. Jill Southam, the Centre's administrator, sorted out the conference logistics with her customary eciency. The Vice-Chancellor of Warwick University, Professor Sir Brian Follett, and the then Pro-Vice-Chancellor, Professor Robert Burgess, provided generous hospitality.

Anna Winton, administrator at the Transnational Communities Programme, gave stalwart help at the editing stage. Steven Vertovec, the Programme's Director, was also helpful. So much of the crucial work on globalization and transnationalism in the UK is anchored at these two units that readers are advised to consult their sites at *www.csgr.org* and *www.transcomm.ox.ac.uk* from time to time. Their sponsor, the Economic and Social Research Council, is to be congratulated for making such wise and productive investments in 'blue skies' and applied research.

R. C. and S. M. R.

BIBLIOGRAPHY

AAFS (n.d.) *Lessening the burden for women*, Advocates for African Food Security, pamphlet.

AAWORD (n.d.) *Aims of the organization*, Association of African Women for Research and Development, pamphlet.

Aberle, David (1966) *The Peyote religion among the Navaho*, Chicago: Aldine Aboriginal Policy Round-table on APEC (1997), Discussion Paper No.1 at *http://www.usasask.ca/nativelaw/apect_policy.html*.

Adam, B. (1996) 'Detraditionalization and the certainty of uncertain futures', in Paul Heelas, Scott Lash and Paul Morris (eds) *Detraditionalization: critical reflections on authority and identity*, Oxford: Blackwell, 134–48.

Adriance, M. (1991) 'Agents of change: the roles of priests, sisters, and lay workers in the grassroots Catholic Church in Brazil', *Journal for the Scientific Study of Religion*, 30 (3): 292–305.

Afkhami, Mahnaz and Friedl, Erika (eds) (1997) *Women and the politics of participation: implementing the Beijing platform*, Syracuse: Syracuse University Press.

Afshar, Haleh (ed.) (1998) *Women and empowerment: illustrations from the Third World*, London: Macmillan.

Agnew, J. and Corbridge, S. (1995), *Mastering space: hegemony, territory and international political economy*, London: Routledge.

Aho, James (1991) *The politics of righteousness: Idaho Christian patriotism*, Seattle: University of Washington Press.

Aho, James (1996) 'Popular Christianity and political extremism in the United States', in C. Smith (ed.) *Disruptive religion*, New York: Routledge, 189–204.

Al-Azmeh, Aziz (1993) *Islams and modernities*, London: Verso.

Albrow, Martin (1996) *The global age: state and society beyond modernity*, Cambridge: Polity Press.

Amin, A. (1997) 'Placing globalisation', *Theory, Culture & Society*, 14 (2): 123–37.

Amoure, L. *et al.* (1997) 'Overturning "globalisation": resisting the teleological, reclaiming the politica', *New Political Economy*, 2 (1).

Appadurai, Arjun (1995) 'The production of locality', in Richard Fardon (ed.), *Counterworks: managing the diversity of knowledge*, London: Routledge, 204–25.

Arendt, Hannah (1958) *The human condition*, Chicago: Chicago University Press.

Aron, R. (1968) 'War and industrial society', in L. Bramson and G. W. Goethals (eds) *War*, London: Basic Books.

Arrighi, G. (1996) 'Workers of the world at century's end', *Review*, 19 (3).

Arrington, L. J. and Bitton, D. (1979) *The Mormon experience*, London: George Allen & Unwin.

Asad, Talal (1997) 'On torture, or cruel, inhuman or degrading treatment', in Arthur Kleinman, Veena Das and Margaret Lock (eds) *Social suffering*, Berkeley: University of California Press, 285.

Ashwin, S. (1991) 'The 1991 miners' strike: new departures in the independent workers' movement' *Report on the USSR*, 3 (33): 1–7.

Ashwin, S. (1994) 'Trade unions after the fall of communism in Eastern Europe and Russia' *Journal of Area Studies*, 5: 137–52.

Ashwin, S. (1995) 'Russia's official trade unions: renewal or redundancy?' *Industrial Relations Journal*, 26 (3): 192–203.

Ashwin, S. (1997) 'Shopfloor trade unionism in Russia: the prospects of reform from below', *Work, Employment and Society*, 11 (1): 115–31.

Ashworth, Georgina (ed.) (1995) *A diplomacy of the oppressed: new directions in international feminism*, London: Zed Books.

Bachrach, P. and Baratz, M. S. (1962) 'Two faces of power', *American Political Science Review*, 56: 47–52.

Bagguley, Paul (1995) 'Protest, poverty and power: a case study of the anti-poll tax movement', *The Sociological Review*, 43 (4): 693–719.

Bagguley, Paul (1999) 'Beyond emancipation? The reflexivity of social movements,' in Martin O'Brien, Sue Penna and Collin Hay (eds) *Theorizing modernity: reflexivity, environment and identity in Giddens' Social Theory*, London: Longman.

Bainbridge, William S. (1997) *The sociology of religious movements*, New York: Routledge.

Bakker, Isabella (ed.) (1996) *Rethinking restructuring: gender and change in Canada*, Toronto: University of Toronto Press.

Barbé, D. (1987) *Grace and power: base communities and nonviolence in Brazil*, Maryknoll, NY: Orbis Books.

Barker, Eileen V. (1984) *The making of a Moonie*, Oxford: Blackwell.

Bastide, Roger (1978) *The African religions of Brazil*, Baltimore: Johns Hopkins University Press.

Basu, Amrita (ed.) (1995) *The challenge of local feminisms: women's movements in global perspective*, Boulder, CO: Westview.

Baxi, Upendra (1982) *The crisis of the Indian legal system*, Delhi: Vikar.

Baxi, Upendra (ed.) (1986) *Inconvenient forum and convenient catastrophe: the Bhopal case*, Bombay: N. M. Tripathi.

Baxi, Upendra (1993) *Marx, law and justice*, Bombay: N. M. Tripathi.

Baxi, Upendra (1996) ' "Global neighbourhood" and the "universal otherhood": notes on the Report of the Commission on Global Governance', *Alternatives*, 22: 525–49.

Baxi, Upendra (1999) 'Voices of suffering, fragmented universality and the future of human rights', in Burns H. Weston and Stephen P. Marks (eds) *The future of international human rights*, Ardsley, NY: Transnational Publishers, 101–56.

Baxi, Upendra (2000) *The future of human rights,* Delhi: Oxford University Press.

Baxi, Upendra and Amita, Dhadha (eds) (1990) *Valiant victims and lethal litigation*, Bombay: N. M. Tripathi.

Baxi, Upendra and Paul, Thomas (eds) (1985) *Mass disasters and multinational liability: the Bhopal case*, Bombay: N. M. Tripathi.

Beck, Ulrich (1992) *The risk society*, London: Sage Publications.

Beck, Ulrich (1996) *The reinvention of politics*, Cambridge: Polity Press.

Beck, Ulrich (1998) 'Politics of risk society', in Jane Franklin (ed.) *The politics of the risk society*, Cambridge: Polity Press, 9–22.

Beck, Ulrich, Giddens, Anthony and Lash, Scott (1994) *Reflexive modernization*, Cambridge: Polity Press.

Beckford, James A. (1973) 'A Korean evangelistic movement in the West.' *The contemporary metamorphosis of religion?* Acts of the 12th Conférence internationale de la Sociologie des Religions, The Hague, 319–35.

Beckford, James A. (1975) *The trumpet of prophecy: a sociological study of Jehovah's Witnesses*, Oxford: Blackwell.

Beckford, James A. (1977) 'The Watchtower movement worldwide', *Social Compass*, 24 (1): 5–31.

Beckford, James A. (1985) *Cult controversies: the societal response to new religious movements*, London: Tavistock.

Beckford, James A. (ed.) (1986) *New religious movements and rapid social change*, London: Sage Publications.

Beckford, James A. (1989) *Religion and advanced industrial society*, London: Unwin–Hyman.

Beinin, J. and Stork, J. (eds) (1997) *Political Islam: essays from Middle East Report*, Berkeley, CA: University of California Press.

Bergman, J. (1984) *Jehovah's Witnesses and kindred groups: a historical compendium and bibliography*, New York: Garland.

Berhane-Selassie, Tsehai (n.d.) 'Decade conference: a soap opera in the sun?' *Spare Rib*, 16–21.

Beyer, Peter (1990) 'Privatization and the public influence of religion in global society', *Theory, Culture and Society* 7 (2–3): 373–95.

Beyer, Peter (1992) 'The global environment as a religious issue: a sociological analysis', *Religion*, 2: 1–19.

Beyer, Peter (1994) *Religion and globalization*, London: Sage Publications.

Bhabha, H. (1994) *The location of culture*, London: Routledge.

Bhatt, Chetan (1997) *Liberation and purity: race, new religious movements and the ethics of postmodernity*, London: UCL Press.

Bijker, W. E. and Law, J. (1997) 'Postscript: technology, stability and social theory', in W. E. Bijker and J. Law (eds) *Shaping technology/building society: studies in socio-technical change*, Boston: MIT Press, 290–308.

Blackholm, Yvonne (1990) Personal interview, Vienna, 27 February.

Blackwood, Caroline (1985) *On the perimeter*, New York: Penguin.

Bloomer, Olive (1990) Personal interview, Vienna, 27 February.

Boggs, Carl (1993) *Intellectuals and the crisis of modernity*, Albany, NY: SUNY Press.

Boggs, Carl (1995) 'Rethinking the sixties legacy: from New Left to New Social Movements', in Stanford M. Lyman (ed.) *Social movements: critiques, concepts, case-studies*, Basingstoke: Macmillan, 331–5.

Borer, T. A. (1996) 'Church leadership, state repression, and the "spiral of involvement" in the South African anti-Apartheid movement, 1983–1990', in C. Smith (ed.) *Disruptive religion*, New York: Routledge, 125–43.

Borgers, F. (1996), 'The challenge of economic globalization for US labor', *Critical Sociology*, 22 (2).

Boyer, R. and Drache, D. (eds) (1995) *States against markets: the limits of globalization*, London: Routledge.

Bradney, Anthony (1993) *Religions, rights and laws*, Leicester: University of Leicester Press.

Bramble, Barbara J. and Porter, Gareth (1992) 'Non-governmental organizations and the making of US international environmental policy', in Andrew Hurrell and Benedict Kingsbury (eds) *The international politics of the environment*, Oxford: Clarendon Press, 313–53.

Brennan, Katherine (1989) 'The influence of cultural relativism on international human rights law: female circumcision as a case study', *Law and Inequality*, 7 (July): 367–98.

Bromley, David G. and Shupe, A. D. Jr (1979) *The Moonies in America*, Beverly Hills, CA: Sage Publications.

Brouwer, S., Gifford, P. and Rose, S. D. (1996) *Exporting the American gospel: global Christian fundamentalism*, New York: Routledge.

Brown, R. (1997) 'Think local, act global: Political strategy and transnational conflict', Paper at Warwick University conference 'Non-state actors and authority in the global system', 31 October–1 November.

Brown, Wendy (1995) *States of injury: power and freedom in late modernity*, Princeton: Princeton University Press.

Browne, E. G. (1891) *A traveller's narrative, written to illustrate the episode of the Báb*, Cambridge: Cambridge University Press.

Buchanan, Allen (1982) *Marx and justice: the radical critique of liberalism*, London: Methuen.

Bull, M. and Lockhart, K. (1989*) Seeking a sanctuary: Seventh-day Adventism and the American dream*, San Francisco: Harper & Row.

Bunch, Charlotte and Carrillo, Roxanna (1990) 'Feminist perspectives on women in development', in Irene Tinker (ed.) *Persistent inequalities: women and world development*, New York: Oxford University Press, 70–82.

Bunch, Charlotte and Castley, Shirley (1980) '*Developing strategies for the future: feminist perspectives. Report of the International Feminist Workshop held at Stony Point, New York, April 2025, 1980*', New York: International Women's Tribune Center.

Bunch, Charlotte, Carrillo, Roxanna and Guineem, Ied (1985) 'Feminist perspectives: Report of the feminist perspectives working group to the closing plenary', *Women's Studies International Forum*, 8 (4): 243–7.

Burgat, François (1997) 'Ballot boxes, militaries, and Islamic movements' in Martin Kramer (ed.) *The Islamism debate*, Tel Aviv: The Moshe Dayan Center for Middle Eastern and African Studies, Tel Aviv University.

Burgat, François and Dowell, W. (1993) *The Islamic movement in North Africa*, Austin: University of Texas Press.

Burgess, S. M. and McGee, G. B. (eds) (1988) *Dictionary of Pentecostal and charismatic movements*, Grand Rapids, MI: Zondervan.

Burke, Edmund, III (1998) 'Orientalism and world history: representing nationalism and Islamism in the twentieth century', *Theory and Society*, 27/4 (August), 489–507.

Byrne, Paul (1988) *The Campaign for Nuclear Disarmament*, London: Croom Helm.

Byrne, Paul (1997) *Social movements in Britain*, London: Routledge.

Callaway, Helen (1986) 'Reflections on Forum '85 in Nairobi, Kenya', *Signs: Journal of Women, Culture and Society*, 11 (3): 599–602.

Candelaria, M. (1990) *Popular religion and liberation: the dilemma of liberation theology*, Albany, NY: SUNY Press.

Casanova, Jose (1994) *Public religions in the modern world*, Chicago: University of Chicago Press.

Cassels, Jamie (1993) *The uncertain promise of law: lessons from Bhopal*, Toronto: University of Toronto Press.

Castells, Manuel (1996) *The rise of the network society*, vol I of *The information age: economy, society and culture*, Oxford: Blackwell.

Castells, Manuel (1997) *The power of identity*, vol II of *The information age: economy, society and culture*, Oxford: Blackwell.

Caulkin, S. (1997) 'Amnesty and WWF take a crack at Shell', *The Times*, 11 May.

Caute, David (1988) *The year of the barricades: a journey through 1968*, New York: Harper & Row.

Centre for Women's Studies (1997) *Women and the politics of peace*, Zagreb: Centre for Women's Studies.

Cerny, P. (1990) *The changing architecture of politics: structure, agency and the future of the state*, London: Sage Publications.

Chatterjee, P. and Finger, M. (1994) *The earth brokers: power, politics and world development*, London: Routledge.

Chen, Martha Atler (1996) 'Engendering world conferences: the international women's movement and the UN', in T. Weiss and L. Gordenker (eds) *NGOs, the UN and global governance*, Boulder, CO: Lynne Rienner.

Chryssides, George D. (1991) *The Fadvent of Sun Myung Moon*, Basingstoke: Macmillan.

Clapp, J. (1997) 'Threats to the environment in an era of globalization: an end to state sovereignty?' in T. Schrecker (ed.) *Surviving globalism: the social and environmental challenges*, Basingstoke: Macmillan.

Clarke, J. and Gaile, G. (1997) 'Local politics in a global era: thinking locally, acting globally', *Annals* (The Annals of the American Academy of Political and Social Sciences), No. 551, May.

Clarke, S., Fairbrother, P., Burawoy, M. and Krotov, P. (1993) *What about the workers? Workers and the transition to capitalism in Russia*, London: Verso.

Clarke, S., Fairbrother, P. and Borisov, V. (1995) *The workers' movement in Russia*, Cheltenham: Edward Elgar.

Cockburn, Cynthia (1998) *The space between us: negotiating gender and national identities in conflict*, London: Zed Books.

Cohen, Robin (1997) *Global diasporas: an introduction*, London: UCL Press.

Cohen, Robin and Kennedy, Paul (2000) *Global sociology*, Basingstoke: Macmillan.

Commonwealth Secretariat (1985) *Record of the workshop on ladies in limbo revisited: Belize City, Belize. 11–15 November 1985*, London: Women and Development Programme, Commonwealth Secretariat.

Commonwealth Secretariat (1989) *Engendering adjustment for the 1990s: Report of a commonwealth expert group on women and structural adjustment*, London: Commonwealth Secretariat.

Comte, Auguste (1893) *The cours de positive philosophie*, London: Kegan Paul Trench, Trübner.

Conca, K. (1993) 'Environmental change and the deep structure of world politics' in B. Lipschutz and K. Conca (eds) *The state and social power in global environmental politics*, New York: Columbia University Press.

Connolly, William E. (1991) *Identity/difference: democratic negotiations of political paradox*, Ithaca, NY: Cornell University Press.

Cook, Alice and Kirk, Gwyn (1983) *Greenham women everywhere: dreams, ideas and actions from the women's peace movement*, London: Pluto Press.

Cornfield, Daniel (1997) 'Labor transnationalism?' *Work and Occupations*, Special Issue on Labor in the Americas, 24 (3): 278–87.

Corporate Watch (1997) No. 4 June.

Cottingham, Jane (1989) 'ISIS: a decade of international networking', in Ramona R. Rush and Donna Allen (eds) *Communications at the crossroads: the gender gap connection*, Norwood, NJ: Ablex, 238–50.

Cover, Robert (1975) *Justice accused: antislavery and the judicial process*, Mineola, NY: Foundation Press.

Cover, Robert (1987) 'Foreword: nomos and narrative', *87 Harvard Law Review*, 62nd issue.

Cox, Robert W. (1987) *Production, power and world order: social forces in the making of history*, New York: Columbia University Press.

CSW (1989) *Peace: full participation of women in the construction of their countries and in the creation of just social and political systems*, Vienna: Commission on the Status of Women, 33rd session, E/CN.6/1989/7.

CSW (1990) *Progress at the national, regional and international levels in the implementation of the Nairobi forward-looking strategies for the advancement of women*, Vienna: Commission on the Status of Women, 34th session, 26 February–9 March 1990. E/CN.6/1990/5.

CSW (1991) *National, regional and international machinery for the effective integration of women in the development process, including non-governmental organizations*, Vienna: Commission on the Status of Women, 35th session, 27 February–8 March 1991. E/CN.6/1991/3.

Cumper, Peter (1996) 'Religious liberty in the United Kingdom', in J. D. Van der Vyver and J. Witte, Jr (eds) *Religious human rights in global perspective*, The Hague: Martinus Nijhoff, 205–41.

Daniel, E. Valentine (1997) *Chapters in an anthropology of violence: Sri Lankans, Sinhalas, and Tamils*, Delhi: Oxford University Press.

D'Antonio, W. V. and Pike, F. B. (eds) (1964) *Religion, revolution, and reform*, London: Burns & Oates.

Darwin, Charles (1985) *The origin of species by means of natural selection*, London: Penguin.

Das Veena (1994) 'Moral orientations to suffering' in L. C. Chen, N. Ware and A. Klienman (eds) *Health and social change*, Cambridge, MA: Harvard University Press.

Das, Veena (1995) *Critical events: an anthropological perspective on contemporary India*, Delhi: Oxford University Press.

Das, Veena (1997) 'Language and Body: transactions in the construction of pain', in *Social Suffering*, 93.

Davidson, Scott (1993) *Human rights*, Buckingham, Open University Press.

DAWN (1990) *Interregional meeting and general report*, Rio de Janeiro, Brazil: Development Alternatives with Women for a New Era.

Day, G. and Robbins, R. (1987) 'Activists for peace: the social basis of a local peace movement', in C. Creighton and M. Shaw (eds) *The sociology of war and peace*, Basingstoke: Macmillan, 37–46.

de Gruchy, J. (1979) *The church struggle in South Africa*, Grand Rapids, MI: Eerdmans.

De Martino, G. (1991), 'Trade-Union, isolation and the catechism of the left', *Rethinking Marxism*, 4 (3).

Deacon, B., Hulse, M. and Stubbs, P. (1997) *Global social policy. international organizations and the future of welfare*, London: Sage Publications.

Debord, Guy (1970) *The society of spectacle*, Detroit, MI: Black & Red.

Debord, Guy (1990) *Comments on the society of spectacle*, London: Verso.

della Porta, D. and M. Diani (1999) *Social movements: an introduction*, Oxford: Blackwell.

Devetak, Richard and Higgott, Richard (1999) 'Justice unbound? Globalization, states and the transformation of the social bond', *International Affairs*, 75 (3), 483–98.

Dicken, Peter (1992) *Global shift: the internationalization of economic activity*, London: Paul Chapman.

Dickson, Lisa and McCulloch, Alistair (1996) 'Shell, the Brent Spar and Greenpeace: a doomed tryst?' *Environmental Politics*, 5 (1): 122–9.

DIESA (1991) *The world's women, 1970–1990: trends and statistics*, New York: United Nations, Department of International Economic and Social Affairs.

Dobbelaere, Karel (1981) 'Secularization: a multi-dimensional concept', *Current Sociology*, 29 (2): 1–216.

Dodds, F. (1997) (ed.) *The way forward: Beyond Agenda 21*, London: Earthscan.

Donini, Antonio (1996) 'The bureaucracy and the free spirits: stagnation and innovation in the relationships between the UN and NGOs', in T. Weiss and L. Gordenker (eds) *NGOs, the UN and global governance*, Boulder, CO: Lynne Rienner, 83–101.

Doran, P. (1993) 'Ecology as spectacle' *Paradigms*, 7 (1): 55–6.

Dunlop, J. (1958) *Industrial relations systems*, New York: Holt.

Dunn, J. (1985) 'Unimagined Community: the deceptions of socialist internationalism', in J. Dunn (ed.) *Rethinking modern political theory. Essays 1979–83*, Cambridge: Cambridge University Press.

Durkheim, Émile (1967) *Moral education*, trans. E. K. Wilson and H. Schnurer, New York: The Free Press.

Dyck, Noel (ed.) (1985) *Indigenous peoples and the nation state: Fourth World politics in Canada, Australia and Norway*, St Johns, Newfoundland: Institute of Social and Economic Research, Memorial University of Newfoundland.

Earth First! Action Update (1997) No. 41, July and August.

Eickelman, Dale F. (1997) 'Trans-state Islam and security', in Susanne Hoeber Rudolph and James Piscatori (eds) *Transnational religion and fading states*, Boulder, CO: Westview, 27–46.

Eickelman, D. and J. Piscatori (1990) *Muslim travellers: pilgrimage, migration and the religious imagination*, Berkeley: University of California Press.

El Saadawi, Nawal, Mernissi, Fatima and Vajrathon, Mallica (1978) 'A critical view of the Wellesley Conference', *Quest: a Feminist Quarterly*, 4 (2): 101–7.

Elson, Diane (1995) 'Trade unions and international markets: the view of the World Bank', presented to ESRC seminar on 'The Internationalisation of Capital: Labour's Responses', Manchester International Centre for Labour Studies, University of Manchester.

Elson, Diane and Pearson, Ruth (1984) 'The subordination of women and the internationalisation of factory production', in K. Young, C. Wolkowitz and R. McCullagh (eds) *Of marriage and the market: women's subordination internationally and its lessons*, London: Routledge, 18–40.

Enderwick, P. (1985) *Multinational business and labour*, London: Croom Helm.

Esping-Andersen, Gøsta (1993) 'Post industrial class structures: an analytical framework', in G. Esping-Andersen (ed.) *Changing classes; stratification and mobility in post industrial societies*, London: Sage Publications.

Ethical Consumer Magazine (1997/1998) January, special issue on ethical consumerism.

Exchange (1980) *Exchange report: women in the Third World*, newspaper.

Fabig, H. and Boele, R. (1999) 'The changing nature of NGO activity in a globalizing world', *IDS Bulletin,* 30 (3): 58–68, Brighton: Institute of Development Studies.

Featherstone, M. (1995) *Undoing culture: globalization, postmodernism and identity,* London: Sage Publications.

Feminist Forum (1984) *Women's studies international forum,* 7 (6): i–xii.

Feminist Forum (1985a) *Women's studies international forum,* 8 (1): i–x.

Feminist Forum (1985b) *Women's studies international forum,* 8 (6): i—xix.

Feminist Forum (1987) *Women's studies international forum,* 10 (2): i–viii.

Finger, Matthias (1993) 'Foxes in charge of the chickens', in W. Sachs (ed.) *Global ecology: a new arena of political conflict,* London: Zed Books.

Finger, Matthias and Kilcoyne, James (1997) 'Why transnational corporations are organizing to "save the global environment"', *The Ecologist,* 27 (4): 138–42.

Fischer, K. and Schot, J. (eds) (1993) *Environmental strategies for industry,* Washington: Island Press.

Forum '85 (1985) *NGO Planning Committee. Final Report: Nairobi, Kenya.* New York: International Women's Tribune Center.

Freeman, R. (1992) 'Is declining unionisation of the US good, bad or irrelevant?' in L. Mishel and P. Voos (eds) *Unions and economic competitiveness,* New York: Sharp, 143–69.

French, J., Cowie, J. and Littlehare, S. (1994) *Labor and NAFTA: a briefing book,* Durham, NC: Duke University.

Friedman, J. (1994) *Cultural identity and global process,* London: Sage Publications.

Fuentes, Annette and Ehrenreich, Barbara (1983) 'Women in the global factory', *INC Pamphlet No. 1,* New York: Institute for New Communications, South End Press.

Fukuyama, F. (1992) *The end of history and the last man,* New York: Oxford University Press.

Gabriel, Christina and Laura Macdonald (1994) 'NAFTA, Women and organising in Canada and Mexico: forging a 'feminist internationality', *Millennium: Journal of International Studies,* 23 (3), 535–62.

Gallin, D. (1994) 'Inside the New World Order: drawing the battle lines', *New Politics,* Summer.

Ghamari-Tabrizi, B. (1998) *Islamists and the quest for an alternative modernity,* unpublished paper, Sociology Department. University of California, Santa Cruz.

Gibson-Graham, J. K. (1996) *The end of capitalism (as we knew it). A feminist critique of political economy,* Oxford: Blackwell.

Giddens, Anthony (1990) *The consequences of modernity,* Cambridge: Polity Press.

Giddens, Anthony (1991) *Modernity and self identity: self and society in the late modern age,* Cambridge: Polity Press.

Giddens, Anthony (1994) *Beyond left and right: the future of radical politics,* Cambridge: Polity Press.

Gill, S. (1995) 'Theorising the interregnum: the double movement and global politics in the 1990s', in B. Hettne (ed.) *International political economy: understanding global disorder,* London: Zed Books.

Gill, S. and Law, D. (1988) *The global political economy,* Hemel Hempstead, Herts: Harvester/Wheatsheaf.

Gills, B. (1997) 'Globalisation and the politics of resistance', *New Political Economy,* 2 (1) March.

Gindin, S. (1995) *The Canadian autoworkers: the birth and transformation of a union,* Toronto: James Lorrimer.

Global Labour Summit (1997) A new global agenda. Visions and strategies for the 21st century, Copenhagen, 31 May–1 June, <*http://www.labournet.org.uk/discuss.html*>.

Glover, D. (1999) 'Defending communities. Local exchange trading systems from an environmental perspective', *IDS Bulletin,* 30 (3): 75–82, Brighton: Institute of Development Studies.

Gold, Daniel (1991) 'Organized Hinduisms: from Vedic truth to Hindu nation', in M. Marty and S. Appleby (eds) *Fundamentalisms observed,* vol 1, Chicago: University of Chicago Press, 531–93.

Golden, R. and McConnell, M. (1986) *Sanctuary: the new underground railroad,* New York: Orbis.

Gordenker, Leon and Weiss, Thomas (1995) (eds) *NGOs, the UN and global governance,* Boulder, CO: Lynne Rienner.

Gouldner, Alvin (1976) *The dialectic of ideology and technology: the origins, grammar and future of ideology,* Basingstoke: Macmillan.

Gray, John (1998) *False dawn: the delusions of global capitalism,* London: Granta.

Greer, Germaine (1975) 'Phoney manifesto comes under fire', *Xilonen,* June 20, Mexico City.

Grewal, Inderpal and Kaplan, Caren (eds) (1994) *Scattered hegemonies: postmodernity and transnational feminist practices,* Minneapolis: University of Minnesota Press.

Guarnizo, Luis Eduardo and Smith, Michael Peter (1998) 'The locations of transnationalism', in M. P. Smith and L. E. Guarnizo (eds) *Transnationalism from below,* New Brunswick, NJ: Transaction Publishers, 3–34.

Guha, R. and Martinez-Alier, J. (1997) 'The merchandising of biodiversity', in R. Guha and J. M. Alier
    (eds) *Varieties of environmentalism: essays in North and South,* London: Earthscan.
Gupta, Akhil and Ferguson, James (1992) 'Beyond "culture": space, identity, and the politics of
    difference', *Cultural Anthropology,* 7, 6–23.
Gurvitch, Georges (1973) *Sociology of law,* London: Routledge & Kegan Paul.
Gusfield, Joseph R. (1981) 'Social movements and social change: perspectives of linearity and fluidity',
    Research in Social Movements, Conflict and Change, 4: 317–39.

Hall, Stuart (1996) 'Introduction: who needs identity?' in Stuart Hall and Paul du Gay (eds) *Questions of
    cultural identity,* London: Sage Publications.
Hammond, Phillip E. (1963) 'The migrating sect: an illustration from early Norwegian immigration',
    Social Forces, 41: 275–83.
Hannum, Hurst (1996) *Autonomy, sovereignty and self-determination: the accommodation of conflicting
    rights,* Philadelphia: University of Pennsylvania Press.
Harris, Adrienne and King, Ynestra (eds) (1989) *Rocking the ship of state: toward a feminist peace politics,*
    Boulder, CO: Westview Press.
Harvey, David (1996) *Justice, nature and the geography of difference,* Oxford: Blackwell.
Hashimoto, Hideo and McPherson, William (1976) 'Rise and decline of Soka Gakkai, Japan and the
    United States', *Review of Religious Research,* 17 (2): 82–92.
Haslegrave, Marianne (1990) Personal interview, Vienna, 27 February.
Haufler, V. (1995) 'Crossing the boundary between public and private', in V. Rittberger (ed.) *Regime
    theory and international relations,* Oxford: Clarendon Press.
Haufler, V. (1997) 'Private sector international regimes: An assessment', Paper at Warwick University
    conference 'Non-state actors and authority in the global system', 31 October–1 November.
Haworth, N. and Ramsay, H. (1984) 'Grasping the nettle: problems in the theory of international labour
    solidarity', in Peter Waterman (ed.) *For a new labour internationalism,* The Hague: ILERI.
Heelas, Paul (1996) 'On things not being worse and the ethic of humanity', in Paul Heelas, Scott Lash
    and Paul Morris (eds) *Detraditionalization,* Oxford: Blackwell, 200–22.
Hegedus, Z. (1989) 'Social movements and social change in self-creative society: new civil initiatives in
    the international arena', *International Sociology,* 4 (1).
Held, David (1995) *Democracy and the global order,* Cambridge: Polity Press.
Helleiner, E. (1994) 'From Bretton Woods to global finance: A world turned upside down', in R. Stubbs
    and G. Underhill (eds) *Political economy and the changing global order,* Basingstoke: Macmillan.
Herdt, Anne (1990) Personal interview, Vienna, 1 March.
Herod, A. (1997) 'Labor as an agent of globalization and as a global agent', in K. Cox (ed.) *Spaces of
    globalization, reasserting the power of the global,* New York: The Guildford Press.
Herod, A. (1998) 'Labor's transnational spatial strategies and the geography of capitalism', in A. Herod
    (ed.) *Organizing the landscape: geographical perspectives on labor unionism,* Minneapolis: University of
    Minnesota Press.
Hewitt, P (1998) 'Technology and democracy', in Jane Franklin (ed.) *The politics of the risk society,*
    Cambridge: Polity Press, 83–9.
Heyniger, Line Robillard (1985) 'The International Conference on Research and Teaching related to
    Women', *Women's Studies International Forum,* 8 (2): 157–60.
Hiro, D. (1998) 'The cost of an Afghan victory', *The Nation,* 268 (6) 17–20.
Hirst, P. and Thompson, G. (1996) *Globalization in question,* Cambridge: Polity.
Hodges, Tony (1976) *Jehovah's Witnesses in Central Africa,* London: Minority Rights Group.
Hodgson, M. (1974) *The venture of Islam,* Chicago: Chicago University Press.
Hoffman, Andrew (1996) 'Trends in corporate environmentalism: The chemical and petroleum
    industries: 1960–1993', *Society and Natural Resources,* 9: 47–64.
Hollenweger, Walter (1972) *The Pentecostals,* London: SCM Press.
Horowitz, D. (1985) *Ethnic groups in conflict,* Berkeley: University of California Press.
Hoskens, Fran (1978/79) 'WIN – Women's International Network – News', *Isis International Bulletin,*
    10 (Winter): 38.
Hoskyns, Catherine (1996) *Integrating gender: women, law and politics in the European Union.* London:
    Verso.
Humphreys, D. (1997) 'Environmental accountability and transnational corporations', Paper presented
    to the International Academic Conference on 'Environmental Justice: Global ethics for the 21st
    century', University of Melbourne, Victoria, Australia, 1–3 October.
Hunter, Allen (1995) 'Globalization from below: promises and perils of the new labour internationalism',
    Social Policy 25 (4), 6–13.

Huntington, Samuel P. (1996) *The clash of civilizations and the remaking of world order*, New York: Simon & Schuster.

ICEM (1996) *Power and counterpower: the union responses to global capital*, London: Pluto Press.
ICFTU (1996) *Policies adopted by the 16th World Congress of the ICFTU*, Brussels: International Confederation of Free Trade Unions.
ICFTU (1996a) *The global market – trade unionism's greatest challenge*, Brussels: International Confederation of Free Trade Unions.
ICFTU (1996b) *Behind the wire: anti-union repression in the export processing zones*, Brussels: International Confederation of Free Trade Unions.
ICFTU (1997) *Fighting for workers' rights in the global economy*, Brussels: International Confederation of Free Trade Unions.
ICFTU–Phare Democracy Programme (1995) *Promotion and defence of trade union rights in Central and Eastern Europe,* Brussels: International Confederation of Free Trade Unions.
IFC Environmental and Social Policies and Procedures at *http://www.ifc.org/envir/html/rev-2a.txt*.
ILO Human Rights Fact Sheet (1998) at *http://www-ilo-mirror.who.or.jp*.
Ilyin, V. (1996) 'Russian trade unions and the management apparatus in the transition period', in S. Clarke (ed.) *Conflict and change in the Russian industrial enterprise,* Cheltenham: Edward Elgar, 65–106.
Inoue, N. (1997) 'Globalization's challenge to indigenous culture', in N. Inoue (ed.) *Globalization and indigenous culture*, Tokyo: Institute for Japanese Culture and Classics, 7–19.
Inter-Parliamentary Union (1988) *Participation of women in political life and in the decision-making process*, Series 'Reports and Documents', no. 15, Geneva: International Centre for Parliamentary Documentation.
Ionescu, D. (1992) 'Trade Unions in Romania abandon political neutrality', *RFE/RL Research Report,* 1 (12): 12–15.
Isaksson, Eva (ed.) (1988) *Women and the military system*, New York: St. Martin's Press.
ISIS and DAWN (1988) *Confronting the crisis in Latin America: women organizing for change*, Isis International and DAWN, Development Alternatives with Women for a New Era, Book Series 1988/2.
IWTC (1984) *Women organizing: A Collection of IWTC newsletters on women's organizing and networking strategies*, New York: International Women's Tribune Center.

Jackson, Robert (1995) 'The construction of "Hinduism" and its impact on religious education', unpublished paper presented at a conference, Goslar, Germany.
Johns, R. (1994) 'International solidarity: space and class in the U.S. labor movement'. PhD diss., Department of Geography, Rutgers University, New Brunswick, NJ.
Johnston, Hank and Klandermans, Bert (eds) (1995) *Social movements and culture*, London: UCL Press.
Jones, Lynne (ed.) (1983) *Keeping the peace*, London: Women's Press.
Jordan, June (1989) *Moving towards home: political essays*, London: Virago Press.
Jordan, W. K. (19321940) *The development of religious toleration in England*, 4 vols, London: Allen & Unwin.
Judge, A. and Skjelbaek, K. (1975) 'Transnational associations and their functions', in A. S. R. Groom and P. Taylor (eds) *Functionalism: theory and practice in international relations*, London: Athlone Press, 190–224.

Kapstein, E. (1996) 'Workers and the world economy', *Foreign Affairs*, May/June.
Karl, Marilee (1986) 'Networking the global women's movement', in M. Karl and X. Charnes (eds) *Women, struggles and strategies: Third World perspectives*, Rome: ISIS International.
Kassell, Paula and Kaufman, Susan J. (1989) 'Planning an international communications system for women' in R. Rush and D. Allen (eds) *Communications at the crossroads: the gender gap connection*, 222–37.
Kaufmann, R. (1964) *Millénarisme et acculturation*, Brussels: Institute of Sociology of the Free University of Brussels.
Kazanov, M. (1995) *After the USSR: ethnicity, nationalism and politics in the commonwealth of independent states*, Madison, WI: University of Wisconsin Press.
Keck, Margaret E and Sikkink, Kathryn (eds) (1998) *Activists beyond borders: advocacy networks in international politics*, Ithaca, NY: Cornell University Press.
Kidron, Beeban and Richardson, Amanda (n.d) *Carry Greenham Home*, film made by Women Make Movies, New York.

Kisslinger, T. (1997) 'Human rights movement enters the information age', in the electronic *Human Rights Tribune*, Wired wURLd section, 4, nos 2–3. at *http://www.hri.ca/publicat/tribune/feature/wired 1.shtn.*

Klandermans, B. (ed.) (1991) *Peace movements in Europe and the United States*, London: JAI Press.

Kleinman, Artur and Kleinman, Joan (1997) 'The appeal of experience; the dismay of images: cultural appropriations of suffering in our times', in *Social Suffering*, 1.

Knox, P. (1995) 'World cities in a world system', in P. Knox and J. P. Taylor (eds) *World cities in a world system*, Cambridge: Cambridge University Press.

Kodama, K. (1989) 'The peace movements for the future', in K. Kodama *et al.* (eds) *The future of the peace movements*, Lund: Lund University Press.

Korten, D. (1995) *When corporations rule the world*, London: Earthscan.

Kramer, Gudrun (1993) 'Islamist notions of democracy', *Middle East Report*, 23 (4): 2–8.

Kriesberg, Louis (1997) 'Social movements and global transformation', in Jackie Smith, Charles Chatfield and Ron Pagnucco (eds) *Transnational social movements and global politics*, Syracuse: Syracuse University Press, 3–18.

Kürti, N. (1997) 'Globalisation and the discourse of otherness in the "new" Eastern and Central Europe', in T. Modood and P. Werbner (eds) *The politics of multiculturalism in the new Europe*, London: Zed Books, 29–53.

Kurtz, L. (1995) *Gods in the global village*, Thousand Oaks, CA: Pine Forge Press.

Kymlicka, Will (1995) *Multicultural citizenship: a liberal theory of minority rights*, Oxford: Oxford University Press.

Laclau, E. and Mouffe, C. (1985) *Hegemony and socialist strategy: towards a radical democratic politics*, London: Verso.

Lanternari, Vittorio (1963) *The religions of the oppressed*, New York: Alfred Knopf.

Lavalette, M. and Kennedy, J. (1996) *Solidarity on the waterfront: the Liverpool lock-out of 1995/6*, Liverpool, Liver Press.

Lee, Kelly, Humphreys, David and Pugh, Michael (1998) 'Privatization in the United States System: patterns of influence in three intergovernmental organizations', *Global Society*, 1 (3), 42–54.

Levine, Daniel (1986) *Religion and political conflict in Latin America*, Chapel Hill, NC: University of North Carolina Press.

Lewis, Shelby (1988) 'Pan-African Women's Forum', *Women in Action*, 4: 23–4.

Lewis, William (1997) 'Shell to face shareholder vote on ethics', *Financial Times,* 12 April.

Liebman, C. S., and Don-Yehiya, E. (1984) *Religion and politics in Israel*, Bloomington, IN: Indiana University Press.

Litfin, Karen (1993) 'Ecoregimes: Playing tug of war with the nation-state', in R. Lipschultz and K. Conca (eds) *The state and social power in global environmental politics*, New York: Columbia University Press.

Lloyd, John (1998) 'Interview with Manuel Castells', *New Statesman*, 5 June, 13–14.

Logan, M. (1995) 'Untangling the "Net's" web' *Human Rights Tribune*, Wired wURLd section, 3(3): 7–13.

Long, F. J. and Arnold, J. (1995) *The power of environmental partnerships management institute for environment and business*, New York: Harcourt Brace.

Lorwin, L. (1953) *Labor and internationalism*, New York: Macmillan.

Lubeck, P. (1987) *Islam and urban labor: the making of a Muslim working class in Northern Nigeria*, Cambridge: Cambridge University Press.

Lubeck, P. (1997) 'Globalization and the Islamist movement: explaining communal conflict in Muslim majority states', in B. Crawford and R. Lipschutz (eds) *The causes of cultural conflict*, Ithaca, NY: Cornell University Press.

Lynch, Cecelia (1998) 'Social movements and the problem of globalization', *Alternatives*, 23, 149–73.

Lycklama à Nijeholt, Geertje, Vargas, Virginia and Wieringa, Saskia (1998) *Women's movements and public policy in Europe, Latin America and the Caribbean*, New York: Garland.

McAdam, Doug (1982) *Political processes and the development of black insurgency, 1930–1970*, Chicago: University of Chicago Press.

McBride, Dorothy and Mazur, Amy (eds) (1995) *Comparative state feminism*, London: Sage.

McCarthy, John D. and Zald, Mayer N. (1977) 'Resource mobilization and social movements: a partial theory', *American Journal of Sociology*, 82 (6): 1212–41.

McCully, P. (1997) *Silenced rivers: the ecology and politics of large dams*, London: Zed Books.

McKay, George (1996) *Senseless acts of beauty: cultures of resistance since the sixties*, London: Verso.

MacKenzie, Donald A. (1990) *Inventing accuracy: a historical sociology of nuclear missile guidance*, Cambridge, MA: Massachusetts Institute of Technology Press.

MacPhee, Susan C. (1990) *Talking Peace: The Women's International Peace Conference*. Charlottetown: Ragweed Press.

McShane, D. (1993) 'Labor standards and double standards in the New World Order', in J. Brecher, J. B. Childs and J. Cutler (eds) *Global visions: beyond the New World Order*, Boston: South End Press.

Madan, T. N. (1991) 'The double-edged sword: fundamentalism and the Sikh religious tradition', in M. Marty and S. Appleby (eds) *Fundamentalisms observed*, Chicago: University of Chicago Press, 594–627.

Mair, Lucille Mathurin (1985) International Women's Decade: a balance sheet, *Third J. P. Naik Memorial Lecture*, New Delhi: Centre for Women's Development Studies, 15 December 1984.

Mandelbaum, D. G. (1972) *Society in India*, 2 vols, Berkeley, CA: University of California Press.

Mann, M. (1987) 'War and social theory: into battle with classes, nations and states', in Colin Creighton and Martin Shaw (eds) *The sociology of war and peace*, Basingstoke: Macmillan, 54–72.

Mann, M. (1993) *The sources of social power, vol 2: A history of power in industrial societies*, Cambridge: Cambridge University Press.

Manuel, George and Posluns, M. (1974) *The Fourth World: an Indian reality*, Toronto: Collier–Macmillan.

Manza, J. and Brooks, C. (1997) 'The religious factor in US presidential elections, 1960–1992', *American Journal of Sociology*, 103 (1): 38–81.

Marchand, Marianne and Runyan, Anne Sisson (eds) (Forthcoming) *Gender and global restructuring*, London: Routledge.

Martin, D. A. (1990) *Tongues of fire*, Oxford: Blackwell.

Martin, Hans Peter and Schumann, Harold (1998) *The global trap: civilisation and the assault on democracy and prosperity*, London: Zed Books.

Martin, W. G. and Beittel, M. (1998) 'Towards a global sociology?' *The Sociological Quarterly*, 39 (1): 139–61.

Massey, D. (1995) 'The conceptualization of place', in D. Massey and P. Jess (eds) *A place in the world? Places, cultures and globalization*, Oxford: Oxford University Press.

Mathiason, John (1990) Personal interview, Vienna, 5 March.

Mattausch, J. (1989a) *A commitment to campaign: a sociological study of CND*, Manchester: Manchester University Press.

Mattausch, J. (1989b) 'The peace movement: some answers concerning its social nature and structure', *International Sociology*, 4 (2): 217–25.

Mattausch, J. (1991) 'CND: the first phase, 1958 to 1967', in B. Klandermans (ed.) *Peace movements in Europe and the United States*, London: JAI Press.

Melucci, Alberto (1989) *Nomads of the present: social movements and individual needs in contemporary society*, Philadelphia: Temple University Press.

Melucci, A. (1994) 'A strange kind of newness: what's "new" in the New Social Movements', in E. Larana, H. Johnston and J. R. Gusfield (eds) *New social movements: from ideology to identity*, Philadelphia: Temple University Press.

Melucci, Alberto (1996) *Challenging codes: collective action in the information age*, Cambridge: Cambridge University Press.

Meyer, Mary K. and Prügl, Elisabeth (eds) (1999) *Gender politics in global governance*, Lanham: Rowman and Littlefield.

Mitchell, J. (1997) *Companies in a world of conflict*, London: RIIA/Earthscan.

Mitchell, Richard P. (1969) *The society of the Muslim Brothers*, London: Oxford University Press.

Mittelman, J. (1998) 'Globalisation and environmental resistance politics', *Third World Quarterly*, 19 (5): 847–72.

Mlango, Susie (1990) Personal interview, Vienna, 5 March.

Moghadam, Valentine M. (1996) 'Feminist networks North and South' *Journal of International Communication*, 3 (1): 111–26.

Monks, J. (1998) *The state of the unions*, presentation, LSE Industrial Relations Department.

Monthly Review (1997) *Rising from the ashes? Labor in the age of 'global capitalism'*, Special issue, ed. by Ellen Meiksins Wood, Peter Meiksin and Michael Yates, 49 (3), New York.

Moody, K. (1997) *Workers in a lean world: unions in the international economy*, London: Verso.

Moody, R. (ed.) (1988) *The indigenous voice: visions and realities*, vols 1 and 2, London: Zed Books.

Morris, Aldon (1996) 'The black church in the civil rights movement: the SCLC as the decentralized, radical arm of the black church', in C. Smith (ed.) *Disruptive religion*, New York: Routledge, 29–46.

Munck, R. (1988) *The new international labour studies*, London: Zed Books.

Munck, R. and Waterman, P. (eds) (1998) *Labour worldwide in the era of globalisation,* Basingstoke: Macmillan.

Murphy, D. and Bendell, J. (1997) *In the company of partners,* Bristol: Policy Press.

Nanda, Ved P. and Bailey, Bruce C. (1988) 'Export of hazardous waste and hazardous technology: challenge for international environmental law', *Denver Journal of International Law and Policy,* 17 (1): 155–206.

Nash, June (1996) 'Religious rituals of resistance and class consciousness in Bolivian tin-mining communities', in C. Smith (ed.) *Disruptive religion,* New York: Routledge, 87–102.

Nepstad, S. E. (1996) 'Popular religion, protest and revolt: the emergence of political insurgency in the Nicaraguan and Salvadoran churches of the 1960s–80s', in C. Smith (ed.) *Disruptive religion,* New York: Routledge, 105–24.

Newell, P. and Paterson, M. (1998) 'Climate for business: Global warming, the state and capital', *Review of International Political Economy,* 5 (4): 679–704.

Newland, Kathleen (1991) 'From transnational relationships to international relations: Women in Development and the International Decade for Women', in Rebecca Grant and Kathleen Newland (eds) *Gender and international relations,* Buckingham: Open University Press.

Nias, P. (1983) 'The poverty of peace protest', unpublished MA thesis, Bradford University Postgraduate School in Peace Studies.

Nzomo, Maria (1991) Personal interview, Vancouver, 23 March.

O'Brien, R. (1996) 'Contesting globalization: A Response from the ICFTU 16th World Congress', Paper for Conference on The Globalization of Production and the Regulation of Labour, University of Warwick, 11–13 September 1996.

O'Brien, R. (1997) 'Subterranean hegemonic struggles: international labor and the three faces of industrial relations', School of English and American Studies, University of Sussex.

Ohmae, K. (1990) *The borderless world,* London: Collins.

Pagnucco, Ron (1996) 'A comparison of the political behaviour of faith-based and secular peace groups', in C. Smith (ed.) *Disruptive religion,* New York: Routledge, 205–22.

Panos Institute (1998) 'North South disparities – "The Internet and the South: superhighway or dirt track?"' at *http://www.oneworld.org/panos/panos internet press.html.*

Parkin, F. (1968) *Middle class radicalism: the social bases of CND,* Manchester: Manchester University Press.

Paterson, M. (1997) 'Globalisation, ecology and resistance'. Paper for 'Putting the "P" into IPE' conference, Birmingham University, 26–27 September.

Peck, J. (1996) *Work place: the social regulation of local labour markets,* London: Guildford Press.

Penton, James M. (1985) *Apocalypse delayed: the story of Jehovah's Witnesses,* Toronto: University of Toronto Press.

Pereira de Queiroz, Maria Isaura (1989) 'Afro-Brazilian cults and religious change in Brazil', in J. A. Beckford and T. Luckmann (eds) *The changing face of religion,* London: Sage Publications.

Peterson, V. Spike, and Runyan, Anne Sisson (1993) *Global gender issues.* Boulder, CO: Westview Press.

Polanyi, K. (1944) *The great transformation,* Boston: Beacon Press.

Portugal, Ana Maria (1990) 'History of the meetings', *Women in Action,* 3/4: 18–19.

Priestley, J. B. (1962) *Margin released,* London: The Reprint Society.

Project Five-O (1990) *Project Five-O: An example of coalition-building for the advancement of women'. Workshop, NGO Consultation, 1990*: 'Making the Forward-looking Strategies Work', Vienna, 23 February.

Prudtatorn, Niramon (1987) 'Women and the military system symposium', *Women's World,* 13 (March): 8.

Psacharopoulos, G. and Patrinos, A. (eds) (1994) *Indigenous people and poverty in Latin America: an empirical analysis,* Washington, DC: World Bank.

Rai, Shirin M. (2000) *International perspectives on gender and democratization,* Basingstoke: Macmillan.

Rainforest Action Network (1998) *'Action Alert 135'.*

Ramsay, H. (1997) 'Solidarity at last? International trade unionism approaching the millennium', *Economic and Industrial Democracy,* 18 (4): 503–37.

Regini, M. (1992) 'Introduction: the past and future of social studies of labor movements', in M. Regini (ed.) *The future of labor movements,* London: Sage Publications.

Richards, A. (1987) 'Oil booms and agricultural development: Nigeria in comparative perspective', in M. Watts (ed.) *State, oil and agriculture in Nigeria,* Berkeley: University of California Press.

Richards, A. and Waterbury, J. (1996) *A political economy of the Middle East*, Boulder, CO: Westview.

Rifkin, J. (1995) *The end of work: the decline of the global labor force and the dawn of the post-market era*, New York: Putnam Books.

Ritzer, G. (1993) *The McDonaldization of society*, London: Pine Forge Press.

Robertson, Roland (1985) 'The sacred and the world system', in P. E. Hammond (ed.) *The sacred in a secular age*, Berkeley, CA: University of California Press, 347–58.

Robertson, Roland (1989) 'Globalization, politics and religion', in James A. Beckford and Thomas Luckmann (eds) *The changing face of religion*, London: Sage, 10–23.

Robertson, Roland (1990) 'Mapping the global condition: globalization as the central concept', in Mike Featherstone (ed.) *Global culture: nationalism, globalization and modernity*, London: Sage, 15–30.

Robertson, Roland (1992) *Globalization: social theory and global culture*, London: Sage Publications.

Robertson, Roland (1993) 'Community, society, globality, and the category of religion', in E. Barker, J. Beckford and K. Dobbelaere (eds) *Secularization, rationalism and sectarianism*, Oxford: Oxford University Press, 1–17.

Robertson, Roland and JoAnn Chirico (1985) 'Humanity, globalization and worldwide religious resurgence: a theoretical exploration', *Sociological Analysis*, 46 (3): 219–42.

Rodman, K. (1997) 'Think globally, sanction locally: non-state actors, multinational corporations and human rights' Paper at Warwick university conference on 'Non-state actors and authority in the global system', 31 October–1 November.

Rodman, K. (1998) 'Think globally, punish locally: Non-state actors, MNCs and human rights sanctions', *Ethics and International Affairs*, vol 12.

Rodney, Pat (1990) Personal interview, Toronto, 8 November.

Rogerson, Alan (1969) *Millions now living will never die: a study of Jehovah's Witnesses*, London: Constable.

Rootes, Christopher (1997) 'Environmental movements: acting globally, thinking locally?' ECPR paper, Berne, Switzerland, 27 Feb–4 March.

Rose, Paula (1995) 'The NATO alerts network', in Georgina Ashworth (ed.) *A diplomacy of the oppressed*, London: Zed Books.

Rosenau, J. (1990) *Turbulence in world politics: a theory of change and continuity*, Hemel Hempstead, Herts: Harvester/Wheatsheaf.

Rosenau, J. and Czempiel, E. O. (eds) (1992) *Governance without government*, Cambridge: Cambridge University Press.

Roseneil, Sasha (1995) *Disarming patriarchy: feminism and political action at Greenham*, Buckingham: Open University Press.

Rowbotham, S. and Mitter, S. (1994) 'Introduction', in S. Rowbotham and S. Mitter (eds) *Dignity and daily bread: new forms of economic organising among poor women in the Third World and the First*, London: Routledge.

Rowell, Andrew (1995) 'Oil, Shell and Nigeria: Ken Saro-Wiwa calls for a boycott', *The Ecologist*, 25 (6): 210–13.

Rowell, Andrew (1996) *Green backlash: global subversion of the environment movement*, London: Routledge.

Rowell, Andrew (1997) 'Crude operators: the future of the oil industry', *The Ecologist*, 27 (3): 99–106.

Roy, O. (1994) *The failure of political Islam*, Cambridge, MA: Harvard University Press.

Runyan, Anne Sisson (1988) *Feminism, peace, and international politics: an examination of women's organizing internationally for peace and security*, unpublished dissertation at American University, Washington.

Runyan, Anne Sisson (1999) 'Women and the neo-liberal frame', in M. K. Meyer and E. Prügl (eds) *Gender politics in global governance*, Lanham, MD: Rowman & Littlefield, 210–20.

Rupprecht, Carol Schreier (1982) 'The First International Interdisciplinary Congress on Women: Haifa, Israel, December 28, 1981–January 1, 1982', *Women's Studies International: A Supplement to Women's Studies Quarterly*, (July): 42–7.

Rupprecht, Carol Schreier (1985) 'The Second International Interdisciplinary Congress on Women', *Signs: Journal of Women in Culture and Society*, 10 (3): 606–14.

Rupprecht, Carol Schreier (1988) 'Third International Interdisciplinary Congress on Women', *Signs: Journal of Women in Culture and Society*, 14 (1): 235–42.

Rush, Ramona R. and Ogan, Christine L. (1989) 'Communication and development: the female connection', in R. R. Rush and D. Allen (eds) *Communications at the crossroads: the gender gap connection*, Thousand Oaks, CA: Sage, 265–78.

Rutherford, Jonathan (1990) 'A place called home: identity and the cultural politics of difference', in J. Rutherford (ed.) *Identity: Community, culture, difference*, London: Lawrence & Wishart.

Sachs, Wolfgang (1994) 'The blue planet: an ambiguous modern icon', *The Ecologist*, 24 (5): 170–5.

Sachs, Wolfgang (1997) 'Ecology, justice and the end of development', *Development*, 24 (2) (June).

Santos, Bouaventura de Sousa (1995) *Towards a new commonsense: law, science and politics in the paradigmatic transition*, New York: Routledge.

Sassen, Saskia (1996) *Losing Control? Sovereignty in an age of globalization*, New York: Columbia University Press.

Saurin, J. (1996) 'International relations, social ecology and the globalisation of environmental change' in J. Vogler. and M. Imber (eds) *The environment and international relations*, London: Routledge, 77–99.

Scheingold, Stuart (1974) *The politics of rights: lawyers, public policy, and political change*, New Haven, CT: Yale University Press.

Schmidheiny, Stephan (1992) *Changing course: a global business perspective on development and the environment*, Boston, MA: MIT Press in association with the Business Council for Sustainable Development.

Schoenberger, E. (1989) 'Multinational corporations and the new international division of labour: a critical appraisal', in S. Wood (ed.) *The transformation of work? Skill, flexibility and the labour process*, London: Unwin Hyman.

Scholte, J. A. (1997) *Global capitalism and the state*, mimeo, The Hague, Institute of Social Studies.

Scott, A. (1991) *Ideology and the new social movements*, London: Unwin.

Seidman, G. (1994) *Manufacturing militance. Workers' movements in Brazil and South Africa, 1975–1985*, Berkeley, CA: University of California Press.

Sen, Gita and Caren Grown (1987) *Development, crises, and alternative visions: Third World women's perspectives*, New York: Monthly Review Press.

Shiva, V. and Holla-Bhar, R. (1993) 'Intellectual piracy and the neem tree', *The Ecologist*, 23 (6), 23–7.

Shklar, Judith (1990) *The faces of injustice*, New Haven, CT: Yale University Press.

Shoghi Effendi (1955) *The world order of Bahá'u'lláh*, Wilmette, IL: Baha'i Publishing Trust.

Shreier, Sally (1988) *Women's movements of the world: An international directory and reference guide*, London: Longman.

Shterin, Marat S. and Richardson, James T. (1988) 'Local laws restricting religion in Russia. Precursors of Russia's new national law', *Journal of Church and State*, 40 (2): 319–41.

Simpson, John (1991) 'Globalization and religion: themes and prospects', in R. Robertson and W. Garrett (eds) *Religion and global order*, New York: Paragon, 1–17.

Sivard, Ruth Leger (1985) *Women: a world survey*, Washington: World Priorities.

Sklair, Leslie (1994) 'Global sociology and global environmental change', in T. Benton and M. Redclift (eds) *Social theory and the global environment*, London: Routledge.

Sklair, Leslie (1998) 'A transnational capitalist class?' Paper to the ESRC Transnational Communities Programme Seminar, Faculty of Anthropology and Geography, University of Oxford, 1998, posted at *www. transcomm.ox.ac.uk*.

Smith, A. G. (1998) 'Fishing with New Nets: Maori internet information resources and the implications of the internet for indigenous peoples' Private communication, *Alastair.Smith@vuw.ac.nz*.

Smith, Christian (1991) *The emergence of liberation theology: radical religion and social-movement activism*, Chicago: University of Chicago Press.

Smith, Christian (ed.) (1996) *Disruptive religion: The force of faith in social movement activism*, New York: Routledge.

Smith, D. E. (1963) *India as a secular state*, Princeton, NJ: Princeton University Press.

Smith, D. E. (ed.) (1971) *Religion, politics and social change in the Third World*, New York: Free Press.

Smith, D. E. (ed.) (1974) *Religion and political modernization*, New Haven, CT: Yale University Press.

Smith, Jackie (1997) 'Characteristics of the modern transnational social movement sector', in J. Smith, C. Chatfield and R. Pagnucco (eds) *Transnational social movements and global politics*, Syracuse: Syracuse University Press, 42–58.

Smith, Jackie *et al.* (1997) 'Social movements and world politics: a theoretical framework', in J. Smith, C. Chatfield and R. Pagnucco (eds) *Transnational social movements and global politics*, Syracuse: Syracuse University Press, 59–77.

Smith, Michael Peter and Guarnizo, Luis Eduardo (eds) (1998) *Transnationalism from below*, New Brunswick, NJ: Transaction Publishers.

Smith, N. C. (1990) *Morality and the market: consumer pressure for corporate accountability*, London: Routledge.

Smith, Peter (1985) 'A Baha'i view of human rights', Paper presented at a UNESCO conference on Religion and Human Rights, Dubrovnik.

Smith, Peter (1987) *The Babi and Baha'i Religions: From messianic Shi'ism to a world religion*, Cambridge: Cambridge University Press.

Smith, Robert C. (1998) 'Transnational localities: community, technology and the politics of membership within the context of Mexico and US migration', in Michael Peter Smith and Luis Eduardo Guarnizo (eds) *Transnationalism from below*, New Brunswick, NJ: Transaction Publishers, 196–238.

Spyropulos, G. (1991) *Sindicalismo y sociedad. Problemas actuales del sindicalismo en el mundo*, Buenos Aires: Humanitas.

SSW (1989b) *Women and decision-making*, Vienna: UN Office at Vienna. EGM/EPPDM/1989/WP.1.

Stamp, Patricia (1987) *Understanding technology transfer, community and gender in Africa*, Ottawa: International Development Research Centre.

Steele-Orsini, Marie-Antoinette and Wuthrich, William (1984) 'Les organizations non gouvernmentales dans le systeme international: Leurs statut et fonctions aupres des Nations Unies', *Relations internationales*, 40 (hiver): 505–22.

Stevis, Dimitris (1998) 'International labor organizations, 1864–1997: the weight of history and the challenges of the present', *Journal of World-Systems Research*, 4 (1): 52–75.

Stienstra, Deborah (1994) *Women's movements and international organizations*, London: Macmillan.

Stienstra, Deborah (1999a) 'Gender, women's organizing and the "net"', in J. Allison and G. A. Oclassen, Jr (eds) *Conflict, cooperation and information*, New York: SUNY Press.

Stienstra, Deborah (1999b) 'Working globally for gender equality' in A. Van Rooy (ed.) *Canadian Development Report 1999*, Ottawa: North–South Institute.

Stienstra, Deborah (Forthcoming) 'Entering the gated community: Gender, women's movements and international society', in P. Conge (ed.) *Power and Imagery* [publisher to be announced].

Stoker, G. (1988) 'Governance as theory: Five propositions', *International Social Science Journal*, March, 17–27.

Strange, S. (1996) *The retreat of the state*, Cambridge: Cambridge University Press.

Sullivan, Denis J. (1994) *Private voluntary organizations in Egypt: Islamic development, private initiative, and state control*, Gainesville, FL: University Press of Florida.

SustainAbility (1996) *Strange attractor: the Business–ENGO Partnership*, Strategic review of BP's relationships with environmental NGOs, Summary of findings: Trends, July.

Tabb, W. K. (ed.) (1986) *Churches in struggle: liberation theologies and social change in North America*, New York: Monthly Review Press.

Tatla, Darshan Singh (1999) *The Sikh diaspora*, London: UCL Press.

Taylor, Phillip A.M. (1965) *Expectations westward*, Edinburgh: Oliver & Boyd.

Taylor, R. (1983) *The British nuclear disarmament movement of 1958–65 and its legacy to the left*, PhD Thesis, Dept. of Politics, Leeds University.

Taylor, R. and Pritchard, C. (1980) *The protest makers: the British disarmament movement of 1958–65, twenty years on*, Oxford: Pergamon Press.

The Ecologist (1997) 'Big Mac attacks: lesson from the burger wars', 5 September/October, 27.

The Ecologist (1998) 'The Monsanto files', *The Ecologist*, 28 (5): 249–318.

The Economist (1995) 'Multinationals and their morals', 12 December, p 8.

The Economist (1998a) 'Gypsies in America: from open road to the Internet', 7 April, p 59.

The Economist (1998b) 'Indians, oil and the Internet', 6 June, p 66.

Third World Quarterly, 19 (5): 847–72 Special Issue.

Thomas, Jeff and Cook, Keith (1998) *Brent Spar – a triumph for whom?*, Open University MSc Science supplement 392141, Milton Keynes: The Open University.

Thompson, D. and Larson, R. (1978) *Where were you brother? An account of trade union imperialism*, London: War on Want.

Thompson, E. P. and Smith, D. (1980) *Protest and survive*, Harmondsworth: Penguin.

Tillich, Paul (1958) 'Existential analysis and religious symbols', in W. Herberg (ed.) *Four existential theologians*, Garden City, NJ: Doubleday.

Tilly, Charles (1978) *From mobilization to revolution* Reading, MA: Addison-Wesley.

Tilly, Charles (1981) *As sociology meets history*, New York: Academic Press.

Tilly, Charles (1995) 'Globalization threatens labor's rights', *International Labor and Working Class History*, no .47 (Spring), 1–23.

Tinker, Irene (1976) 'Introduction: the seminar on women in development', in Tinker *et al.* (eds) *Women and world development*, New York: Praeger, 1–6.

Tóth, A. (1993) 'Great expectations – fading hopes: trade unions and system change in Hungary', *Journal of Communist Studies*, 9 (4): 85–97.

Touraine, Alain (1981) *The voice and the eye: an analysis of social movements*, Cambridge: Cambridge University Press.

Touraine, Alain (1986) 'Unionism as a social movement', in S. M. Lipset (ed.) *Unions in transition: entering the second century*, San Francisco: ICS Press.
Turner, Bryan (1994) *Orientalism, postmodernism and globalism*, London: Routledge.

UN (1985) *State of the world's women 1985*, New York: United Nations Publications Office.
Union of International Associations (1989/90) *Yearbook of international organizations*, vol 1. Munich: K. G. Saur.
Union of International Associations (1990/91) *Yearbook of international organizations*, vol 1. Munich: K. G. Saur.
UNNGLS (1990) *Beyond the debt crisis: structural transformations. Final report of the international women's seminar, 23–25 April 1990*, New York: United Nations Non-Governmental Liaison Service.

Vallier, I. (1970) *Catholicism, social control, and modernization in Latin America*, Englewood Cliffs, NJ: Prentice-Hall.
van Vugt, J. P. (1991) *Organizing for social change: Latin American Christian base communities and literacy campaigns*, New York: Bergin & Harvey.
Vernon, Raymond (1991) 'Sovereignty at bay: twenty years after', *Millennium*, 20 (2): 191–5.
Vertovec, Steve and Cohen, Robin (1999) 'Introduction', in S. Vertovec and R. Cohen (eds) *Migration, diasporas and transnationalism*, Cheltenham: Edward Elgar, xiii–xxviii.
Verzola, Roberto (1998) 'The third wave of colonialism' Private correspondence, *rverzola@phil.gn. apc.org*.
Vidal, J. (1996) *McLibel: Burger culture on trial*, Basingstoke: Macmillan.
Vidal, J. (1997) 'Industry terrified at the outbreak of ethics', *The Guardian*, 23 April.
Viezzer, Moema (1990) Personal interview, Toronto, 27 November.
Villa-Vicencio, C. (1990) *Civil disobedience and beyond: law, resistance, and religion in South Africa*, Grand Rapids, MI: Eerdmans.
Vogel, D. (1978) *Lobbying the corporation: citizen challenges to business authority*, New York: Basic Books.
Vogler, C. (1985) *The nation state: the neglected dimension of class*, Aldershot: Gower.
Voyé, L. (1997) 'Religion in modern Europe: pertinence of the globalization theories?' in N. Inoue (ed.) *Globalization and indigenous culture*, Tokyo: Institute for Japanese Culture and Classics, 155–86.

Wakeman, Frederic E. (1988) 'Transnational and comparative research', *Items*, 42 (4): 85–7.
Walker, Anne S. (1991) Personal interview, New York, 1 February.
Wallerstein, Immanuel (1983) *Geopolitics and geoculture: essays on the changing world system*, Cambridge: Cambridge University Press.
Wallis, Roy (1976) *The road to total freedom: a sociological analysis of scientology*, London: Heinemann.
Walton, John and Seddon, David (1994) *Free markets and food riots: the politics of global adjustment*, Oxford: Blackwell.
Walzer, Michael (1996) *The revolution of the saints. a study in the origins of radical politics*, London: Weidenfeld & Nicolson.
Wapner, P. (1995) *Environmental activism and world civic politics*, New York: SUNY Press.
Wapner, P. (1997) 'Governance in global civil society', in Oran Young (ed.) *Global governance*, Cambridge, MA: MIT Press.
Waterman, Peter (1993) 'Social movement unionism: a new model for a New World Order', *Review*, 16 (3): 245–78.
Waterman, Peter (1998) *Globalization, social movements and the new internationalisms*, London: Mansell.
Waters, M. (1995) *Globalization*, London: Routledge.
WCNYGN (1990) *Making the 'Forward looking Strategies' work: Report of the NGO consultation, Vienna, 1990*, Vienna: UN NGO Women's Committees of New York, Geneva and Vienna.
Weil, Lise and Nelson, Linda (1990) 'An international feminist book fair', in Joan Turner (ed.) *Living the changes*, Winnipeg, MB: University of Manitoba Press, 205–6.
Welford, Richard (ed.) (1996) *Corporate environmental management: systems and strategies*, London: Earthscan.
Welford, Richard (1997) *Hijacking environmentalism: corporate responses to sustainable development*, London: Earthscan.
Welford, Richard and Starkey, R. (eds) (1996) *The Earthscan reader in business and the environment*, London: Earthscan.
Wellesley Editorial Committee (1977) *Women and national development: the complexities of change*, Chicago: University of Chicago Press.

Whitaker, Jennifer Seymour (1975) 'Women of the World: Report from Mexico City', *Foreign Affairs*, 54 (1): 173–81.

White, B. (1996) 'Globalization and the child labour problem', Economic Research Seminars, The Hague: Institute of Social Studies.

White, J. R. (1970) *The Soka Gakkai and mass society*, Stanford, CA: Stanford University Press.

Wickham, Carrie Rosefsky (1997) 'Islamic mobilization and political change: The Islamic trend in Egypt's professional associations,' in Joel Beinin and Joe Stork (eds) *Political Islam: essays from Middle East Report*, Berkeley, CA: University of California Press.

Willems, E. (1967) *Followers of the New Faith*, Nashville, TN: Vanderbilt University Press.

Willetts, P. (1982), 'Pressure group as transnational actors', in P. Willetts (ed.) *Pressure groups in the global system: the transnational relations of issue-orientated non-governmental organizations*, London: Frances Pinter.

Wills, J. (1997) 'Taking on the Cosmo Corps? Experiments in trans-national labour organization', Draft paper for Globalisation: Regulation and Resistance session, RGS–IBG Conference, Exeter, January 1997.

Wils, L. (1996) 'The workers' movement and nationalism', in P. Pasture, J. Verberckmoes and H. de Witte (eds) *The lost perspective? Trade unions between ideology and social action in the New Europe*, Aldershot: Avebury.

Wilson, Bryan R. (1967) 'The migrating sect', *British Journal of Sociology*, 18 (3): 303–17.

Wilson, Bryan R. (1970) *Religious sects*, London: Weidenfeld & Nicolson.

Wilson, Bryan R. (1973) *Magic and the millennium*, London: Heinemann.

Wilson, Bryan R. (1976) *Contemporary transformations of religion*, Oxford: Oxford University Press.

Wilson, Bryan R. (1995) 'Religious toleration, pluralism and privatization' *Kirchliche Zeitgeschichte* 8 (1): 99–116.

Wilson, Bryan R. and Dobbelaere, K. (1994) *A time to chant: the Soka Gakkai Buddhists in Britain*, Oxford: Oxford University Press.

Wilson, E. O. (1995) *On human nature*, Harmondsworth: Penguin.

Wilson, John (1973) *Introduction to social movements*, New York: Basic Books.

Windmuller, J. and Pursey, S. (1998) 'The international trade union movement' in *Comparative Labour Law and Industrial Relations in Industrialised Market Economies*, Kluwer Law International: The Netherlands, 83–109.

Women's Support Network (1996) *Development Plan 1996–99*, Belfast.

World Bank (1995) *World Development Report 1995. Workers in an integrating world*, New York: Oxford University Press.

Worsley, Peter (1957) *The trumphets shall sound: a study of 'cargo cults' in Melanesia*, London: MacGibben & Kee.

Wuthnow, Robert (1987) 'Indices of religious resurgence in the United States', in R. T. Antoun and M. E. Hegland (eds) *Religious resurgence: contemporary cases in Islam, Christianity and Judaism*, Syracuse, NY: Syracuse University Press, 15–34.

Yearley, Steven (1992) *The green case: a sociology of environmental issues, arguments and politics*, London: Routledge.

Yearley, Steven (1993) 'Standing in for nature: the practicalities of environmental organizations', in K. Milton (ed.) *Environmentalism: the view from anthropology*, London: Routledge, 59–72.

Yearley, Steven (1995) 'The transnational politics of the environment', in J. Anderson *et al.* (eds) *A global world? Re-ordering political space*, Oxford: Oxford University Press, 209–47.

Yearley, Steven (1996) *Sociology, environmentalism, globalisation*, London: Sage Publications.

Young, N. (ed.) (1987) *Campaigns for peace*, Manchester: Manchester University Press.

Young, Oran R. (1997) *Global governance: drawing insights from the environmental experience*, Cambridge MA: MIT Press.

Young, Oran R., Demko, George and Ramakrishna, Kilaparti (1991) 'Global environmental change and international governance', Summary and recommendations of a conference held at Dartmouth College Hanover, NH, June.

Yuval-Davis, Nira (1995) 'The Cairo conference, women and transversal politics', *Women Against Fundamentalism Journal*, no. 6, February, 19–21.

Zirakzadeh, Cyrus Ernesto (1997) *Social movements in politics: a comparative study*, London: Longman.

Zubaida, S. (1989) *Islam, the people and the state*, London: Routledge.

INDEX